THE HONG KONG CONUNDRUM

THE HONG KONG CONUNDRUM

PANGS OF TRANSITION

RUP NARAYAN DAS

KNOWLEDGE WORLD
KW Publishers Pvt Ltd
New Delhi

ISBN 978-93-91490-68-3 Hardback
ISBN 978-93-91490-69-0 ebook

Published in India by Kalpana Shukla

KNOWLEDGE WORLD
KW Publishers Pvt Ltd
4676/21, First Floor, Ansari Road
Daryaganj, New Delhi 110002
Phone: +91 11 43528107
Marketing: kw@kwpub.in
Editorial: production@kwpub.in
Website: www.kwpub.in

Printed and Bound in India

Dedicated to the memory of
Professor Late Gargi Dutt
and
Late V.P. Dutt

Contents

Preface

The peaceful surrender of Hong Kong to China on the midnight of 30 June 1997 after almost one hundred and fifty six years of colonial rule was a unique event in the annals of world history. Rarely before had one power surrendered a rich treasure to another. Even those who favoured the status had to admit that the hand over was a remarkable diplomatic achievement despite the challenges ahead.

The credit for finding a solution to the peaceful reunification of Hong Kong, a capitalist enclave, with mainland China, a socialist country, through the formula of 'one country, two systems' goes to Deng Xiaoping, China's most pragmatic leader. Deng, however, breathed his last before Hong Kong's merger with the mainland. Thus, the future of Hong Kong under the People's Republic of China had aroused considerable interest among Sinologists the world over. The hiatus between promises and performance of the system of 'one country, two systems', has been laid bare within less than past 25 years of Hong Kong's reversion to China.

The book attempts to focus attention on the viability of 'one country, two systems' within the contours and parameters of the Basic Law of Hong Kong and the constitution of the People's Republic of China in the context of political and economic compulsions. The publication of the book coincide at a time when Hong Kong's reversion to China completes 25 years on 1st July 2022, moving the half way mark of 50 years of the promise of "one country, two systems".

The book consists of nine chapters, each chapter consisting of sub-sections. First chapter throws light on what the Chinese call the unequal treaties which ceded Hong Kong to Britain. This chapter discusses, *inter alia*, the opium war fought between the imperial China and Britain and the Treaties of 1842, 1860 and 1898, and the position and stand of the People's Republic of China with regard to these treaties.

The second chapter delineates the evolution of colonial administration in Hong Kong, which was primarily aimed at facilitating trade and commerce in the colony. The third chapter highlight the rise of Hong Kong as a leading commercial and trading center of the world. This chapter also focuses on the symbiotic relationship between Hong Kong and China. It is needless to say that Hong Kong and China over the years have developed a symbiotic relationship. It is for these specific reasons that Beijing had been historically interested in the stability and prosperity of Hong Kong.

The fourth chapter attempts to reconstruct the protracted negotiation between Britain and China which was initiated with the visit of Margaret Thatcher, the then British Prime Minister, to Beijing in September, 1982. This chapter discusses the diplomatic parleys between the two countries culminating in the signing of the historic Sino-British Joint Declaration of 1984 and later the 'Basic Law', the mini constitution of Hong Kong.

The Joint Declaration set at rest the worries and anxieties of the people of Hong Kong and for that matter the concern of the world at large. The Sino-British Joint Declaration, hailed as a feat of diplomatic craftsmanship, settled once for all that Hong Kong would be transferred to People's Republic of China in 1997 and satisfied the national pride of the Chinese. It also provided a breather to Hong Kong entrepreneurs who felt jittery about the stability and prosperity of Hong Kong. The Joint Declaration and the Basic Law, however, failed to resolve many attendant problems such as the pace of democracy and representative institutions in Hong Kong and the nationality status of ethnic minorities such as Indians in Hong Kong.

The fifth chapter, therefore, seeks to analyse democratization and political participation in Hong Kong. The sixth chapter highlights the nationality issue of ethnic minorities particularly the Hong Kong Indians. The seventh chapter is on pangs of transition. The eighth chapter is the conclusion, which is a prognosis on the basis of foregone chapters. A post script has been added as ninth chapter which updates the developments.

The book is essentially analytical in nature. The study is based on primary as well as secondary sources of material. It may be mentioned here in this connection that the field trip to Hong Kong sponsored by the School of International Studies, Jawaharlal Nehru University was found immensely beneficial which enabled the researcher access to some rare publications not available in India. It also afforded me an opportunity to meet and interview a cross section of people – university professors, scholars, journalists, diplomats and common people.

I must record here my appreciation of the assistance received from various sources. First, I am deeply indebted to my supervisor, Prof. (Ms.) late Gargi Dutt for her valuable guidance, inspiration, encouragement and unfailing moral support without which this work would not have seen the light of the day. I am equally grateful to Professor late V. P. Dutt, her husband, the doyen of Chinese studies in India for his inspiration and encouragement.

I am also grateful to Ms Kalpana Shukla, the publisher for accepting my proposal to publish the manuscript. I am also thankful to Mr Sushanta Gayen for enduring the long gestation period. Last but not least, the publication of the book is made possible to a large extent due to constant prodding by my wife Sanjukta. I dedicate the book to the memory of late Ms. Gargi Dutt and her husband late Professor V.P. Dutt for their support and inspiration.

March 2022
New Delhi

Rup Narayan Das

List of Abbreviations

BDTC	British Dependent Territory Citizen
BNO	British National Overseas
BLDC	Basic Law Drafting Committee
DPP	Democratic Progressive Party
HKSR	Hong Kong Special Administrative Region
KMT	Kuo-min-tang
NPC	National People's Congress
LEGCO	Legislative Council
OMELCO	Office of Members of Executive and Legislative Council
PLA	People's Liberation Army
PRC	People's Republic of China
SEZ	Special Economic Zone

CHAPTER 1

Opium Trade and Unequal Treaties: The Birth of Hong Kong

Hong Kong, once a cluster of hilly islands, was born out of trading relations between Britain and China, and its rise and development has been determined by geographical and economic factors. The erstwhile British colony consisted of three parts: the first is the Island of Hong Kong, occupying 29 square miles, ceded by the treaty of Nanking in 1842; the second is the small peninsula of Kowloon, which was acquired by Great Britain through the Convention of Peking, 1860; and the third is the New Territories, acquired through the Convention of Peking, 1898.

Although British contacts with China began in the 17th century – with the commencement of the Royal Charter of 1600 that accorded the monopoly of British trade to the east of Cape of Good Hope – until the second half of the 18th century, there was not much expansion of British commerce in East Asia. It may, however, be mentioned that British contact with China had preceded commercial interaction between the two countries. Much before commercial contact was established with China, Christian missionaries had already arrived there. Among various factors that accelerated the British trade with China was the success of the 'seven years' war (1756-63), the loss of American colonies which spurred greater interest in commerce in the Far East and the expansion of British rule in India. This in turn ensured the opportunity of a dominant place for the British in India's trade with China.

The formation of the British East India Company paved the way for trade and commerce between China and Britain. Guangzhou (called Canton earlier), the chief port of China on the periphery of Hong Kong, had for centuries been in contact with the countries of South-east Asia, India, and the Arabs. Since the 16th century, when the Portuguese obtained permission to establish a trading colony at Macao on the western shore of the Pearl estuary, the city had also been in touch with Europe. The western countries aspired for a pie of China's fabled resources. For many years, several of them had been permitted to open and operate factories or warehouses in Guangzhou, the only Chinese city where foreigners were allowed to reside. They sold woolens, cottons, furs, and a few manufactured goods. At the end of 1830s, the merchants of four foreign powers maintained factories in Guangzhou – the British, the Americans, the French, and the Dutch. The British East India Company had by then abandoned its official monopoly of Anglo-Chinese trade, and so there were some 30 British firms operating from Guangzhou. In theory at least, they were supervised by a Chief Superintendent of Trade, appointed by the British government.[1]

Later, the pattern of trade changed to dealing with illicit Indian opium. The growth and sale of opium was officially organised in British India, and traders brought vast quantities of it to Guangzhou, selling it at an exorbitant profit to Chinese buyers. As a matter of fact, there was not much else British traders could sell to the Chinese, who were self-sufficient in most things and scornful of western innovations. So, opium traffic was pursued vigorously. The drugs illegally sold to China were worth twice as much as all the legal commodities put together, and without them, the British imports of Chinese tea could have been paid for only in spice. Opium became, so it is said, not only the principal export of the Indian Empire, but actually the single largest international commerce anywhere in the world.[2]

In the earlier times, the East India Company's merchants dealt in a variety of exports from China, including raw silk and nankeens, Chinaware, and tea. But since 1813, the Company had confined its exports to the profitable trade in tea, leaving out trade in other goods to private merchants. Tea was unknown in England when the East India Company was first given its Charter in 1600, but later in the 17th century, small quantities were imported from India. In 1664, the Company gave King Charles II two pounds of tea as a curiosity. But by early 18th century, the new drink had become so popular that its annual consumption in England amounted to 1.2 million pounds. It was a trade which the British government was glad to encourage, since a modest excise duty of 12.5% had been gradually raised to the considerable figure of 100%. Soon, tea became so important in English life that an act of Parliament ordered the Company to always to keep one year's supply in stock, and the Treasury's receipts from tea duty amounted to one-tenth of the country's total revenue.[3]

To pay for its imports of tea, the Company initially sold woolens, lead iron, and Cornish tin in the Chinese market. After a long struggle, Manchester cotton manufacturers succeeded in selling calicos at a profit in China by 1827. But the trade was uneven, as Britain was more anxious for China tea than the Chinese were for British goods. While the value of British exports to China averaged only $3.5 million a year, the East India Company annually imported about $7 million worth of Chinese goods. The $3.5 million balance was made up with American silver currency, originally brought to China by the East India Company. After 1805, the East India Company ceased carrying silver to Canton because it could instead rely upon private merchants or free traders who sold mechanical instruments, Indian cottons, and exotica from South East Asia to the shopkeepers of Canton.[4]

These private merchants were forbidden by the Chinese government to export their cash profits from Canton, so they turned the silver over to East India Company in return for exchange bills which could be cashed in London or India. The East India Company, of course, used the silver to continue purchasing the vast quantities of tea, which it sold in England. Three developments altered this balance system of economic interests: the increasingly private corruption of Chinese customs superintendents called *Hoppo*, the growing credit instability of Anglo-Chinese monopolists, and the rise of the free trade in opium.[5]

OPIUM TRADE

The emergence of opium as the single most important item of export to China, offsetting the import of a large quantity of tea from China, was one of the major reasons of friction between Britain and Imperial China. The history of opium in China can be traced back at least to the 17th century, when the opium-producing poppy was first mentioned in Chinese literature; but at first it was used medicinally and taken by the mouth. It was only after tobacco was introduced into Fukien and Formosa in 1620 that the Chinese began to smoke opium, at first mixed with tobacco and later by itself, the evil effects of which were clearly seen in the ensuing century. In 1729, when the Chinese grown product was already being supplemented by small quantities of foreign opium imported by Portuguese traders, opium-smoking was formally prohibited by an imperial edict, but the ban was so widely ignored that another edict increasing the penalties for disobedience was issued in 1796. Four years later, both the import of opium and its home cultivation were entirely prohibited, the ban was too late. The opium trade was then in the hands of vested interests, both in India and China, and it had long passed the point at which edicts could have much effect on it.

The Indian opium enterprise consisted of two segments: the Malwa opium, and the Bengal opium. The Bengal opium monopoly was established during the British rule in India, an offshoot of India-China trade under the East India Company, while the Malwa opium enterprise was not established by the East India Company. It was created in the beginning of the 19th century by some private British and Parsee traders. The poppy was grown within Indian princely states in Rajasthan and the northern part of the Deccan where the Company's rule could not reach before the 1820s. Opium was smuggled out of India via the Portuguese ports at Goa, Daman, and Diu.[6]

THE MALWA OPIUM

The East India Company had no share in the profit of the Malwa opium prior to 1820. It could not prevent this opium from reaching China and competing with the Company's opium in the Chinese markets. Therefore, the Company's initial attitude towards the Malwa opium was hostile. Bombay, which could have been the ideal port for the export of Malwa opium, was out of bounds for it. However, by 1820, the situation changed. For one thing, the Company's troops had humiliated most of the Indian provinces in the Malwa opium-producing area, which enabled the Company to have a more effective control of affairs within the princely states. On top of it, the Board of Customs, Salt and Opium of the Bengal government inquired into the matter in 1820 and discovered three advantages of Malwa opium over the Bengal brand in the Chinese market. In the first place, the Chinese could get 75% pure extract from Malwa, but only 57% from the Bengal one. Secondly, the Malwa cakes were small and flat, thus easier to smuggle into China than the large and globular Bengal cake. Thirdly, the Malwa chest adopted the Chinese picul weight (a picul equals 133 1/3 pounds), which was more convenient for Chinese counting the two-factory mounds (weighing 149 pounds) Bengal chest.[7]

The discovery of Malwa opium coincided with a change in the Company's attitude towards it. The Company gave up its earlier hostile policy and opened the gates of Bombay to facilitate the export of Malwa opium to China. Subsequently, the Malwa opium enterprise was brought under the Company's monopoly. In 1820, Malwa opium – valued at Rs 32,15,317 – passed Bombay on its way to China. In the next two decades, Bombay's average annual export of Malwa opium to China was Rs 41 lakh in 1821-1830, and more than rupees one crore in 1831-1840. The combination of two opium enterprises formed a formidable trade offensive against China. Between 1770 and 1789, exports rose from 1,400 chests to 4,000, and by 1860s, the government was planning to supply nearly 50,000 chests. In 1814-15, its value stood at Rs 1.2 million; in 1834-35, it was Rs 10.8 million; and by 1849-50, it increased to Rs 50.7 million.[8]

The alluring prospects opened up by the development of Indian opium-cultivation were too tempting for the Company's integrity. It still kept opium out of its own ships, but it had a heavy responsibility for increasing its exports to China. For the Company controlled opium sales in India, and it licensed British and Indian merchants engaged in the 'country trade' between India and China to carry opium in their ships. Moreover, the permits were due to be forfeited if the 'country ships' carried any opium to China other than which was bought at the Company's sales in Calcutta. In this way, the East India Company was making considerable profit out of opium without having any direct role in its distribution in China. So, it had a vested interest in the continuance of the trade. The colonial government in India also found the opium trade too profitable to be discarded, and in London, the British government shared this view. By 1832, the opium duty was providing one-eighteenth of British India's gross revenues.

THE BENGAL OPIUM

The years between the anti-opium edicts of 1729 and 1800 in China had been the years of Britain's conquest of India and her consequent acquisition of the poppy-growing area of Bengal. Both the Government of India (consisting of British officials) and the directors of the East India Company had realised that China's addiction to opium provided a great trade opportunity, and they had decided to keep it to themselves. So, in 1773, Bengal Governor Warren Hastings made opium-growing a government monopoly and decreed that its cultivation could be undertaken only with the government's permission. The permission was given to the East India Company, which became solely responsible for the production and sale of Indian opium, and on which a substantial duty was paid to the Indian Government. The East India Company played a peculiar part in the development of opium trade with China. As far as its own ships were concerned, it had really obeyed the imperial government's ban on opium imports. Indeed, the first reference to opium in the Company's records was in 1733, four years after the first edict, when the commanders of the Company's ships were warned that China was threatening to confiscate opium cargoes.[9]

This indeed was the consideration which determined Britain's approach towards opium trade for several years. Whatever other factors had to be considered, it was imperative that British-India needed its opium revenue. The trade was also of general economic benefit to the British because it had restored the balance of payments. As noted earlier, previously Britain had to send silver to China to pay for its substantial imports of tea and silk, which far exceeded in value the relatively few British exports. The benefits that accrued from opium trade forged the alliance of the East India Company, the British and Indian governments, and even the House of Commons.

The vested interests supporting the opium trade within China were those of foreign merchants, the Chinese middlemen, and Chinese officials who enjoyed their regular 'squeeze'. These vested interests had existed for years, but some other developments precipitated the opium crisis to a flashpoint. The introduction of high speed boats reduced the time taken for the voyage between Calcutta (the port of origin of opium) and its destination (the French port of Lintin). The distance was covered in about 17/18 days. This greatly facilitated the transport of opium, the demand for which had greatly increased in China. Opium flowed from all of India to Canton, and by 1836, total imports came to $18 million, making it the world's most valuable single commanding trade of the 19th century.[10]

The growing demand for opium greatly disturbed the Imperial Chinese government, not only because of its influence on the balance of trade, but also because of its deleterious effects on the health and minds of people. While during the first decade of the 19th century, China had gained about $26 million in her world balance of payments, from 1828 to 1838, $38 million flowed out of the Chinese empire. It was opium that turned the balance and ended by financing much of England's further decolonisation of India. More than siphoning of money, the adverse effects of opium consumption on the people was a matter of concern for the Imperial government, and particularly for the reformist- minded Emperor Tao-Kuang, who had occupied the throne in 1820. Tao-Kung was determined not only to stop consumption of opium, but also its unhindered entry into China.

THE CANTON SYSTEM

The practice of the Canton system by which China's European trade (which also included trade with the British East India Company) was conducted from 1760 to 1834, was hierarchical subordination – first of the foreign traders to the licensed Chinese monopolists, known collectively as 'Cohong'; and second, of the 'Cohong' members to the imperially appointed Superintendent of Maritime Customs at Canton, known to westerners as 'Hoppo'. In legal-political parlance, power was exerted downward in this hierarchy. The Imperial officials at Canton – not only the 'Hoppo', but also the Governor of

Kwangtung and the Governor-General (Viceroy) of Kwangtung and Kwangsi – issued orders and regulations to members of the Cohong, with the warning that they might jail them or disgrace them for non-compliance. Besides, they customarily avoided any direct contact with the British East India Company's Select Committee at Canton, preferring to transmit their orders to them via the 'Hong' merchants. The system grew up as an expression of China's traditional effort to achieve stability in foreign relations by permitting a limited trade to those who either presented tributes or were quarantined at the entrepots on the frontiers.[11]

In conducting legitimate trade in China, the foreign traders had to deal in the first instance with 'Hoppo' who gave 'chop' (permits) for foreign ships to enter Canton river to carry on their trade. He was an important person in the Imperial echelon who was paid harbour and trading dues by foreigners, and he sent the proceeds to Peking after subtracting his own share. This share was so substantial that the Hoppo was given no salary, but traders had to even pay for the privilege of his appointment. 'Hoppo', however, did not concern himself with actual business transactions. These were left to the 'Cohong'. All dealings, whether import or export, had to go through the 'Cohong' who had been given the exclusive privilege of trading with the foreigners. In trading affairs, they were the sole intermediaries between the Chinese mandarins and the foreign merchants. While the foreign traders had to submit their petitions to the Manchu government through the Hong merchants, the latter were often the conveyers of the authorities' orders and advice. The Cohong, thus, had the onerous task of ensuring that the inhabitants of the factories (the place where the traders conducted their business) scrupulously observed various rules and regulations imposed on them. The Canton system, thus, entrusted the foreign traders entirely to the diligence and supervision of the Hong merchants to insulate between foreign traders and the Chinese masses. The Hong merchants, during the post-1760 period, enjoyed an elevated status in the commercial and social life of Canton after the imposition of the Canton system. Their selection also became stricter. Only those who were known to official circles for a long time and qualified for the prescribed eligibility of 'Yin-shih Kung-Cheng' (rich and judicious) had a chance of becoming Hong merchants.[12]

Among other obligations, the Hong merchant's duty in remitting the import and export duties to the government made his position precarious, having to fight on two fronts with both the foreign traders and the Manchu authorities for his own legitimate profit vis-à-vis the deduction of custom duties. The foreign traders would always suspect he was charging a higher sum than he was obliged to remit to the imperial treasury; while, on the other hand, the Hoppo's office was always inclined to extract maximum revenue from him, even at the expense of his rightful gains. The Canton trade really was highlighted by his financial vulnerability in resisting pressures from both the fronts.

IRRITANTS IN SINO-BRITISH TRADE

The Canton system had greatly facilitated the trade between the Chinese and foreign traders at Canton. Overseas traders were welcomed in China so long as they observed the rules and restrictions imposed on them. Though the Chinese never invited the western traders to come to their shores, and held that they had no need of western goods, they were nevertheless glad to find a market for their own tea, silk, Chinaware, and other products. Funds of both the imperial treasury and the private fortunes of many mandarins were substantially increased by duties and docking fees charged on foreign traders.

Nonetheless, the Chinese always insisted that western traders must be kept under the region's control, and they must go only where the imperial government permitted them to do their business. In earlier times, foreign vessels had traded at several Chinese ports like

Canton in Kwangtung, Amoy in Fukien, Ningpo in Chekiang and Kaun-Yun in Kiangsu.[13] Among them, Canton was the first within the reach of foreign ships coming from the South China Sea. It had the longest history in foreign trade (2,000 years) and was better equipped for receiving foreign traders. The Portuguese settlement at nearby Macao also lent more attraction to it. The British had singled out Canton for obvious reasons. An imperial edict of 1757 drastically changed the situation. From that year until 1842, Canton was the only place where foreign trade was permitted.

Racial segregation also greatly annoyed the European traders who were not allowed to live in the Chinese enclave of Canton, but had to reside in factories in suburbs specially assigned to them, and even there only during the trading season which continued from October to April. The drawback of the factory life in old Canton was that the Chinese had drawn up stringent rules designed to keep foreign traders at bay. These rules went back to 1780, and after being revised in 1819, they were confirmed by an imperial edict in 1819. Some such restrictions were the ban on rowing in rivers, limiting the foreigners' excursions outside the factory area to just three days a month, and even these thrice monthly outings had to be made in the company of a Chinese interpreter who was responsible for the good behaviour of foreigners. Yet another irksome issue was that merchants could not bring their wives to the factories. Women were evidently regarded as dangerous, since the rule under which they were banned stated that 'neither women, guns, spears not of any can be brought to the factories.[14] Merchants who came to Canton with their wives had to leave them at Macao and join them at the Portuguese colony at the end of the trading session.

While these restrictions greatly irritated the foreigners and their governments, the differences between the Chinese and Europeans with regard to the meaning, interpretation, and perception of Chinese laws and customs further strained relations between them. For example, according to the Chinese penal code, foreigners who decided to live in China were subject to trial and punishment if they were guilty of offences. But both the British and the Americans had unfortunate experiences when their nationals were subjected to Chinese jurisdiction which was different from Anglo-Saxon jurisprudence. For example, the Chinese law did not differentiate between 'murder' and 'homicide'. In fact, in 1784, when a gunner of the ship *Lady Hughes* accidentally killed a Chinese in the course of firing a salute, his surrender was demanded, and after some demur, he was handed over to Chinese authorities. He was condemned to death and was strangulated. Following this incident, the British refused to hand over any of their own nationals for trials, and the Chinese officials in practice did not dispute this measure of extra-territoriality, though they never explicitly recognised it as a right.[15]

In the British Government view, however the main drawback in Anglo-Chinese relations was the Chinese intransigence to establish any formal diplomatic contacts. Though Britain and China had traded with each other for long years, there was no British Ministry at the Imperial Court and the Imperial government had no representative in London. Thus, the lack of official contact between the two governments often led to mutual suspicion and bickering between the two. In the meanwhile, private merchants in Canton were growing increasingly restive about the restrictions imposed on them. In 1830, a petition was sent to the House of Commons, describing their life in China as humiliating and pleading for action to mitigate conditions in which both British subjects and other foreigners lived and carried their business. All the practical difficulties and irritants compelled the British Government and the Parliament to consider ways and means to acquire an enclave in the region for the protection and promotion of British commercial interests. This development took place at a time when Adam Smith's ideas of freewheeling trade were gaining ground in Britain.

APPOINTMENT OF NAPIER

It was against this backdrop that in 1833, the Company's monopoly at Canton was ended by an act of Parliament, and British commercial interests were put under the Chief Superintendent of Trade responsible to the Foreign Office. A year later, British Foreign Secretary Palmerton appointed Lord William John Napier, a former naval officer, as the Superintendent of Trade in 1834. Napier was sent to Macao with diversing instructions that reflected his government's reluctance to choose between war (which would disrupt the existing trade) and passive compliance (which would confirm the monopolistic single-port trading policy of China). On the one hand, Napier was told that he must not endanger Britain's existing relations with China, but then almost as an afterthought, Palmerton added, "Your lordship will announce your arrival at Canton by a letter to the Viceroy.[16]

Traditionally, direct contact between Chinese officials and foreigners was not encouraged under the Canton trading system. Palmerston's instructions were, as such, at variance with the Chinese imperial practices, which aroused displeasure. Unaware of these niceties, Napier arrived in Canton on July 25, 1834, to present his credentials to the imperial authority. The Viceroy at Canton, Lu Kun, instructed that no letter from the 'barbarian headman' should be received, unless it was transmitted through the Hong merchants, who were the authorised contact persons between merchants and the mandarin, and only then it was superscripted with Chinese characters, signifying that it was a 'petition' from an inferior to a superior.

Lu's point of view was quite understandable. There was no instance earlier of direct communication on equal terms between a Chinese Viceroy and a representative of foreign merchants. Though

Lu knew that Napier was a high-ranking functionary, he was not going to compromise his own position to gratify a westerner in terms of protocol and propriety. He would accept a petition, which could be forwarded to the Emperor for consideration and a ruling on future procedure and protocol, but there could be no question of communication on equal terms. The Chinese authorities also did not take favourably the decision of Napier to reside at Canton to observe Chinese customs and conventions. Napier had no intention of waiting humbly for the Emperor to convey his pleasure. He had even less intention of allowing his letter to a mere provincial Viceroy to be superscripted as 'petition'. The arrogance and obdurate attitude of Napier hurt Viceroy Lu Kun, who ordered Napier to return to Macao at once. Napier did not relent, which in turn impelled Lu to halt the trade when Napier still remained there. Lu ordered the trading factories to be blocked and cut off from supplies. Napier then, contrary to Palmerston's instructions, ordered two war ships to fight their way up to Pearl River, and asked for troops. Meanwhile, Lu Kun blocked up the river, assembled 68 war junks, and secured the Emperor's permission to use force.

The belligerence of the Chinese Viceroy was too much for Napier to digest. He was not reconciled to yield to Chinese dictate, compromising the esteem and dignity of His Majesty's government. He was faced with the problem of asserting British authority against an obdurate Viceroy, who further proceeded to garrison the factory area. To add to Napier's personal predicament, he was struck with malaria. Notwithstanding his ill-health, Napier decided to strike with the help of two British frigates which were in Chinese waters. He gave orders to Captain Charles Elliot, his naval aide, to force the passage of Borgue and dock at Whampoa. As their frigates made their way up to the estuary, they were fired on by the Chinese ships. The frigates successfully reached Whampoa on September

11, 1834. Napier, however, could not sustain his resolve because of his deteriorating health. He himself had realised the futility of his position. So long as he stayed in Canton, there was little hope Lu would lift his embargo on British trade, and in the weak state of his own health, he had no desire to remain there. On his surgeon's advice, he decided to go back to Macao. At the same time, he ordered the two frigates to retreat from Whampoa to Lintin Island. Napier reached Macao on September 26, 1834. Three days later, Lu lifted the trade embargo. But Napier had no further role in determining British policy towards China. He succumbed to fever on October 11. His mission ended in failure, though he had taken the first step on the trajectory his successors followed in subsequent years. On Napier's death, his deputy John F Davis took over the reins of the Trade Commission, and it was clear he had no intention of trying to settle Chinese problems by show of force. In his three months as Acting Chief Superintendent, Davis maintained his nuanced policy and tried to avoid unnecessary clashes with the Chinese. When he resigned in January 1835, the same policy was continued by his successor Sir George Robinson.

Robinson had very well realised the importance of Hong Kong and its natural harbour as a potential resting place for merchants and their ships. He had suggested as early as January 1836 that British interests would best be served by occupying one of the islands in the vicinity, thereby stepping away from Canton. In April 1836, he named Hong Kong as such an island, and in November the same year, in a dispatch he announced that he was moving his office there. A measure of the disapproval associated with such a policy can be gauged from the fact that on receipt of his January communication, London had decided to do away with Robinson's post of Chief of Superintendent of Trade, and directed him to hand over his files to his successor Captain Charles Elliot.[17]

PRELUDE TO OPIUM WAR

After being formally appointed as chief of the Commission on June 15, 1836, Elliot took up his position at a critical time, when Emperor Tao-Kuang and his advisors were becoming more and more concerned about the ill-effects of opium trade. By November 1836, they had effectively banned opium trade. Instructions were communicated to the foreign merchants at Canton through the Cohong. They, however, did not take the orders earnestly. This time, the merchants were proved wrong. After mulling over, the imperial authorities firmly decided to initiate stringent action to enforce the decree banning opium. It was against this tenuous background that Elliot attempted to establish direct communication with higher imperial officials. In pursuance of their nuanced policy, both Davis and Robinson had stayed at Macao during their tenure of office, but Elliot decided that unless he went to Canton, he could not establish direct contact with the Chinese authorities. This was the course he had proposed in his correspondence with the British government. It was but natural, therefore, that on the day of his appointment, he wrote to the Chinese Viceroy asking for a passport to Canton. He put on his letter the superscription 'Pin', which marked it as a petition, and he submitted it through the Hong merchants.[18]

The Imperial Viceroy was happy to respond to the petition, and he conveyed to the interlocutor that the words and subject matter of the petition were reverential and submissive. He replied that he would ask for an Imperial edict allowing Elliot to go to Canton. Elliot's submissive petition, however, greatly annoyed the Foreign Office. The British Foreign Office expected Elliot to deal with the Chinese authorities on an equal footing. The Imperial edict permitting Elliot to go to Canton was duly received. He went to the sites called 'factories' where merchants lived, and met them. But his real aim of going to Canton was not achieved. The letter to the Viceroy still had to be sent through the Hong merchants. His attempts to make the Viceroy communicate with him directly and on equal terms did not fructify.

Elliot realised there would soon be trouble over opium, since the imperial government's concern with the problem could no longer be taken casually. His counselling and considered views had the desired effect on the Foreign Office. The Foreign Secretary felt the time had come for British gunboats to be seen in Chinese waters. He suggested to the Admiralty that Rear Admiral Sir Frederick Maitland, Commander-in-Chief of the East India Station, would himself visit China and that warships should be sent there regularly to afford protection to British interests. By the time Admiral Maitland visited China in 1835, Elliot's warning of serious trouble over opium were being amply manifested. The imperial instructions were carried out in letter and spirit.

The Chinese Viceroy thought it prudent to demonstrate to the foreign community in Canton that the anti-opium edicts were being fully enforced. So, in December 1838, he gave instructions that a Chinese opium-seller was going to be executed by strangling in front of the factories where the foreign merchants did their physical exercises. The site chosen was near the American flag staff, from which the United States Consul hauled down his flag in protest, and when the merchants saw the apparatus for the execution being set up on their own exercise ground, they were outraged. A large crowd gathered outside the factories where the merchants tried to drive off the executioners with sticks. The Chinese retaliated by pelting stones and drove out the merchants inside the factory gates. The incident ended with the arrival of the Chinese troops, who dispersed the mob. The opium seller was executed later in another part of Canton.

APPOINTMENT OF LIN TSE-HSU (LIN ZEXU)

It was in these circumstances that in December 1838 Lin Tse-hsu was asked by the Chinese Emperor to go to Canton as High Commissioner, with plenipotentiary powers and Supreme Command of Canton's naval forces to investigate port affairs and find out ways and means to suppress the opium trade. Lin was a native of Foochow. He had qualified the Imperial Civil Service with distinction. He subsequently studied at the Hanlin Academy. As a civil servant, he rose rapidly and was soon recognized as an able administrator known for his scholarship and erudition, honesty, integrity and dedication. In 1804, at the age of 19, he had acquired his first higher degree. Then he served for five years as the governor's secretary, and later worked as a Hanlin Compiler for three years. After that came routine promotions in various capacities at a slightly faster pace than normal as a judge, provincial treasure, conservancy director and so forth, until at the relatively young age of 47, he was made a Governor. Within five years, he rose to the post of Governor-General.

Lin Tse-hsu became a provincial governor before he was 50, and in 1838, he was appointed as the Viceroy of Hupeh and Hunan. He had campaigned against opium which was lauded by Emperor Tao-Kuang. Lin strongly urged for complete suppression of opium smoking, and his arguments made a very strong impression, because he had acted on them in his own provinces. It was his crusade against opium which persuaded Tao-Kuang that at last there was a man who could firmly deal with the menace of the drug. Therefore, when he was appointed as Commissioner of Canton, he had the message and mandate of the Emperor.

SEIZURE AT CANTON

Even before arriving in Kwangtung, Lin-hsu ordered the arrest of some Cantonese offenders, and the investigation of some imperial officials implicated in the opium traffic. Lin was convinced that Canton was the den of corruption and crime. He was determined to stem the rot. On March 18, 1839, he took the first step by informing the Hong merchants that they had three days to persuade the foreign merchants to surrender their opium stocks to the Chinese government and sign bonds promising never to handle the drug again. Otherwise, one or two Hongists would be executed and the rest would lose their property. At last, the merchants agreed to a token surrender. But Lin insisted for full surrender, and believed that the key supplier he sought was Lancelot Dent, head of the second largest country firm and president of the British Chamber of Commerce. On March 22, therefore, Lin issued an order for Dent's arrest and seized two Chinese merchants as hostages to be decapitated in the Englishman's stead unless he turned himself over to the local authorities.[19]

This news quickly reached Captain Elliot at Macao, who immediately assumed the worst. Ordering his available warship to move to Hong Kong and prepare for hostilities, he left Macao on March 23 with a small escort and quickly arrived the next day at the Canton factories. The Chinese, in the meantime, had enforced the trade embargo, labour boycott, blocked the factories, and held 350 foreigners in thrall for the next 47 days. Elliot for all his courage, was in a desperate situation. His overriding concern was for the survival of those under his charge and it was not difficult to imagine that thousands of Chinese troops cordoned around the factories were preparing to attack them all while he stood by helplessly. Thus, on March 26, when Lin made it clear that the English would be released whenever he got his opium, Elliot had a sigh of relief. The next day, he summoned all country traders to surrender their stocks of drug to him. Within a very short time, Commissioner Lin destroyed part of the stock and was sufficiently convinced of British good faith to lift the blockade, allowing the foreigners to leave Canton if they so desired.

Lin, however, wanted to ensure that the opium trade was stopped completely. Therefore, he insisted that the trading community to give an understanding not to indulge in the opium trade or else face trial and execution. Elliot found it not only unacceptable but also humiliating. How the British nationals could subject themselves to Chinese laws, he reacted. The issue was of extra-territoriality. For the British merchants, it was not so much the abstract principle of jurisdiction as the actual fear of personal arrest that kept them from signing the bonds. Since the country traders did not yield, they could not afford to remain in Canton, and Lin suddenly decided to block them again.

Accordingly, Elliot asked the Portuguese authority at Macao for sanctuary. The Portuguese governor had no interest for the British and did not wish to become embroiled with Commissioner Lin; but he finally acceded to Elliot's request on humanitarian ground. Thus, by July 4, the entire English community had moved to Macao. Lin Tse-hsu was not surprised by this. He reasoned that the lure of trade would bring them back, and then they would have to sign the bonds. With this assumption, he devoted himself to his literary pursuit.

THE LIN WEI-HEI INCIDENT

Meanwhile, what ignited fuel to the fire was the Lin Wei-hei incident. It was on July 7 that sailors went ashore to a small village on the Kowloon side of the Hong Kong anchorage. After a heavy drinking bout, they found they could get no more wine in the village and showed their tantrum by attacking its inhabitants. During the fight, a Chinese called Lin Wei-hei was killed. His death stirred a new phase in the Anglo-Chinese crisis and precipitated the situation.

The incident not only symbolised the extra-territorial issue, but also became a major irritant, straining the relationship between Imperial China and Britain. Lin Tse-hsu was concerned that as long as the English could remain comfortably in Macao, they would keep resisting him and defying his authority. He, therefore, carried his factory boycott tactics one step further on August 15 by cutting Macao off from production and supplies, while simultaneously ordering the English out. On August 24, Elliot and his countrymen took their ships and anchored across the bay near Hong Kong.[20]

BATTLE OF CHUENPI

The transfer of British merchants from Macao to the Hong Kong anchorage did not in any way stop their lucrative opium trade and the whole floating community was soon in better spirits owing to the arrival of British naval forces. With the support of the frigates, Elliot went to Kowloon and in defiance of Lin's orders, he was able to arrange regular supplies of food from the local peasantry. When some Chinese war ships tried to stop the delivery of these supplies, Elliot opened fire on them. This incident took place on September 4, 1839. It was the first British naval action against the Chinese, and is regarded as the beginning of the first Opium War.

To Lin, this was clear proof of Elliot's complicity in the opium trade. He, therefore, decided to be tough with Elliot and the merchants. He deployed his warships to assemble at Chuenpi. As the imperial flotilla began to reach at Chuenpi, Elliot assumed they were preparing to attack the trading vessels moving under his flag. Therefore, he sailed upriver on November 3, 1839, to disperse the Chinese fleet. The two British frigates were more than a match for 29 war junks under Admiral Kuan. The British frigates destroyed four Chinese war junks and damaged several others. The whole Chinese fleet then withdrew to the other side of the Borgue.

While the Ching dynasty reacted nervously to the first shots of the Opium War, Elliot awaited instructions from England and reinforcements from the British regiments in India. Elliot's dispatches relating to the seizure of the factories and the forced surrender of British-owned opium was carefully considered at the Foreign Office. The Queen's speech at the opening of Parliament in 1840 showed that the British Government supported Elliott's decision to bring the war to its logical conclusion. In February 1840, Palmerston sent a formal ultimatum to the Imperial Government, demanding restoration of the confiscated goods or their monetary equivalent, repercussions for the imprisonment of British merchants and the Chief Superintendent of Trade and Security of British trade in future. The war, he declared, would go on until China met Britain's demands and signed a treaty in which they were incorporated. In February 1840, Palmerston also formally appointed two plenipotentiaries to command the expedition: Capitan Elliot and his cousin, Admiral George Elliot.

In making these demands, Palmerston did not dispute China's right to prohibit opium imports. The Queen of England, he explained, wished her subjects in foreign countries to obey the laws of those countries, but Her Majesty could not allow them to be treated with violence, and when wrongs were done to them, she would see that they obtained redress. China, he suggested, should have punished her own officials who carried the opium trade, instead of seizing peaceable British merchants. This was the reason why the British Government was insisting on reparations.

The responsibility for mounting an expeditionary force to carry on the war in China was entrusted with Lord Auckland, the Governor-General of India, who began by summoning the 18th Regiment (the Royal Irish) from Ceylon (Sril Lanka) and the 26th Cameroonians from Fort William, Calcutta. These two regiments, together with the 49th (Hertfordshire), some volunteer companies from the native regiments, two Madras Artillery companies, and two of sappers and miners made up the land forces, some 4,000 men in all; the naval vessels numbered about 20, including three battleships, two frigates, other warships, and some steamers. It was a single enough force to fight against an empire with tremendous manpower. Component units of this expeditionary force against China were ordered to assemble at the end of April at Singapore which had been acquired for Great Britain by Sir Stamford Raffles in 1819, and was seen as valuable, not only as trading post but also as an advanced base for military action in the Far East.

OPIUM WAR AND BRITISH PARLIAMENT

The crisis in Canton and the British response to it, especially the conduct of Elliot, had triggered intense debate in British Parliament and the public. Some of the Whigs strongly articulated a more hawkish action. Dr William Jardine, the wealthiest trader in Canton, had returned to London in January 1839, in time to exploit the opium seizure issue. As the head of a merchant delegation, he backed a clever pamphlet campaign which depicted the 'Siege in Factories' as another 'Black Hole' of Calcutta, and insult to the prestige of Great Britain. He was also instrumental in organising the support of 300 Midland textile firms to ask Palmerston to intervene at Canton. Dr Jardine who lived in Calcutta knew about the horror of 'Black Hole' tragedy of 1756 in which the Nawab of Bengal Siraj ud-Daulah had kept British prisoners in a dungeon in Fort William.

It was against this backdrop that on April 7, 1840, Sir James Graham of the Tory Opposition moved a resolution criticising the government for initiating the war. The Tories were of the view that the war was unjust, and was caused by the short-sightedness of the Queen's advisers. Defending the government's action, Thomas Babington Macaulay, the youngest member of the cabinet replied:

> "The Englishmen who have been blocked at Canton," he declared to the gallery, "belong to a country unaccustomed to defeat, to submission or to shame; to a country which had exacted such reparation for the wrongs to her children as had made the ears of all who heard it to tingle; to a country which had made the Dey of Algiers humble himself in the dust before her insulted Consul; to a country which had avenged the victims of the Black Hole on the field of

> Plassey; to a country which had not degenerated since the great Protector vowed that he would make the name of Englishman as much respected as ever had been the name of Roman citizen. They knew that surrounded as they were by enemies and separated by great oceans and continents from all help, not a hair on their heads would be harmed with impunity."

To this, Gladstone replied on behalf of the Tories:

> "A war more unjust in its origin, a war more calculated to cover this country with permanent disgrace, I do not know and I have not read of. The right Honourable gentlemen opposite spoke of the British flag waving in glory at Canton. That flag is hoisted to protect an infamous contraband traffic; and if it were never hoisted except as it is now hoisted on the coast of China, we should recoil from its sight with horror."

By the narrow margin of nine votes – 271 against 262 – Sir James Graham's resolution was defeated and Palmerston was thus given formal approval by the House of Commons for the prosecution of the war. With the approval of the Parliament, the British transports and warships sailed from Singapore on May 30, 1840, on their way to China.

Palmerston's instructions to Admiral Elliot were that he should block Canton, occupy Chusan and deliver a letter addressed to the Minister of the Emperor of China, and then sign a treaty with a duly accredited representative of the Imperial Government. A draft treaty was enclosed with the instructions and also with the letter to the emperor's minister. On July 4, British ships entered the harbour of Chusan. At first, Chinese authorities there thought that the ships had come there to trade, and there was great rejoicing in the small port at the thought of the profits to be gained. But Chusan was attacked and the port city occupied. Elliot's next task was to deliver Palmerston's letter to the Imperial Government, and he therefore sailed still further north to river Peiho. The very sight of the British warships alarmed Emperor Tao-Kuang when they arrived at the Taku forts at the mouth of the Peiho in August, 1840. The advancement of the British warships compelled the Chinese envoy Chi-Shan, who later succeeded Lin Tse-hsu, to receive Captain Charles Elliot and George Elliot. Chi-Shan had no other option but to agree to the demands of Elliot. He helplessly agreed to the Convention of Chuenpi on January 20, 1841. This agreement called for the cession of Hong Kong, a $6 million indemnity, direct official interaction on an equal basis, and the opening of Canton trade on English terms. The Convention of Chuenpi was however, repudiated by their respective governments. Emperor Tao-Kuang indignantly rejected it for obvious reasons. The Convention cost Chi-Shan his job.

On the British side, the Chuenpi agreement was found equally objectionable on the ground that Elliot had agreed to evacuate Chushan immediately in return for the cession of Hong Kong, and that the indemnity was inadequate. Palmerston criticised Elliot for accepting the 'barren island' of Hong Kong without securing the opening of other ports further north. Palmerston was so annoyed with Elliot's decision that he removed him from the post in May. However, Elliot continued in the post till his successor Sir Henry Pottinger assumed charge in August 1841. Hong Kong was, however, occupied on January 26, 1841, by the British. The island was thus at once available as a base for troops and partial storehouse for opium.

On the Chinese side, the emperor was so annoyed with Chi-Shan that he was replaced by I-shan, a Manchu, and a cousin of the Emperor. I-Shan was given two deputies – Lung-wen and Yang-Fang. The Chinese were in no mood to accept and honour the Treaty of Chuenpi, and they resumed hostility against the British, which greatly provoked Elliot. It was against this backdrop that war broke out in February 1841. Sensing that the Chinese were not going to honour the terms and conditions of the Treaty, Elliot decided to strike with the help of existing naval forces available with him. In the skirmishes that broke out on February 26, 1841, Chinese Admiral Kuen was killed. Meanwhile, the British naval forces were beefed up with the arrival of Major-General Sir Hugh Gough in Hong Kong. Gough occupied one of the forts overlooking Canton itself. Twelve days later, the British troops occupied the factory area.

With Canton so precariously threatened, Yang Fang, the Chinese General, reluctantly agreed for armistice negotiation. Thus, in the middle of the First Opium War, trade was resumed and the British flag flew again over Hong Kong. In May, Elliot was back in the British factory, but he was sure the Chinese were only waiting for an opportunity to strike once again. On May 21, therefore, as a precaution, Elliot advised all foreign merchants to leave the factories. Elliot's apprehension proved true when a big Chinese garrison encamped outside the city. The Chinese opened fire on the British ships lying off Canton. The war was resumed with a general naval action, in which more than 70 Chinese junks were destroyed. I-Shan and his two deputies realised very well that it was futile to fight the British, and they agreed for a negotiation. On May 27, a Convention was signed in which the three Chinese Commissioners and all extra provincial troops agreed to leave the city, and a 'ransom' of $6 million was promised within the week to save Canton from destruction.

CHINESE PROTEST AND RESENTMENT

Although Elliot was happy with the ransom, his military counter part Major General Gough differed with his perception. The uneasy truce did not endure. Intermittent hostility broke out between the British forces and the Chinese. Although I-Shan and his two deputies submitted to the dictates of Elliot, the opium war created resentment of the Chinese who rose in revolt and waged a people's war against the 'foreign devil'. The villagers armed themselves and formed the 'Ping Ying Tuan' or 'Quel the British corps'. When the battle of Canton began, people in the surrounding area joined in of their own accord. Peasants tilling the fields also launched spontaneous attacks against the invaders. People continued their determined resistance, and a fierce struggle flared up in Sanyualin, a village 2.5 kilometers to the north of Canton city. The battle of Canton directly affected the villagers. The atrocities committed by the British troops and the surrender of Ching officials infuriated people of Sanyualin and the surrounding area. When British troops went to the village on the morning of May 29, 1841, the local people put up a stiff resistance, and killed seven or eight of them.[21] Like the 'Sepoy Mutiny' of 1857, which is regarded as the first war of Independence in India, the Sanyualin incident can be regarded as the first organised and spontaneous Chinese revolt against British imperialism. It was indeed the precursor of the republican revolutionary movement in China.

TREATY OF NANKING

It was against this backdrop of determined and resolute resistance by the Chinese people that Pottinger reached Hong Kong on August 10, 1841. Pottinger was to direct an expeditionary force coming via the Indian Ocean and Singapore. With reinforcements from India, Pottinger launched an attack on the Chinese forces. The ill-armed Chinese were no match for the British and Indian troops. Thus, the attack on Nanking was called off and hostilities were suspended on August 17. After the suspension of hostilities, Pottinger summoned Chi-Ying (the Manchu Commissioner for Western Affairs) and his colleagues to *HMS Cornwallis* to accept the terms of treaty which were almost exactly those which Palmerston had prescribed some two years earlier. Main provisions of the treaty were: (1) An indemnity of $2,10,00,000 to be paid in installments. (2) The opening for trade of the five ports of Canton, Amoy, Foochow, Ningpo, and Shanghai. (3) Equal interaction between officials of corresponding rank. (4) British Consuls at each port. (5) Abolition of the Cohong monopoly. (6) A uniformly moderate tariff to be imposed on both imports and exports, and (7) Cession of the island of Hong Kong to be British territory.[22]

The opening of new ports brought greater prosperity to British opium traders that they had enjoyed before the war. The exchange of ratification of the treaty took place on June 26, 1843, when Chi-Ying paid a ceremonial visit to Hong Kong. On the same day, the island of Hong Kong with its dependencies was publicly proclaimed a British Colony. The treaty, which at last brought China into direct contact with the Western world, has been called the first of the unequal treaties imposed on China in the 19th century. It was unequal, indeed in the sense that most of its immediate benefits accrued to Britain.

THE ACQUISITION OF KOWLOON

Though the Treaty of Nanking put Anglo-Chinese relations on a new footing and dented the Chinese policy of exclusiveness, China did not intend to give the westerners all they wanted. More fighting and another peace treaty were needed to secure the settlement. In Canton and its neighbourhood, where villagers had rallied against the foreigners in the early period of the war, the treaty was very unpopular and there was resentment and protest. The ease with which the British had won their victory aroused a spirit of defiance for the Chinese, and particularly the Cantonese did not consider that they had been decisively beaten in a war which from the first to the last had engaged so few of China's armed forces.

According to the Treaty of Nanking, foreigners should have been allowed not only to have their own factories at Canton, but also to move freely within the Chinese city. This part of the treaty was not accepted by the Chinese. Foreigners were confined strictly to the factory areas. The Chinese city was closed to them, and there was instant trouble if any of them tried to rent a house on it. There were also many unruly elements in Canton and the neighbourhood, and British merchants had no guarantee for their personal safety. In spite of the Treaty of Nanking, unusual distrust and ill-feeling persisted between the Chinese and the English, and there were sporadic hostilities and skirmishes.

In 1858, while Canton was still under the effective control of an Allied Commission (composed of British and French troops), supported by an Anglo-Chinese garrison, an agreement was made whereby the Governor-General of two Guangs (i.e. Guangdong and Guangxi provinces), acting on behalf of the Chinese Government, granted a lease to Henry Smith Parks, the peninsula opposite Hong Kong island, which is the heart of Kowloon. The lease provided that so long as the British Government punctually paid the Chinese Government the annual rental of 500 silver taels, "no claim can ever be made for the return of the said ground."

The lease was, however, quickly superseded by the Convention of Peking, which was signed at Peking (Beijing) on October 24, 1860. The primary objective of the Convention was the enlargement of British commercial, diplomatic, and extra-territorial privileges in China. However, the opportunity was taken to compel the Chinese Government to formalise the status of the Kowloon peninsula by an outright cession of the territory to the Queen. However, the lease did not wholly disappear from view, for it is referred to in the text of the Convention by reference to the map which was annexed to it. The English text of Article VI of the Convention of Peking reads as follows:

> 'With a view to the maintenance of law and order in about the harbour of Hong Kong, His Imperial Majesty the Emperor

> of China agrees to cede to Her Majesty the Queen of Great Britain and Northern Ireland, and to her heirs and successors, to have and hold as a dependency of Her Britannic Majesty's colony of Hong Kong, that portion of the township of Kowloon, in the province of Kwangtung, of which a lease was granted in perpetuity to Harry Smith Parks, Esquire companion of the Bath, a member of the Allied Commission at Canton, on behalf of Her Britannic Majesty's Government, by Lan Tsung Kwang, Governor-General of the two Kwang.'

It further declared that 'the lease in question is hereby cancelled; that the claims of any Chinese to any property on the said portion of Kowloon shall be duly investigated by a mixed commission of British and Chinese officers; and the British Government to any Chinese whose claims shall be by the said Commission established should his removal be deemed necessary by the British Government.[23]

THE CONVENTION OF PEKING, 1898

The Convention of Peking, 1898, represented the successful conclusion of a well-organised campaign by the British commercial interests in Hong Kong. It was Paul Chater, a prominent Armenian businessman who helped to found the business enterprises in Hong Kong who clamoured for the acquisition of additional land. The Sino-Japanese war (1894-95), however, impelled Sir William Robinson, the then Governor of Hong Kong, for the acquisition of additional territory in Hong Kong. The victory of Japan in the Sino-Japanese war demonstrated with profound results the military weakness of China, and consolidated the successful modernisation of Japan.

When great powers like Russia, Germany, France, and Japan scrambled for a slice of territory in the Far East, to Great Britain it was primarily a matter of preserving her predominance in the Chinese market and framing a suitable policy to prevent, if possible, dismemberment of the Chinese empire. As the predominant power in China, Britain stood to lose most from the growing ambition of others. The issue before her was to preserve, in an age of competition, what she had gained in an age of monopoly. Acquisition of the New Territories was also pleaded on the ground that it was necessary to ensure efficient administration, protection, and for obtaining more land for cemeteries.

Making a strong plea for the acquisition of additional territories, Chater observed, "China is now at the lowest ebb, but 50 years, possibly 20 years hence, judging from the progress Japan has made, China will probably enable her to make use of the vast natural strength. If then the boundaries of Hong Kong are no more extensive than they are now, where will we be with a Chinese fleet in Kowloon Bay, and the hills and islands... at their mercy any moment.[24] Chater also referred to civil advantages from such an extension of territory. He pleaded that with the acquisition of New Territories, the Colony's population would have space to spread, industries would have space and water supplies, and Hong Kong might become independent as regards cattle, poultry, and vegetables. Robinson had arranged considerable support for his views on the subject, but there was originally little response from the Colonial Office. Pressure for the rectification of boundaries was, however, increasing for the armed services, and at the newly arrived and potentially hostile Japan.

OCCUPATION OF THE NEW TERRITORIES

The day chosen for the formal taking of possession of the New Territories was April 17, 1899. A public holiday was declared in the colony. But the population of the new British possession was less enthusiastic about the proceedings than was hoped for in the city of Victoria. From 2.50 pm on Sunday, April 16, the inhabitants of the New Territories became subjects of British jurisdiction. They conveyed their disrespect a short time later, however, by renewal of hostilities which had disrupted the great event.

THE WALLED CITY HONG KONG

While the British government was still undecided on the question of acquisition of the New Territories, the existence of the Walled City within the administrative jurisdiction of Chinese authorities often irked the colonial administration in Hong Kong. The Walled City was once a fort and administrative centre to the immediate north-west of a Chinese town called Kau Lung Gai (Kowloon City). This town was frequently condemned during 1890 as an obstacle to law and order in British Kowloon, and Hong Kong citizens seeking rectification on the Colony's boundaries constantly referred to it as an evil that should be overcome. It had a dubious distinction for gambling. The demoralising influence of gambling dens and the potential danger that it posed to Hong Kong perturbed the colonial administration and the citizens of Hong Kong. To the imperial Chinese government, the fort was an important center for civil and military administration. In 1898, the walled city was about a quarter of a mile from the seashore. Its fortified stone wall, built from 1843 to 1847 with an average height of 13 feet, and an average width of above 15 feet was almost the shape a parallelogram, and enclosed an area of 6½ acres. Inside were several public buildings, a reputed school, and a number of residences along with wide streets.[25]

If the walled city of Kowloon represented irreconcilable differences between China and the mercantile interests in Hong Kong, the vexed question of smuggling was an even more potent source of friction. China relied on the various taxes and duties levied on traded goods generally, but specifically opium, for much of her imperial and local revenues, and she had a commensurate interest in the proper collection of such fees. But Hong Kong's openness as a free port contiguous to Kwangtung favoured the development of smuggling operations so large and well-organised that Chinese revenue inevitably suffered, and all schemes designed to protect that revenue inevitably endangered the freedom of Hong Kong trade. The Chinese attempted to prevent the avoidance of duty on goods by establishing blockades. This originally consisted of two parts. In 1868, the Canton Viceroy opened stations near Kowloon for collection of Likin (a form of inland trade tax) on Chinese carried opium, and in 1871, the Hoppo at Canton established depots where the treaty tariff duty on opium could be paid. These depots later became the New Territories.

The Convention of Peking, 1898, extended the northern boundary of the Colony from just over two miles to 60 miles. On May 19, 1898, a draft agreement was prepared, and on June 9, the final treaty was signed. At first, the residents of Hong Kong were jubilant though somewhat dismayed at the reservation of Chinese jurisdiction in Kowloon city. Britain had no great difficulty in goading the imperial Chinese authorities to accept the extension in principal. But Yamen, the Chinese minister, contemplated a very limited grant of territory and hoped that British demands would go no further. When these demands did go further, involving over 350 square miles of territory, Chinese authorities suggested various other counter proposals to balance the British claim, and it was only through British compromise on other matters that they eventually agreed to lease the whole area.

The major compromise was over the Walled City and the reservation of its piers. Mac Donald, the British negotiator, conceded these with reluctance, but he had to do so if the main demand was to be achieved without friction and resort to threats. Other concessions were the railway clause and the right of Chinese vessels of war to use the waters of Mirs Bay and Deep Bay. The promise to take steps against smuggling was unpopular but essential for the speedy conclusion of the negotiations. Finally, the ministers successfully resisted Mac Donald's demand for an absolute cession by agreeing that other nations with Chinese leaseholds would follow suit. The Chinese managed therefore, to salvage something from the negotiations, though in practice the British 'concessions' have meant very little. A curious omission from the agreement was any mention of rent. In fact, no rent was paid by France, Germany, and Russia for their respective leaseholds.[26]

CULTURAL WAR, TRADE WAR, OR OPIUM WAR?

Although the war between China and Britain broke out primarily due to the contentious issue of opium, there are scholars who contest this view.[27] One of the earliest critics of the Opium war theory was John Quincy Adams, the Sixth President of the United States of America. In his address to the Massachusetts Historical Society in December 1841, Adams criticised those who argued that the British expeditionary force had been sent to China to fight for the interest of opium trade. The few thousand "Chests of opium imported by British merchants into China and seized by the Chinese government for having been imported contrary to law" were, according to him, no more the cause of war, than the throwing overboard of tea in Boston harbour was the cause of the North American Revolution."

Adams opined: "The cause of (opium) war is the Kowtow: the arrogant and insupportable pretensions of China that she will hold commercial interactions with the rest of mankind not upon terms of equal reciprocity, but upon the insulting and degrading forms of relations between lord and vassal."

One more scholar who shares the perception of Adams was WAP Martine, a US missionary-scholar who was the chief instructor of Peking's Foreign Language School. In his book, The *Awakening of China*, Martin observed that the opium war was "the result of a series of collisions between the conservative of the extreme Orient and the progressive spirit of the Western world." No less a person than the distinguished Sinologist John K Fairbank, in his classic work *Trade and Diplomacy on the China Coast,* also reflected the Occidental bias of the 'cultural war theory'. According to him, opium provided the occasion rather than the sole cause of the war." In hindsight, it seems that the cultural war theory of the Anglo-Chinese war of 1839-1842 bears a streak of resemblance with Samuel P Huntington's paradigm of 'Clash of Civilizations' which continues to dominate academic debate in recent times.

The second type of Western scholars are not willing to be so uncharitable to the victims of aggression. The late professor Victor Purcell of Cambridge University was one of the few British scholars who deeply understood Chinese sentiments and aspirations. Although he also subscribed to the cultural conflict theory and the middle kingdom there, he had no intention of singling out traditional China as the cause of the opium war. While conceding that "it was opium which finally brought China and Britain into collision, Purcell warns his readers not to forget, other subjects of dispute between the two nations, which eventually might have had the same outcome. The two examples of such subjects mentioned are 'the refusal of China to deal with other nations on equality', and the Sino-British differences in judicial conception and practices. To all this, Purcell adds another dimension. "England in 1840 was trade obsessed", and this obsession was created by the quest for 'foreign markets' as a result of the vastly increased "efficiency and output of her factories due to Industrial Revolution."[28]

Purcell's observations are a distant echo of the radical opinions expressed by George Marion. According to him, it was the triumph of industrial capitalism in Great Britain over merchant capitalism that led to drastic changes in the situation of China trade. The rush of private British traders to China, after the abolition of the East India Company's trade monopoly made the Chinese arrangements for foreign trade at Canton look very inadequate. He concluded that it was the Industrial Revolution, the principle of free trade, and the practice of free competition which had contributed to British intolerance of the commercial policies of China.

Hsin-Pao Chang offers another example of such a perspective. Chang observed that in the broad sense, the opium war was a clash between two cultures. One was agricultural, Confucian, stagnant, and waist-deep in the quicksand of a declining dynastic cycle. The other society was industrial, capitalistic, progressive, and restless. When the two met, conflicts were inevitable, and the defeat of China was equally inevitable.

THE CHINESE POSITION

Whatever may be the reason of the origin of the opium war, the Chinese have consistently questioned the validity of the treaties. China, for her part, while apparently having as strong an interest as Britain in maintaining the status quo, had from time to time felt the necessity of making her views explicit, thereby placing it on record that although Britain had been in possession of Hong Kong, China did not accept any British claim, express or implied, to permanent possession or sovereignty. The most formal statement of the Chinese legal position was contained in a letter dated March 10, 1972, addressed by the Chinese Ambassador to the United Nations to the Chairman of the Special Committee on Colonialism, with the object of removing Hong Kong and Macao from the list of territories falling within the Committee's terms of reference. It contained the following observation.

'The question of Hong Kong and Macao belong to the category of questions resulting from a series of unequal treaties which the imperialists imposed on China. Hong Kong and Macao are part of Chinese territory occupied by the British and Portuguese authorities. The settlement of the question of Hong Kong and Macao are entirely within China's sovereign right and do not at all fall under the category of colonial territories covered by the declaration on granting independence to colonial countries and people. With regard to the question of Hong Kong and Macao, the Chinese government has constantly held that they should be settled in an appropriate way when conditions are ripe.'[29]

The UN Decolonization Special Committee passed a resolution on June 15 the same year, suggesting the UN General Assembly to delete Hong Kong and Macao from the colony list. On November 8, 1972, the 27th UN General Assembly adopted a resolution approving the Special Committee's report.

NOTES

1. Jan Morris, *Hong Kong Epilogue to an Empire* (Penguin Books, 1990), p. 21.
2. Ibid p. 22.
3. Edgar Holt, *The Opium War in China* (London, 1964), pp. 36-37.
4. Frediric Wakeman, "The Canton Trade and the Opium War" in Dennis Twitchett and John K. Fairbank, (eds.), *The Cambridge History of China* (London, 1978) vol. X, p. 164.
5. Ibid. p. 164.
6. Tan Chung, *China and the Brave New World: A Study of the Origins of the Opium War* (Delhi, 1976), pp. 83-84.
7. Ibid., *Citing Bengal Commercial Reports* Vol. 13-52, p. 85.
8. K. N. Choudhury, "Foreign Trade and Balance of Payment (1757-1947)"; In Dharma Kumar (eds.), *The Cambridge Economic History of India* (New Delhi, 1970) Vol. 11, p. 846.
9. Holt op cit., p. 63.
10. Wekeman, n. 4, p. 172.
11. Ibid. p. 163.
12. Tan Chung, n. 6, p. 56.
13. Ibid. p. 43.
14. Hold, p. 35.
15. G.B. Endacott, *Government and People in Hong Kong* (1840-1962): *A Constitutional History of Hong Kong*, (Hong Kong, 1964) p. 9.
16. Wakeman n. 2, p. 175.
17. Flex Patrickuff, *Hong Kong at Cross Roads*, (London 1990), p. 16.
18. For details please see Arthur Wally, *The Opium War Through the Chinese Eyes*, (London, 1958).

19. Wakeman n. 4, p. 190-194.
20. Holt, n. 3, pp. 96-100.
21. *The Opium War.* (Foreign Languages Press, Beijing, 1976) pp. 52-63.
22. For detail please see Annexure 1.
23. Anthony Dicks, "Treaty, Grant Usage or Sufferance?" *China Quarterly* (London) Nu. 95. (September, 1983), pp. 427-55.
24. Peter Westley-Smith, *Unequal Treaty 1897-1997: China, Great Britain and Hong Kong's New Territories* (Hong Kong, 1980) p. 13.
25. Ibid., p.18.
26. Ibid., p.40.
27. For a details account of academic controversy please see Tan Chung, n. 6, pp. 1-2.
28. Ibid., quoting Victor Purcell China (London), pp. 53-54.
29. Joseph Y.S. Cheng and Richard Wong (eds.), *Hong Kong in Search of a Future* (Hong Kong, 1984), p. 54.

CHAPTER 2

Evolution of Colonial Administration in Hong Kong

After acquiring Hong Kong through the treaty of Nanking in August 1842, the colonial government focused on developing the administrative edifice of the governance structure of the colony. The succeeding British governors contributed in their own way for development of the administrative system with the twin objectives of maintaining law and order and in facilitating trade and commerce. Its founding governor Sir Henry Pottinger declared that the island would very soon become 'a vast emporium of commerce and wealth'.[1] While creating a congenial and conducive environment for promotion of trade and commerce, the interests of the ethnic Chinese were kept in mind. The colonial administration thus was not a despotic one, rather a benevolent one, if we set apart the causes and consequences of the 'Opium War'.

Lord Stanley, the Secretary of State for War and the Colonies, in a letter to Pottinger in June 1843 articulated his views that the function and purpose of Hong Kong was to serve as a diplomatic, commercial, and military post. Pottinger was told that he was mandated with three functions with regard to Hong Kong, viz., (i) negotiate with the Chinese Emperor, (ii) to superintend the trade of British subjects in China, and (iii) to regulate the internal economy of the colony. After possession of the territory, interim measures for the administration of the colony were pronounced in a series of letters and instructions, all dated January 4, 1843, addressed by Lord Aberdeen, the British foreign secretary to Pottinger. These dispatches directed him to make necessary arrangements for defence, and for the erection of forts for the protection of ships and of barracks to house the garrison. He was further told that if, as a result of the establishment of a free port and the introduction of these liberal arrangements by which foreigners would be encouraged to come, a great commercial entrepot was created, then His Majesty's Government would feel justified in securing the Crown the increased values the land would then have.[2]

Pottinger temporarily administered the territory through executive fiats in his capacity as Plenipotentiary and Superintendent of Trade. His opinion on the nature and structure of the government was sought, but before he could respond, decisions had to be taken by the British Government, partly because of the slow communication, and partly because some form of constitution had to be put in place when the cession of the island became operational after the exchange of ratification of the treaty. It was against this backdrop that Pottinger was asked to assume legislative power forthwith. A constitution for the colony was also drawn up. It was embedded in two documents – the Hong Kong Charter, dated April 4, 1843, and the Instructions to Sir Henry Pottinger.

COMPOSITION OF LEGISLATIVE AND EXECUTIVE COUNCILS

The first major task before Pottinger was the constitution of the Legislative Council and Executive Council in the territory in similar patterns as in other British colonies with minor variations to suit the local societal conditions. The Charter authorised the Governor to proclaim the territory as a separate colony and entrusted him the task to set up a Legislative and Executive Council. The Charter outlined the Constitution in a very rudimentary form. The Legislative Council was to consist of the Governor and such other persons to be nominated by him at the Royal pleasure. The Governor, with the advice of the Legislative Council, was empowered to make laws for peace, order, and good government of the colony subject to some limitations. It had to be exercised in accordance with any instructions given by the Secretary of State. It was subject to power of disallowance by the Crown by any ordinance either in whole or part, and Parliament retained the power of concurrent legislation over the colony. Not much was said about the Executive Council, except that it was to advise and assist the Governor.

These two documents established the constitution of the colony following the usual pattern of the Government and Executive and Legislative Council with control from London exercised by means of instructions to the Governor. The salient features of the constitutional arrangement for Hong Kong were that the Governor was given overriding power over the Executive and Legislative Council, which could discuss only such matters as he considered to place before them, and he could introduce and put into effect legislation contrary to their wishes, provided the Secretary of State was informed. The Governor could, therefore, act at his own volition as long as he enjoyed the confidence of the Secretary of State of the desirability of his policy. The Councils were deliberately kept small in number to enable the Governor to work with a few key officials most closely associated with him in the administration. There could be little formal debate or formality of any sort in a Council of three persons, with a quorum of two. The Councils were set up as matter of form but in reality, the Secretary of State exercised effective control through the Governor.

After proclamation of the Charter, the Legislative Council was constituted in August 1843. The nominated members were A.R. Johnston, J.R. Morrison, and William Caine. Johnston was earlier the Deputy Superintendent of Trade in the Office of the Superintendent of Trade at Guangzhou which was reorganized in 1836. He had also administered Hong Kong during the temporary absence of Pottinger. Morrison, the son of Robert Morrison, the first Protestant missionary to China, had also worked as Chinese Secretary and Interpreter to the Superintendent of Trade after the death of his father in 1834. William Caine had come to China with his regiment, the Cameroonians, in the 1840 expedition. He had experience in India as Deputy Judge-Advocate General at the East India Company. All the three were officials in the service of the Crown. They were also appointed members of the Executive Council and an accompanying proclamation allowed them to prefix their names with 'Honourable'.

Pottinger was succeeded by Sir John Davis on May 7, 1844, as Governor, Superintendent of Trade and Plenipotentiary. Davis earlier had lived in China for more than 30 years as a senior functionary of the British East India Company. As such, he had already earned a very good understanding and knowledge about China. He came to Hong Kong with a battery of civil servants recruited in England for senior positions in the colony's administration. Thus, almost after one year of the proclamation establishing the colony, there was a team of officials from which suitable members of the two Councils were selected. A major contribution of Davis was separation of the membership of the Executive and Legislative Councils. Under Pottinger, the Executive and Legislative Councils were together in the sense that the same officials were members of both the Councils.

Davis was succeeded by Sir George Bonhan who arrived in the colony in March 1848. The most important reform in Bonham's administration was the addition of two unofficial members to the Legislative Council in 1850. These important constitutional changes effected by Bontham were attributed to the recommendations of the 1847 Select Committee of the House of Commons on the China trade. The Select Committee had evinced considerable sympathy with the views of the merchants who had asked for representation and participation in the administration of the territory. After reviewing the China trade, the Committee recommended that a share in the administration of the ordinary and local affairs of the island should be given to the British residents. It also recommended that drafts of all new laws regulations of an urgent nature should be published for three to six months before they were finally enacted.[3]

In pursuance upon recommendation of the Select Committee, and in deference to the wishes of the British residents, Bonham decided to nominate two unofficial members to each of the two Councils. However, his proposal of nomination to the Executive Council did not find favour with the British government. On his recommendation, David Jardine, the nephew of Dr William Jardin, the founder of Jardine & Matheson; and JF Edgar were nominated to the Legislative Council in June 1850. Bontham's idea was that the nominated members would provide insight and inputs which would be useful to the government, and that residents could make their wishes known through them, and they would assist the government to explain its policy to the community.

Bonham was succeeded by John Bowring who took over the gubernatorial position in the colony in April 1854. A friend of Jeremy Bentham, the political philosopher regarded as the founder of modern utilitarianism, Bowring was greatly inspired by Bentham's political ideas. Bowring wanted to make the local legislature the institution of reform, for which purpose he wanted it to be augmented in membership and made it at least partly elective so as to be representative of the community. To Bowring, reforms of the Legislative Council were an essential condition for the success of his other reforms, which he was contemplating.

Bowring's governorship marked an important stage in the development of the Legislative Council, despite his failure to bring about electoral reform. Some of the major reforms which Bowering initiated included an increase in the number of unofficial members, the opening of the Council meeting to the public and greater control over finances, and importance given to the unofficial members. If the Imperial government had rejected the elections, it was not because it objected to governing the territory in accordance with the wishes of the community, but for the very opposite reason that elections would have given power to a privileged minority which might not have reflected the views of the inhabitants as a whole. The officials, by being divested of the responsibility to a narrow electorate, were able to take a broader view of the common interest, and their support was sought particularly on questions on which they had special knowledge, and their opposition was taken seriously.[4]

FIRST CHINESE MEMBER OF THE LEGISLATIVE COUNCIL

The appointment of the first Chinese member of the Legislative Council was made in 1880 on the initiative of Sir John Pope Hennessy, who was the Governor of the Colony from 1878 to 1882, as part of his policy of co-opting and conciliating the Chinese section of the population. The decision to give the Chinese community greater voice and participation in the Colony's administration was increasingly realised in view of their contribution to the economic prosperity, and augmenting the revenue of the colony through business and commerce. In the all-round expansion of the Colony's fortunes, the Chinese played a significant role. In January 1880, Hennessy appointed Ng Choy, a Chinese barrister as a temporary member of the Legislative Council. He argued that the time had come to place on the Council a man who fairly represented the interests of the Chinese community. It was recognised that Ng Choy was suited well to represent them.

Hennessy followed up his action by a proposal to recognise the Council to provide for permanent Chinese representation. He proposed to increase the Legislative Council to 11 members (six official and five unofficial), plus the Governor. To the stipulated four unofficial members, he suggested the addition of one, who was to be a Chinese. Since this purpose was made only nine days after the appointment of Ng Choy, clearly its objective was to provide him with a permanent seat. The nomination of Ng Choy as a temporary member was supported by the Secretary of State. However, in the colonial office minutes on Hennessy's dispatch, the arguments used against giving Ng Choy a permanent seat was not that if the Governor wanted to consult the Legislative Council secretly or if relations with China became strained, the presence of Ng Choy on the Council might be awkward. It was felt that if a Chinese was appointed to the Legislative Council, it ought to be a Chinese merchant. The importance of the mercantile interest thus received implicit official recognition.[5] Ngo Choy took his seat as the first Chinese member of the Legislative Council on February 19, 1880, and the occasion was marked by a deputation of the leading Chinese members of the Colony, who called at his Government House to congratulate the Governor on the appointment.

Sir John Pope Hennessy was succeeded by Sir George Bowen who arrived in the Colony in April 1883. Ngo Choy's term as a member of the Legislative Council was due to expire on January 21, 1883, and as he proposed to go on leave, a decision about his successor had to be taken. In fact, Ng Choy resigned at the expiry of the tenure of his seat. Bowen did not treat the question of a permanent Chinese member in isolation, but as part of a wider scheme of reforms of the Legislative Council, which he thought required a general overhaul. He considered that popular elections were not feasible in a heterogeneous community as Hong Kong. Instead, he suggested a change in the system of nomination by which members of the Council should be more representative of the public opinion and more responsible to it, by entrusting public bodies such as the Chamber of Commerce and the Bench of Justices of Peace with the power to make nominations. Bowen proposed that one if not two of the six unofficial members should be a Chinese. As the Chinese member of the Council, the Governor nominated Wong Shing who had English education from Hong Kong and the USA. He had been a member of the Chinese legation staff in Washington and was fully qualified to look at Chinese affairs with English and at English affairs with Chinese eyes.[6]

Wong Shing adopted a co-operative attitude which at least had the merit of demonstrating that no risk was likely to result from having a Chinese representative permanently on the Legislative Council. When his six-year term ended in 1890, he asked not to be reappointed. His place was taken by Dr Ho Kai who had been educated in England, where he had been called to the Bar and also had qualified in medicine. He attired as a European and was married to an English woman. On that account, he was not at first acceptable to the Chinese as their representative on the Council.

DEMAND FOR POLITICAL PARTICIPATION

In June 1894, some unofficial members of the Legislative Council, notably Sir Catchik Paul Chater, a prominent British-Indian businessman of Armenian descent from erstwhile Calcutta and the Chinese member Ho Kai initiated a petition signed by the Hong Kong rate payers to the Secretary of State asking for constitutional reform and greater participation of the people in the decision making processes in the colony. They pointed out that though the Hong Kong community had been composed of British merchants, traders and ship owners, they had a small share in the government of the Colony because the Legislative Council was controlled by an official majority, despite the fact that the senior officials often had only a short period of residence in the Colony, and were unable to feel the pulse of the people.

They pleaded that Crown colonies were given more liberal treatment by having unofficial members in the Executive Council and an unofficial majority in the Legislative Council and they must be subjected to the Imperial Parliament and to the Queen in Council, but argued that it was the common right of Englishmen to manage their local affairs and control the expenditure of the colony where imperial considerations were involved. The petitioners made two specific demands – they asked for free election of representatives of the British nationality in the Legislative Council, and a majority of such representative in the Legislative Council. They also asked freedom of debate for the official members.[7] The plea of the petitioners, however, did not find favour with the Colonial office on the ground that Hong Kong was not suited for any form of self-government because it was an imperial station with imperial interests on the borders of a foreign land.

The final outcome was that the composition of the Legislative Council was increased by two – one official member, representing the General Officers community, and one unofficial member. The latter, appointed in July 1889, was Wei Yuk. The first unofficial members of the Executive Council were J Bell, Irving of Jardine Matheson Company, and Catchik Paul Chater. They took their seats on October 22, 1896. Wei Yuk was born in Hong Kong, and was the son of a comprador of the Charter and Mercantile Bank of India, London, and China. He was also the first Chinese to be educated in Britain.

Though the attempt in 1894 to introduce larger reform of the Legislative Council of an elected majority of unofficial members was not successful, it aroused an undercurrent of desire for constitutional change. It was not until the Great War of 1914-18 that the demand for reform was again seriously raised. The important contribution of the colonial peoples to the war was acknowledged, and it buttressed their aspiration to a great degree of self-government within the Empire. Hong Kong could not remain unaffected by the prevailing ideas and impulses aroused by the war and the agitation for reform. There was demand to increase the number of unofficial members of the Executive Council and also for introduction of election to the Legislative Council. There was also a clamour to increase the number of unofficial members to 10 by the addition of four unofficial members, so as to create an unofficial majority in the Legislative Council. The demands were, however, rejected.

Meanwhile, the British government decided on a revision of the Letter of Patent and Royal Instructions in order to bring these constitutional instruments up to date. The instructions were issued on February 14, 1917. The composition of the Legislative Council remained fixed – eight officials including the Governor, and six unofficial members, of whom two were elected by the Chamber of Commerce and unofficial Justices of the Peace respectively, and the remaining four, two being Chinese, were nominated by the Governor.

CONSTITUTIONAL REFORM ASSOCIATION

Although the policy of giving political power to a few British residents in Hong Kong was again jettisoned, the demand for constitutional reform persisted. The continued pressure brought into existence a Constitutional Reform Association of Hong Kong, which was launched in May 1917. Its declared aims were promotion of greater representation of the public on the Executive and Legislative Councils, and putting pressure upon the British Government of the claims of Hong Kong to be represented on any imperial Council or association to be formed and the expression of its views on post-war trade policy, and generally the active support or promotion or criticism of all reforms and all matters of public interest and importance to Hong Kong. All British subjects were to be eligible for membership of the association.

The association did not show much prospect until the war was over. In December 1918, it announced a scheme of reforms based on the petition but revised in particulars. The association proposed for the principle of election instead of nomination by the Governor, except for the two Chinese members. The association also pleaded that the number of unofficial members of the Legislative Council should be increased from six to eight, the number of official members should be reduced from eight to seven, and that the six elected members should be elected, two by the chamber of commerce, one by the unofficial Justice of Peace, and three (one of whom should be a Portuguese) by those like to serve on juries or exempted.

KOWLOON RESIDENTS ASSOCIATION

Another organisation with a partly political objective, the Kowloon Residents Association, was formed in January 1921. Its aim was to form a body of residents who had collective and intimate knowledge of the mundane civic requirements of the local residents. The Constitutional Reform Association continued for a year or two, but soon lost its earlier enthusiasm. In May 1921, a joint meeting of the association was held to protest against the increase of house rate which had to further agitate for elected unofficial members on the Legislative Council. The agitation for reforms soon died down. When constitutional change did come, it was to give greater representation to the Chinese. As time went on, the disparity in numbers between the Chinese and European communities had become greater. The Chinese national feelings were also stirred by the Nationalist Party, the Kuo-min-tang (KMT), which pressed for abolition of extra-territorial rights, the retrocession of foreign concessions, tariff autonomy, and the general revision of the so-called 'unequal treaties'. It was against this backdrop that on July 9, 1926, Sir Chouson Chow, was appointed the first Chinese member of the Executive Council, following the death of Sir Paul Chater who had served on the Council. The appointment was made on personal grounds, but also to neutralise anti-British sentiment in China and inculcate loyalty of the native Chinese populace in Hong Kong.

Yet another signification step taken in the direction of demonstration and civic participation was the creation of the Sanitary Board in 1882. The Sanitary Board acquired unofficial members in

1886, two of whom were first elected in 1888. The Sanitary Board later developed into the Urban Council, and as such its constitutional importance could hardly be over-emphasized. Eventually in 1936, the Sanitary Board became the Urban Council; yet it came into being as a result of criticism from within the Government and not as a result of pressure from outside. The creation of the Urban Council did not stimulate any renewed interest among the electorate in the choice of its elected members. Only one candidate was nominated at the first election held on January 22, 1936. The first contested election did not occur until February 29, 1940, and there was another contest in 1941. The main interest in membership of the Urban Council was in the opportunity of serving an administrative apprenticeship.

HONG KONG UNDER JAPANESE RULE

Constitutional devolution and development of representative institutions suffered a temporary setback with the outbreak of World War II and its expansion to the Asia-Pacific. Hong Kong entered its centenary as a British colony in 1941, but there was no official commemoration. Before the end of the year, the British flag hoisted in the governor's house was replaced by the Japanese flag. According to Japanese military plans, Hong Kong had to be occupied because it was an important support base for the Chinese government as well as the sentinel of the British in the Far East.

The Chinese Nationalist government would have been pleased to see the end of British rule in Hong Kong, if the colony did not fall into Japanese hands. Whereas the British considered the colony an important commercial outpost in the Far East, the Chinese saw it as a symbol of Western imperialist domination and national humiliation. The question of the Colony's political status was therefore considered by the Chinese nationalist government not simply in geographic and economic terms but as a matter of prestige and national dignity. Prior to the outbreak of the Pacific War, the Chinese government had not attempted to challenge British rule in Hong Kong directly, even though one of the objectives of the nationalist leaders had been the recovery of Chinese territories added to foreign powers. The perpetual state of civil war, which prevailed until 1920s, the Chinese communist threat, and the Japanese aggression during the 1930s had dominated the political agenda in Nanjing.[8]

Early in the Pacific War, the British government had considered the possibility of political pressure from the Nationalist Chinese government and the United States. Senior officials from the colonial office suggested in mid-1942 that the British might have to return Hong Kong to Chinese rule as part of a general post-war settlement in the Far East, but the British attitude changed towards the end of the war. As British leaders turned their attention to the question of Britain's place in the post-war international order, the maintenance of British Far Eastern territories was seen as a matter of prestige crucial to the British Empire.[9] The British government's determination to hold on the British Far Eastern territories after the war, was clearly demonstrated during a meeting between Winston Churchill and Stanley Hornbeck, special adviser to the US Department of State in November 1943. Churchill told Hornbeck of Britain's intention to maintain political and administrative control of Hong Kong, using his famous 1942 Manson House speech, in which he declared that he was not His Majesty's Prime Minister "to preside over the liquidation of the British Empire".[10]

The change of government in Britain in 1945 did not fundamentally alter British colonial policy or the British position towards Hong Kong. The new British Labour government envisaged equal status of the colonies with other Commonwealth members and the establishment of democratic forms of government for these colonies. In fact, some section of the British foreign office, in the form of memorandum, suggested a number of possible solutions to the Hong Kong problem, including returning the colony to Chinese sovereignty in return for British administration and introducing democratic changes in the colony, as well as it remaining a free port and municipality of Hong Kong.

At the Yalta Conference in February 1945, at which China was unrepresented and Britain not fully consulted in that part of the discussions which concerned the Far East, Roosevelt urged in private conversations with Stalin that Hong Kong should be given back to China or internationalised as free port. Official opinion in the United States did not favour British retention of Hong Kong. A further factor against the British keeping Hong Kong lay in the hopes aroused by the 1943 treaty undertaking by Britain and the United States to end the 'unequal treaty' system and give up their special privileges and concessions in China. The Chinese hoped this would include Hong Kong, though the treaties made no reference to rendition of ceded territory.[11]

THE ABORTIVE CONSTITUTIONAL REFORM

With Japan's collapse in 1945, the British administration was restored in Hong Kong in May 1946. Sir Mark Young, the British Governor of Hong Kong who was interned in Formosa (Taiwan) assumed British administration in the colony on May 1. Immediately after assuming office in a broadcast, he announced his constitutional reform proposal. The Governor's proposal which came to be known as *Young Plan of Constitutional Reforms* envisaged setting up of municipal councils comprising of both elected and appointed members as well as more direct representation of unofficial members in the Legislative Council.

The *Young Plan* was still-born. Before the municipal bills were published on June 3, criticism from a very influential quarter surfaced. Landale, a senior unofficial member of the Legislative Council, in the course of the 1949 Budget debate objected to money being earmarked for the Municipal Council and urged that reform of the Legislative Council should come first. The whole basis of the *Young Plan* was scuttled by a resolution to the reform of the Legislative Council.

The resolutions were brought up on June 22, 1949, in a slightly amended form by Sir Man Kam Lo in the absence of Landale. On the question of elections, Sir Man Kam Lo argued that since the British occupation, the fundamental conception was that the government should concern itself with the welfare of the Colony as a whole without sectional or racial prejudice or distinctions. He thought no electorate could be devised to do justice to all sections and interests. The unofficial members of the Legislative Council represented the interests of the colony as a whole, and this remained the justification for the nomination of members.[12] The Young Plan was therefore shelved. The attitude of the British government was reflected in a statement given by Sir Alexander Grantham who succeeded Young. In short but succinct sentences, the Governor said, "We cannot permit Hong Kong to be a battleground for contending political parties or ideologies. We are just simple traders who want to get on with our daily rounds and common tasks. This may not be very noble, but at any rate it does not disturb others. We do not feel that we have a mandate to reform the rest of the world.[13]

NOMENCLATURE OF GOVERNMENT

Until June 30, 1997, Hong Kong was a Colony of Britain. Although accepting British administration in Hong Kong, China always objected to Hong Kong being called a Colony, practically, however, Hong Kong remained a British colony. As such, in formal terms, power was concentrated in the hands of a Governor chosen by the British Government, who directed the activities of the civil service and all acts of the government were carried out in his name. According to the constitutional documents of Hong Kong, the Letter Patent and Royal Instructions, the Governor was completely subjected to the control of the British government. The Secretary of State for Foreign and Commonwealth Affairs was empowered to issue directives to the Governor, and if the latter refused to obey, he was subject to removal by the former. In practice, however the Governor had almost complete freedom of action. According to Norman J Miners, an acknowledged authority on Government and Administration in Hong Kong, "the Governor may consult the Secretary of State in London, who in turn may offer suggestions and given advice, but the final decision rested with Governor.[14]

The Governor was formally appointed by the Queen. In practice, however, it was invariably the choice of the Prime Minister. The Governor was also nominally Commander-in-Chief of the British Forces stationed in Hong Kong. The Gurkhas from Nepal and other soldiers of the garrison were entirely under the control of the Major-General who used to be the commander of the British Forces. The two most important constitutional documents of the colony, the Letters Patent and Royal Instructions, empowered the Governor with formidable powers. These two constitutional documents enabled the British Governor to appoint members to the Executive and Legislative Councils and all judges and public officials, make grants of land, grant pardons to convicted criminals and dismiss or suspend any civil servant. In general, he bore complete responsibility for the peace, order and governance of the colony.

The Governor was required to obey the laws of Hong Kong, British laws which were extended to Hong Kong, and any instructions sent to him by the Secretary of State in London. But in practice as far as the domestic affairs of Hong Kong were concerned, the Governor had virtually complete autonomy. The only policy which had been imposed upon the Colony in past was the Secretary of State's insistence since 1965 that all convicted murderers sentenced to death should be reprieved.[15] In matters relating to foreign affairs, the Governor remained under the control of London.

In exercising his vast powers in local matters, the Governor in practice had to act under considerable restraints. On all important decisions, he had to consult the Executive Council, notwithstanding the fact that he could act against the advice given by the majority of its members. The last time a Governor is known to have rejected the view of the Executive Council was in 1948. A history of sort was created in the life of Legislative Council when in July 1995, a no-confidence motion was moved against Governor Chris Patten by the leader of Democratic Party, Martin Lee. The motion read, "As the Governor has seriously damaged the future of rule of law in Hong Kong, this Council expresses no confidence in Mr Christopher Patten, the Governor of Hong Kong" The motion, however, had no legal basis as the Governor was appointed by the Queen. On administrative matters, however, the Governor could hardly ignore the recommendations of the Secretary of State or the head or secretary of the department concerned. Through an extensive network of advisory committees, the colonial government has evolved the healthy convention of discussion and consultation with the general public. This in turn helped the government in articulating the feeling the pulse of the people and in gauging their mood.

EXECUTIVE COUNCIL

The Executive Council consisted of five civil servants, and 10 unofficial members. Four of these officials enjoyed the exclusive privilege of sitting in the Council meeting. These officials included the Chief Secretary, the Commander of British Forces, the Finance Secretary and the Attorney-General. The other officials and the unofficial were chosen by the Governor and were formally appointed to the Council with the approval of Secretary of State. All the unofficial members (except for Mr W Purves, the Chairman of the Hong Kong and Shanghai Banking Corporation and Dr Wang Gangwu, the Vice-Chancellor of University of Hong Kong) were also members of the Legislative Council or had retired from it after many years of service. Since 1986, two members had been selected from among the elected members of the Legislative Council. When

Chris Patten, the last British Governor, assumed power in Hong Kong; he brought about radical changes not only in the composition of both Executive Council and Legislative Council, but also in their relationship. He dispensed with the practice whereby membership of the Executive Council and Legislative Council overlapped in some cases.

LEGISLATIVE COUNCIL

Until 1985, the Legislative Council was entirely composed of civil servants and unofficial members selected by the Governor. There were no members who had won their seats in an election. This was changed in 1985 when 24 elected members joined the Council, 12 from functional constituencies and 12 indirectly elected from District Boards, the Urban Council and Regional Council. Two additional functional constituency members were added to the Council in 1988. In 1991 for the first time, 18 members were directly elected to the Legislative Council from a geographical constituency. In 1995, under Chris Patten's constitutional reform package, all 60 seats were opened to election, out of which 20 belonged to the geographical constituency. In the September election, the Democratic Party led by Martine Lee emerged victorious, securing a majority of the seats.

OFFICE OF MEMBERS OF EXECUTIVE AND LEGISLATIVE COUNCIL (OMELCO)

The Office of Members of Executive and Legislative Councils (Omelco) exists to provide secretarial, translation and research assistance to the appointed and elected members of the two Councils who are not civil servants. Before 1985, it was known as Umelco, the Office of Unofficial Members, but the term unofficial was subsequently dispensed with. Until 1989, a major activity of Omelco was the investigation of grievances and complaints by the members of the public against administrative decisions made by government officers. Most of these were later referred to the office of the Commissioner for Administrative complaints, but Omelco continued to receive a large number of inquiries, proposal for change, appeals against government decisions, and request for assistance.[16]

REGIONAL AND DISTRICT ORGANISATIONS

At the regional level, the Urban Council and Regional Council are responsible for providing municipal service to the population in urban areas and new territories respectively. Both Councils are statutory bodies and are financially autonomous. The major sources of income are fees, charges and rates collected from its areas. The Urban Council work through its executive department, the Urban Service Department where in the case of the Regional Council, its executive department the Regional Services Department.

The Urban Council consists of 40 Councilors, 15 elected from district constituencies, 15 appointed by the erstwhile Governor, and one representative member from each of the 10 District Boards. The Regional Council comprised 36 members. Twelve of them are elected directly from the 12 constituencies, and nine are elected from District Board in the Regional Council area. Its three ex-officio members are the chairman and two vice-chairman of the Heung Yee Kuk. The remaining 12 members are appointed by the Governor.

District Boards are statutory bodies established to provide an effective forum for public consultation and participation at the district level. There are 19 District Boards throughout the territory. They consist of appointed members, elected members from the constituencies and Urban Councilors or rural committee chairman. The elected members are in the majority. The boards have mainly an advisory role with substantial responsibility for the management of district affairs. In monitoring the government's performance and achievements, the District Boards discuss a wide range of matters affecting the well-being of residents in the districts. District Boards have also been allocated public funds for local, recreational and cultural activities and for minor environment work.

CIVIL SERVICE

Hong Kong has a very good reputation of an efficient administration and bureaucracy. The civil service provides the staff for all government departments and others unit of administration. It employs some 18,800 people, or about 7.7% of labour force in Hong Kong. The size of the service is growing by about two per cent a year in line with the expansion of service to the public. Some secretaries of branches are appointed to the Executive Council and the Legislative Council in their individual capacity.[17] Together with the Chief Secretary, the Financial Secretary and the Attorney General; they make up about one-third of the Executive Council membership. Ten civil servants of secretary rank and above earlier used to be members of the Legislative Council.[18]

The Sino-British Joint Declaration of 1984 provided that officers in the rank of Deputy Secretary and above have to be ethnic Chinese. Expatriates, however, in junior ranks could continue. The colonial civil service thus consisted of British Civil Services who occupied senior positions and non-ethnic Chinese including Indians. Under the Basic Law, China's mini-constitution for the Hong Kong Special Administrative Region (HKSR), top Civil Servants are to be appointed by Beijing at the nomination of the Chief Executive. In order to maintain change with continuity, the Chief Executive of HKSR Tung Chu Hwa, had said that he would retain few top civil servants.[19] Among the few such privileged expatriate civil servants who still enjoy the confidence of the Chinese government was Indian Haider Verma.[20]

JUDICIARY AND THE RULE OF LAW

Hong Kong had also earned a great distinction for its independent judiciary and rule of law. Historically, the legal system of Hong Kong was implanted from Britain in mid-nineteenth century as a result of British colonisation of Hong Kong. There are striking institutional similarities between the English and Hong Kong legal systems, prior to the handover. The Joint Declaration and the Basic Law provided that after transfer of sovereignty in 1997, the laws of Hong Kong will remain basically unchanged and the legal system will operate in much the same way as before. It seems that the bulk of Hong Kong law, such as, common law, property law, even criminal law can survive under Chinese rule, with the exception of the constitutional basis of the government which has now shifted from Letters Patent and Royal Instructions to the Basic Law. But in view of lack of constitutionalism in China, it is understandable that the people of Hong Kong have nagging doubts as to the prospect of rule of law in Hong Kong under Chinese rule.

THE INDEPENDENT COMMISSION AGAINST CORRUPTION (ICAC)

The ICAC was originally set up in 1974 after some notorious cases of corruption in the Police force had aroused public opinion to demand effective action. Its main function is to investigate all instances of bribery and corruption which come to its knowledge, both those involving civil servants and also the private sector, and to prepare cases for prosecution or disciplinary action. It also reviews procedures and administrative routines in government departments to minimise the opportunities for corruption practices, and conducts, publicity and propaganda campaigns to enlist the support of the public in the fight against corruption.[21]

The staff of ICAC is recruited without reference to the Public Service Commission, some on loan from the civil service, some directly on contract. Staff are paid at higher rates than equivalent grades in the Civil Service, but are liable to instant dismissal by the Commissioner without appeal if any suspicion arises about their conduct. The ICAC is separate from the civil service. It does not come under the supervision of any of the branch secretaries in the secretariat, apart from financial matters. The Commissioner at its head was directly responsible to the Governor and now to the Chief Executive of HKSR. Although, it is likely that ICAC would continue, but under the new dispensation it would be difficult to keep it aloof from political interference. Only time will prove if it can survive the handover of Hong Kong to Chinese sovereignty. The provisional Legislative Council appointed by China has dropped the word 'independent' and renamed it as the Commission for Clean Government.

NOTES

1. Jan Morris, *Hong Kong: Epilogue to an empire*, (Penguin Books, 1990), p. 26.
2. G.B. Endacott, *Government and People in Hong Kong*. (Hong Kong, 1984) p. 21.
3. Ibid., p. 44.
4. Ibid., p. 60.
5. Ibid., p. 94.
6. Ibid., p. 101.
7. Ibid., pp. 109-125.
8. James, T.H. Tang, 'World War to Cold War: Hong Kong's Future and Anglo-Chinese Interactions, 1941-55. 'Ming K. Chan, (ed.) *Precarious Balance: Hong Kong Between China and Britain* (New York, 1994), p. 109.
9. For details please see Steve Yiu-Sang Tsang. *Democracy Shelved: Great Britain China and Attempts at Constitutional Reforms in Hong Kong*, 1945-1952, (Hong Kong, 1988) pp. 293-309.
10. C. Eade (ed) *Winston Churchill War Speeches (II)*, (London, 1960), p. 344.
11. Endacott, n. 2, p. 181.
12. Ibid, pp. 182-195.
13. Harold Ingrams, *Hong Kong* (London, 1952), p. 151.
14. Norman J. Miners, "Constitution and Administration" in Richard Y.C. Wong and Joseph Y.S. Cheng (eds) *The Other Hong Kong Report 1990*, (Hong Kong 1990) p. 1.
15. Ibid, p. 4.
16. Ibid, p. 12.

17. Ibid.
18. *Hong Kong: The Facts Government Structure*, (Government Printers, Hong Kong 1990), p. 6.
19. *The Asian Age*, New Delhi, 19.2.1997.
20. *The Hindustan Times*, New Delhi 2.7.97.
21. Miners n. 14, p. 25.

CHAPTER 3

Rise of Hong Kong as a Commercial and Trading Centre

Along with the development of an administrative structure, Hong Kong also started emerging as a premier commercial and trading hub in what the British called the 'Far East.' In fact, the primary objective of developing an administrative structure in Hong Kong was, as noted earlier, to give a boost to trade and commerce in the territory once described as 'Barren Island' by no less than the British foreign secretary Lord Palmerston. The colonial government in Hong Kong was a minimalist government. The basic aim of the government was to maintain law and order so as to promote trade and commerce. Before the arrival of the British, the Chinese population of Hong Kong island consisted of mostly fishermen farmers, and stone-cutters. They lived in villages scattered throughout the island. In June 1839, the British fleet and merchant ships began to arrive in Hong Kong. This attracted many boatmen, labourers, artisans, and adventurers from adjacent areas of the mainland, who earned livelihood by supplying the British with provisions and other services.

The proclamation of the British Superintendent of Trade, Captain Charles Elliot in 1841 promised that all Hong Kong inhabitants would enjoy full security and protection; that the Chinese on the island were free to practice their own religions; ceremonies, and social customs; and that in the free port of Hong Kong, all vessels were free from import and export duties. To avoid the disruptive conditions around Canton during the Opium War, a number of European merchants began to relocate their offices to Hong Kong. The whole establishment of Superintendent of Trade was transferred from Macao to Hong Kong in February 1842, which further lured some leading British merchants to shift their trade headquarters from Macao and Canton to Hong Kong. In May 1841, the island had an estimated Chinese population of 5,650, which by March 1842 had increased to 12,361, the total population (including foreigners) being over 15,000.[1] The densely populated Canton region though fertile, experienced constant pressure on land and food resources. Poverty forced many Chinese labourers and artisans to move to Hong Kong in search of employment opportunities. Many of these early migrants were adventures prepared to take risk to work for a living. The Treaty of Nanjing of 1842 (Annexure 1) which concluded the war forced China to cede Hong Kong to Britain in perpetuity.

EMERGENT ENTREPOT

Subsequently, the development of the colony as a trading port was carried out at a brisk pace. Buildings of all kinds were constructed, including commercial houses, government offices, private residences, warehouses, markets, and hospitals. The great demand for labour was quickly met by ample supplies from the Chinese mainland, particularly Guangdong province. The island's population had increased to 23,817 by June 1845.[2] The total sea-going tonnage entering and leaving Hong Kong which was 11,64,640 tonnes in 1859, had increased by 1878 to 52,09,437 tonnes; the population rose from 86,941 (including 85,280 Chinese in 1859) to an estimated 1,39,144 in 1876, of which 1,30,168 were Chinese. The Hong Kong Chamber of Commerce was founded in 1861, and the Hong Kong and Shanghai Banking Corporation in 1865. Modern amenities were introduced, the city was the first lit by gas in 1864, the first large company which became the Hong Kong and Whampoa Dock Company was founded in 1864.[3]

Hong Kong's strategic location, midway between Asia and the Pacific, and its deep natural harbour greatly facilitated it to emerge as an entrepot, attracting traders and businessmen from world over. Hong Kong retained its permanent status as an important entrepot until the Second World War. Over two-third of Hong Kong's trade was with China. However, the outbreak of Korean War in June 1950 inflicted a serious jolt to Hong Kong's trade with China and Hong Kong's role as an important entrepot.

In January 1951, Britain supported a UN resolution introduced by the United States in condemning the People's Republic of China as an aggressor in Korea. In May, the UN General Assembly adopted a resolution on strategic embargo. In June, the British government imposed licence controls on all exports to China and Hong Kong. The Colony, together with Macao, was blacklisted because China could break the embargo by obtaining Western goods through its traditional trading connection with both places. The embargo was extremely serious for the Colony. In addition to economic difficulties, the Colony was burdened by a massive inflow of refugees from China. Such was the adverse effect on Hong Kong's economy that many visiting journalists to the Colony sent home gloomy dispatches that predicted "the early demise of the Colony."[4] Be that as it may, Article 114 of the Basic Law stipulates that the Hong Kong Special Administrative Region shall maintain the status of a free port and shall not impose any tariff, unless otherwise prescribed by law.

MANUFACTURING CENTRE

Besides being an entrepot, Hong Kong has had a reputation of being a manufacturing center. The influx of refugees from the mainland brought capital and labour, which facilitated the manufacturing center. At some point of time, manufacturing was the largest sector of Hong Kong's industrial sector. Later, however, the migration of many large and labour-intensive industries to mainland China resulted in the loss of manufacturing in the territory. Certain factors such as scarcity of land, absence of mineral resources, the high cost of labour, and the proximity to China have ruled out heavy industry or other land and labour-intensive industries in Hong Kong. Prior to the 1980s, Hong Kong produced mainly labour-intensive consumer products such as food, beverages, clothing, textiles, and metal products. Being a resource and land-rich country with a low wage labour force, China became a natural choice for Hong Kong industrialists to continue with their labour and land-intensive industries in China itself. The seamless connectivity between mainland China and Hong Kong creates a synergy between the two. Hong Kong industries largely are small-scale operators. They are involved in certain manufacturing processes pertaining to exporting goods produced in China by Hong Kong owned enterpriseas. This process can involve the packaging of goods produced on the mainland. However, there are still export-oriented industries that produce textiles, electronics, plastics, watches and clocks, etc. The textile industry is the largest, followed by electronics.

A major chunk of the industrial sector in Hong Kong is the construction industry. The constant investment in infrastructure, and private sector investment in housing and commercial establishments makes construction a viable industry in Hong Kong. The industry has at times gone through periods of expansion and contraction for political and economic reasons since the 1980s. The smooth handover of the territory to the People's Republic of China in 1997 spurred the involvement of private and commercial construction projects in 1998 and 1999. Article 120 of the Basic Law enshrines that all lease of land granted, decided upon, or renewed before the establishment of the Hong Kong Special Administrative Region which extends beyond

June 30, 1997, and all rights in relation to such leases, shall continue to be recognised and protected under the laws of the HKSR.

FINANCIAL CENTRE

During the 1970s, Hong Kong emerged as a major financial city of the world. The demand for 'total banking' – a package of integrated banking and other complementary or ancillary financial services had been in existence for some time in Hong Kong and the Asia-Pacific region as their economies became more developed and affluent. These services were more sophisticated and complex and could not be handled entirely by indigenous financial institutions. Multinational banks and other financial institutions were well poised to fill this requirement. Hong Kong possessed nearly all the attributes of a viable financial center which attracted a host of international banking and non-banking financial institutions. In terms of locational and physical features, Hong Kong's advantage is well-established. The city is centrally situated in the Asia-Pacific region, supported by a network of excellent transport and communication facilities. Its proximity to mainland China – of which it is now a territorial part – acted as a magnet for multi-national firms, both financial and non-financial that set an eye on the vast China market. Its time-zone position and flexible working hours enable it to engage in arbitrage operations between the Atlantic and Pacific.[5]

Financially, Hong Kong is embedded with a free exchange market, a prudent financial system and low rates, a simple tax structure, and a relatively stable currency. These have been promised by the Sino-British Joint Declaration of 1986 and the Basic Law. While Hong Kong is by no means a tax haven, its rates – despite some upward adjustments during the post-war period – are substantially lower than those in most other countries.

All these have facilitated the emergence of Hong Kong as the world's third largest financial centre after New York and London, and the fourth largest if measured by the number of off-shore loans that originated there. However, some observers feel that Hong Kong may lose its role as a great financial centre. After all, much of Hong Kong's financial role had derived its attractiveness from its openness to international financial flows in a region of previous tight controls of capital markets. As other cities like Tokyo and Taipei liberalise and seek to become financial centres, Hong Kong is likely to lose its special advantage. The Basic Law of Hong Kong Special Administrative Region, however, protects Hong Kong's uniqueness and financial autonomy. So, there used to be no fear from that count, however, the situation has deteriorated in recent years.

The Basic Law also provides that Hong Kong Special Administrative Region may participate in international organisations and international trade agreements using the name 'Hong Kong, China'. In 1986, Hong Kong became a separate contracting party to the General Agreement on Tariffs and Trade (GATT). When the World Trade Organization (WTO) was established in January 1995 replacing GATT, Hong Kong became one of the founding members. Hong Kong also became a member of the Customs Cooperation Council, subsequently renamed as the World Customs Council in 1987. Hong Kong is also a member of the Asia-Pacific Economic Cooperation (APEC) in 1991. Article 112 of the Basic Law provides that no foreign exchange control policies shall be applied in the Hong Kong Special Administrative Region and that the Hong Kong dollar shall be freely convertible. The government shall safeguard the free flow of capital within and outside the region.

SERVICE CENTRE

The late 1980s and the 1990s witnessed the take-off of the services sectors in Asia-Pacific. Complex cross-border trade and investment deals, government's efforts to create and enforce modern tax systems, the rising role of stock markets and their associates, and a host of other developments created an explosion of demand for high-level, cosmopolitan, regionally-oriented service for accountants, lawyers, information specialists, and consultants. Hong Kong and Singapore are the financial hubs playing a significant role – a role Hong Kong continues to play even under Chinese sovereignty, but it is undergoing considerable stress in the post-handover period, a subject which is discussed at appropriate places in the book.

The economic reforms and opening up of mainland China that began in the late 1970s provided new opportunities for entrepreneurs in Hong Kong. Since then, a large part of the manufacturing sector in Hong Kong had been relocated north of the border to take advantage of the much cheaper labour and land cost. As a result, the manufacturing sector in Hong Kong shrank while the service sector expanded very rapidly. While manufacturing accounted for 23.7% of GDP in 1980, in 1992, it accounted for only 13.7%. In the labour market, manufacturing employed 46% of the workers in 1980, but this share had fallen sharply to only 20.5% in 1993. On the other hand, the services sector had assumed much greater importance in both GDP and employment by early 1990s.[6] Trade in service between the Mainland and Hong Kong is extremely important. Conceptually, the re-export margin that Hong Kong earns through entrepot trade in fact represents the export of services. Such services are embodied in the goods sold, however, and are normally recorded in trade statistics as export of goods rather than export of services. It is estimated that half of foreign law firms in Hong Kong provided legal advice on China's trade.

Hong Kong also provides crucial services as an entrepot and trans-shipment centre for China. It is estimated that in 1990, Hong Kong's trans-shipment of goods to and from China via Hong Kong amounted to 4 to 6% of China's imports and exports by value. Hong

Kong's trading firms also perform a valuable brokerage role for China's direct trade, which is roughly 7% of China's overall trade. Hong Kong is also the foremost gateway for foreigners entering China. Visitors to Hong Kong accounted for roughly two-thirds of China's tourist arrivals as well as expenditure in the early 1990s. Although China has increased its direct air links with other countries since 1979, the percentage of foreign tourists arriving and leaving China via Hong Kong has grown considerably since 1982. The outbreak of Covid-19 and it's aftermath have, however, affected the tourist footfalls in Hong Kong.

MAINLAND CHINA AND HONG KONG

Historically, Hong Kong and the mainland China were separated – both economically and politically – for more than 150 years. And yet, in all these past years, they have depended heavily on each other, especially economically. First, China has been an important source of human capital and supplier of natural resources for Hong Kong during the latter's post-war economic development process. So crucial was Hong Kong's trade with China that it was described as its life-blood. Since the late 1940s, there had been a large influx of mainlanders into Hong Kong, and they have supplied the labour market with an abundance of skilled and unskilled labour. As a result, wages could not rise beyond a point in the territory, compared with other developing countries. Hundreds of wealthy people of Shanghai and foreign business people, who fled to Hong Kong before the Communist takeover, brought capital and business experience. They bought looms from Japan and the United States and set up textile factories. Soon, the Colony started exporting so much clothing that Britain was constrained to put quotas on imports from Hong Kong to protect British industry.[7]

While Hong Kong served China as a window to the outside world, the territory has been dependent on the mainland for foodstuff and even drinking water. Poor land structure has limited Hong Kong's agricultural development. Therefore, 80% of all agricultural stuff and food products are imported, and 50% of these imports come from the mainland. An additional consideration is that raw material and consumer goods from the mainland are 25-50% cheaper than those from other sources.[8] The slow increase in local wages and the low price of imported raw material and food products have contributed to the high competitiveness of Hong Kong's exports in the world market. The mainland has also played an important role in Hong Kong's import and export business over the years. At the end of 1940s, communist China's internal chaos caused it to isolate itself from the rest of the world, and Hong Kong, because of its geographic position, became China's only link with the rest of the world. The volume of trade between Hong Kong and the mainland China grew at an average annual rate of 53% between 1949 and 1951. Re-exports from Hong Kong to the Chinese mainland grew even more, however, and this re-export experience was the foundation of Hong Kong's role as an important entrepot in the world market later on.

After Second World War, China conducted most of its trade through Hong Kong and Hong Kong-China trade recovered to pre-war levels. China's feverish buying prior to, and during the Korean war, and the closure of major Chinese ports after the 1949 revolution, led to Hong Kong's exports to China trebling during the period 1948-50, representing 38 per cent of total Chinese imports. Hong Kong's imports from China also rose to 25% of total Chinese exports in 1950. However, the United Nations embargo on the export of strategic commodities to China on May 18, 1951, following China's entry into the Korean War, led to a sharp fall in Hong Kong's exports to China. The United States' ban on all imports from China also led to a stagnation in Hong Kong's imports from China in the early 1950s and Hong Kong's share of imports fell from 25% in 1950 to 4% in 1955.[9]

In addition to the United States embargo, the Communist takeover of power in China resulted in a drastic cut in the import of consumer goods, and also a reorientation of China's trade to communist countries. Trade between Eastern Bloc countries tended to be state-to-state direct trade, and China arranged most of its purchases of capital goods through East Berlin. Hong Kong's exports to China continued to fall throughout the 1950s. After the Sino-Soviet rift in early 1960s, China reoriented its trade to capitalist countries. However, most of China's imports were wheat and capital goods, which were handled directly by China's state trading companies, and Hong Kong's exports to China continued to fall in the 1960s. In 1970, Hong Kong's exports to China were less than 0.5% of China's imports. The picture of Hong Kong's imports from China was rather different. China's need to earn hard currency meant that it had to continue to export to Hong Kong. Hong Kong's import from China grew in the late 1950s, representing some 11% of China's exports. In the 1960s, following the Sino-Soviet rift, China's exports to Hong Kong grew absolutely as well as relatively. In 1966, just before the Cultural Revolution, Hong Kong's imports from China represented 21% of China's exports and 27% per cent of Hong Kong's imports.[10]

China's total export and import to Hong Kong stagnated in the period 1966-70 due to the Cultural Revolution, and China's share of Hong Kong's imports fell to 16% in 1970. The rapprochement with the United States in the early 1970s brought about another expansion of China's total exports and its exports to Hong Kong during 1970-75. After 1977, trade between China and Hong Kong started to grow rapidly. During the period 1978-1984, the average annual growth rate was 42.8%, of which imports from mainland China grew by an average of 32.2%, and exports to the mainland by an average of 175.6%. Entrepot trade also expanded by an annual average of 149.3% during the same period.[11]

ROLE OF HONG KONG IN CHINA'S MODERNISATION

The trade growth was due to mainland China's modernisation programme, which began with the economic reform of 1978. Changes in economic policies and strategies forced China to depend heavily on foreign capital and technology. Given Hong Kong's geographic location and its rise as an important financial and trade hub in the world market, the territory played a crucial role in the mainland's development and modernisation. Much before China's adoption of open-door policy in the late 1970s, there was active cooperation between Hong Kong government and the authorities in the neighbouring parts of China on a number of issues, notably immigration.

The relationship started to develop more rapidly following the adoption of more liberal economic policies in China, designed to accelerate the pace of economic modernisation by encouraging both foreign trade and foreign investment. Hong Kong was well placed to benefit from these policy changes and to make a major contribution to China's modernisation drive. It had, by a great margin, the best deep-water port anywhere on the China's coast and the only one in South China. Its container port was already the third best in the world. It had skilled and a well-educated work force, which had been built up in a different competitive working environment. Above all, it had well-developed trading and other commercial links with rest of the world, including excellent transport and communication links. These attributes were precisely those China needed access to if its bid for modernisation through contact with the outside world was to succeed. China's modernisation drive thus gave a further impetus to trade between mainland China and Hong Kong.

For a long time, Hong Kong has been China's largest export market, and China has been the largest or the second largest (after Japan) supplier of goods to Hong Kong. In 1980s, 27% of China's exports were to Hong Kong, and imports from China accounted for

25% per cent of Hong Kong's imports. However, coinciding with the liberalisation of China's economic policies, the pattern of trade changed. During China's post-liberalisation period, it imported a substantial quantity of products from Hong Kong. Yet another noticeable feature of bilateral trade between mainland China and Hong Kong was that while Hong Kong had long been China's largest trading partner, in the liberalisation period, China overtook the United States to become Hong Kong's largest trading partner.

Some analysts had predicted that Hong Kong's role in China's foreign trade would diminish with the development of direct trade and economic relationships between China and the developed world. The impressive growth in Hong Kong's re-export trade in China's post open-door policy period was one indication of how misplaced these predictions had been. Although China's infrastructural problems have been solved to a large extent in later years, in the early 1980s, China had an acute infrastructural problem. Hong Kong provided the much-needed infrastructural support to China. So, China's open-door policy, instead of diminishing the importance of Hong Kong, further reinvigorated its importance. The managers of the Chinese economy at every level and those doing business with China knew very well that they could either find or obtain rapidly through Hong Kong anything they needed – from advanced machinery to finance for a major project to consumer items for expatriate staff working in China.

Hong Kong's imports of Chinese goods in 1993 was around $49.8 billion, 94% of which were re-exported to third countries and only 6% being retained in the territory. Although China is by far the foremost supplier of Hong Kong's re-exports, representing 58% of the total, China's share of Hong Kong's imports stagnated since 1987, falling to 6% of the total and behind Japan, the United States, and Taiwan. This was because China had been unable to capture the higher end of Hong Kong's market, which is traditionally dominated by Japan. Hong Kong was the largest financial market (excluding Chinese exports via Hong Kong) for Chinese exports in the late 1960s and early 1970s, when Japan and the United States began to dominate. China continued to regard Hong Kong as its largest market until 1992, when it began reclassifying exports meant for third countries. As a result, in 1993, Hong Kong's imports from China accounted for 54% of China's total export, 51% of which were re-exports, only 3.3% being retained in Hong Kong.

Although China was the largest market for Hong Kong products, Hong Kong was only the fourth largest supplier to China after Japan, the United States, and Taiwan. In 1993, the share of Hong Kong in China's imports was 8%. It may be noted that China regarded Hong Kong as its largest supplier from 1987 to 1992, when Chinese trade statistics began to trace incoming exports from third countries via Hong Kong. In 1993, Hong Kong's total exports (including both re-exports and domestic exports) thus accounted for 42% of China's imports in 1993.[12] Prior to Deng's economic liberalisation, the sum total of Hong Kong-China trade was $3.4 billion. By 1996, it had grown to $134.6 billion. Befor the handover, China accounted for 34% of Hong Kong's total exports, including re-exports. Conversely, Hong Kong handled over half of China's total exports, and almost 58% of Hong Kong's re-exports originate in China. As the key entrepot centre and hub of global finance and networking, Hong Kong has contributed to more than a third of China's huge foreign exchange reserve that now exceeds $ 14 trillion.[13]

CHINA-TAIWAN TRADE VIA HONG KONG

Besides the bilateral trade between mainland and Hong Kong, the territory also occupies considerable importance as a conduit through which China trades with Taiwan. China, however, does not recognise Taiwan. Officially, Taiwan has banned trade with Mainland China since 1949, although certain government agencies are allowed to buy mainland commodities via Hong Kong. However, the products purchased from mainland China are limited to those that are either unavailable locally or whose local supply is inelastic.

The growth of Taiwan-China trade through Hong Kong has been phenomenal, particularly between 1980 and 1984, during which period the indirect trade between the two was 139%.[14] . At one point of time Taiwan was the leading source of Hong Kong's re-exports of the mainland since 1980, and Taiwan's domestic role in the re-export trade is primarily attributed to the competitiveness of its products compared to those from Japan and South Korea. The comparative closer and stronger ties between traders in Taiwan and Hong Kong have also helped promote the trade. In recent years the strained political relations between China and Taiwan has also resonated in their bilateral trade and economic engagement.

In addition, the political policies and tactics adopted by China have also influenced indirect trade, as China wanted to create an impression, both domestically and internationally that the political unification of mainland China and Taiwan has been going on through an expansion of indirect trade through Hong Kong and Macao since 1978. This policy became obvious in 1980 when China removed the export tax on mainland products sold to Taiwan and the import duties on Taiwan goods. Consequently, indirect trade grew by as much as 1,032% that year.[15]

Besides the indirect trade, what is not well known is that despite the official ban on direct trade, there is, in fact, substantial direct trade between Taiwan and the Mainland. This direct trade usually involves the switching of trade documents. Taiwanese exporters claim that their goods are destined for Hong Kong when the goods leave Taiwan; however, on arrival in Hong Kong, trade documents are switched, and the claim is made that the goods are destined for the Mainland. Because the goods are consigned to a buyer on the Mainland, they do go through Hong Kong. Hong Kong Customs and

Hong Kong firms claim legal possession of the goods. Such goods are regarded as trans-shipment or 'cargo in transit' by the Hong Kong government, and are not regarded as part of Hong Kong's trade.

Such trade is called 'direct' trade because it looks like indirect trade in terms of trade documentation, involving two separate sets of trade documents, but it is direct trade in reality because no third party buys the goods involved for resale. By switching trade documents, Taiwanese exporters save on the cost of Hong Kong Custom fees and taxes, which are actually quite minor, amounting to 0.1% of the value of goods traded. This direct trade also has the advantage of confidentiality because Hong Kong Customs had no records of the trade, and it is very difficult for anyone to find out who has sold what to whom.[16]

This direct trade has three modalities – trans-shipment, transit shipment, and illegal direct shipment. Trans-shipment involves the uploading and downloading of cargo from one vessel to another, usually in Hong Kong waters. Because Taiwan does not permit cargo to be carried between Taiwan and the Mainland in the same vessel, and there is no regular shipping between Taiwan and the Mainland, trans-shipment is the dominant mode of direct trade. The Hong Kong government maintains statistics on the volume of trans-shipment by weight but not by value, because trans-shipped goods do not clear Hong Kong Customs.

Transit shipment refers to a process whereby ships stop in Hong Kong waters on their way to and from Mainland, and do not trans-ship their cargo, which proceeds in the same vessel. This practice was developed from October 1988, when Taiwanese law allowed chartered ships and airplanes plying the flags of third countries to sail or fly between Taiwan and the Mainland, as long as they stopped in a third place in the voyage, and their cargo or passengers did not continue in the same vessel or plane. Yet because in practice, it is difficult for Taiwanese authorities to verify which cargo has changed vessels or not, Taiwanese chartered ships generally merely stop in Hong Kong waters, where their contents are treated by the Hong Kong government as cargo in transit, and then continue the journey without trans-shipping their cargoes. This practice offers considerable cost and time savings as no downloading and uploading are involved. The Hong Kong government does not keep statistics on cargo in transit. Illegal direct shipment involving chartered ships flying flags of third countries is common. Although illegal direct shipment obviously saves transportation costs, it is rising because shipping records are public information and the Taiwan government can check if the ships have passed through Hong Kong or the third port. Ships have been fined for illegal direct shipment.

Bilateral trade between Mainland China and Taiwan has political significance as well. It is a bridge to promote political dialogue between Mainland and Taiwan. In fact, it created the groundwork for political contact. No wonder, therefore, that even after Hong Kong's reversion to Chinese sovereignty, China has urged Taiwan not to block trade with Hong Kong. China has been 'magnanimous', claimed the official news agency *Xinhua*, in allowing Taiwan to maintain offices in Hong Kong after the territory's reversion to Chinese sovereignty on July 1, 1997. "Permitting such contact benefits to both Hong Kong and Taiwan shows China's commitment to preserving Hong Kong's autonomy under 'one country, two systems' formula." *Xinhua* also estimated that Taiwan and China passed goods worth $24 billion through Hong Kong through Hong Kong, and trade among all three totaled $33 billion.[17]

HONG KONG'S INVESTMENT IN CHINA

In addition to the bilateral trade between Mainland China and Hong Kong, investment made by Hong Kong in Mainland China also contributed a great deal towards China's development. The major share of Hong Kong's investment in Mainland China, however, went to neighbouring Guangdong province, including in the Shenzhen Special Economic Zone. This region lies to the north of the Lo Wu border crossing from Hong Kong. Once a collection of sleepy villages of less than 50,000 people, over the years Shenzhen has become a bustling manufacturing city of two million. It is accessible by frequent train and bus from Hong Kong, as well as by private boat.

Since China's economic reform began in 1979, Guangdong, with Hong Kong's management, finance, technology, and marketing has achieved an average annual real growth of over 12%.[18] Such spectacular growth is not the fruit of Guangdong's efforts alone, but rather the result of a gigantic joint venture between Hong Kong and Guangdong. Before economic reforms and the associated opening of Hong Kong, Guangdong was one of China's poorer provinces, starved of infrastructure investment by a Beijing leadership whose allegiance was firmly to the interior of China. Guangdong had even lost some infrastructure, removed and relocated to the interior by Beijing on the grounds that China's security required important national assets to be placed safely inland, far from a coast that was vulnerable to the imperialists. Guangdong's principal asset remained a vast network of overseas Chinese businessmen, many of whom had family roots in the villages of Guangdong, and still felt ties to their ancestral homeland.

Hong Kong and Guangdong were a perfect fit. Hong Kong had money, management talent, marketing expertise, worldwide network, and technology. Not only that there is seamless connectivity between the two but also a synergy, one reinforcing the other. Yet success was pushing wages and real estate prices so high that the territory was becoming uncompetitive in most of its traditional industries. Guangdong's land and labour cost only 10% of the Hong Kong rate, but the province was desperately short of all skills, money, and technology that were Hong Kong's forte. Bringing them together is like a force multiplier. Most of the early deals involved, for example, a Hong Kong company providing free machinery and materials to a

Guangdong enterprise in return for the right to manage the enterprise, and to receive a certain amount of final products like jeans, toys, plastic bags for a certain number of years.

Beijing gave Guangdong special privileges to move faster in domestic reforms and in foreign trade than the rest of China, and it gave a very flexible mandate for Guangdong's reforms so that local officials could proceed pragmatically. This created the opening for the great Guangdong-Hong Kong joint ventures. To ease the process of reforming and opening up Guangdong, Beijing created a Special Economic Zone in Shenzhen on the Guangdong border with Hong Kong. Three times larger than Hong Kong, and with a mandate to liberalise far faster than the rest of Guangdong, Shenzhen was to be converted from a collection of backward villages of rice paddy into an industrial power centre. Hong Kong investors dominated the investment in Shenzhen Special Economic Zone. About 80 to 90% of the total investment in Shenzhen is mainly in manufacturing, property, and tourist facilities. A large number of these projects are sub-contracting arrangements whereby certain manufacturing processes are performed in Shenzhen and the rest in Hong Kong. These projects range from textiles and clothing through electronics, toys, and other consumer items, to steel-rolling mills and food and beverage production. Besides manufacturing, the constructions on many commercial and residential buildings, including hotels, were financed by Hong Kong investors.[19] Developments in Hong Kong in past years after reversion of sovereignty to Communist regime has, however, put a question mark on China's bid to replicate the Hong Kong example on Taiwan.

By the early 1990s, the economic integration of socialist Guangdong and capitalist Hong Kong was largely completed. Shenzhen had become a mini-Hong Kong with tall buildings and factories that saturated US markets with clothes, shoes, and toys, streets full of Audis and Mercedes-Benzs, people wearing clothing with designer labels, some of which were even real. The effect and impact of Hong Kong on Shenzhen was so profound that the phenomenon has been described as Hong-Kongisation of Shenzhen. The neo-rich yuppies flaunt their opulence, wearing expensive garments, rings, and gold chains studded with stones and pearls, and holding expensive mobile phones. The red capitalism in Shenzhen exemplified the economic revolution in China. The opulence, however, brought in its trail like conspicuous consumption and moral decay like the incidence of divorce and prostitution. In little more than a decade, the city grew in population from 20,000 to three million.

For the peasantry of Guangdong, this growth brought an instant leap into modern consumerism. An unemployed population with little mobility suddenly found itself plenty of jobs working for Hong Kong companies, and with essentially unlimited opportunities for the energetic. In half a generation, good food, decent housing, nearly universal television, motorcycles, and cosmetics replaced hunger, dreary blue suits, and the trudge to work. By 1990, about half of Guangdong rural households had a radio, a television, and a tape recorder. By the end of 1992, Proctor and Gamble was selling as much Rejoice Shampoo as it could provide; after the United States, Guangdong province was its second largest market. McDonald's hamburger restaurants also profited from the new prosperity in Guangdong; the average McDonald's in America had about 1,400 customers a day, but one in Guangdong set the world record with about 14,123 customers in a single day. When a 7-Eleven store opened in 1972, the riot police had to be called out in full battle to control huge crowds of customers.[20]

Hong Kong's investment in Guangdong accounted for a third of the cumulative utilised Foreign Direct Investment (FDI) in China, of which 80% came from Hong Kong. Out of Hong Kong's total (FDI) in China, 40% went to Guangdong. Hong Kong's industrial investment in Guangdong transformed Hong Kong manufacturing as well as the entire Hong Kong economy. While the manufacturing firms employ up to three million workers in Guangdong, the manufacturing labour force in Hong Kong is only around 650,000. By moving labour-intensive processes to Guangdong, Hong Kong has concentrated on more skill-intensive processes, such as product design, sourcing, production management, quality control, and marketing. The arrangement, known as outward processing, has enabled Hong Kong manufacturing to achieve a very high rate of labour production.[21]The expansion of processing operations in Guangdong has increased the demand for Hong Kong's service industries, including entrepot trade, shipping, insurance, business services, and financial services. Both the Hong Kong manufacturing sector and the Hong Kong economy, in fact, have become increasingly service-oriented. In short, Hong Kong has become the economic capital of an industrialised Guangdong.

Before Deng Xiaoping's tour of Southern China in early 1992 to encourage economic reforms, the largest corporations of Hong Kong were notably absent from the investment profit in China, which was dominated by small and medium-sized labour- intensive manufacturing firms. Deng's tour stimulated a wave of investment by major Hong Kong companies, including listed companies such as Cheung Kong, Hutchison-Whampoa, Sun Hung Kai Properties, New World, and Kowloon Wharf, in projects ranging from real estate to infrastructure and commerce. Subsequently, the price of China play shares[22] in listed companies rose rapidly. In addition, a number of China investment funds were established that invested in industrial and B shares on China stock markets. Small investors, besides investing in China play shares and China funds, also purchased pre-sale apartments in Guangdong in droves.As a result of these developments, Hong Kong's already high shares in China's contracted foreign investment rose from 61% in 1991 to 69% in 1992. This indicates that Hong Kong investors are highly sensitive to investment opportunities in China and were one step ahead of other investors.

CHINA'S INVESTMENT IN HONG KONG

Until 1977, the formal structure of China's economic presence in Hong Kong remained essentially unchanged, compared with the years immediately after 1949 when China was established. At that time, China's principal investments in Hong Kong were confined to bilateral trade and other supporting activities, such as financial and communication services. There were three prominent Chinese-owned companies and agencies, namely China Resources Company, Bank of China, and China Merchants Steam Navigation Company. The China Resource Company, representing the Ministry of Foreign Economic Relations and Trade, is involved in imports and exports, and wholesale and retail business; the Bank of China, representing the Ministry of Finance, is involved in a wide spectrum of banking activities, including the management of foreign exchange earning for China; and the China Merchants Steam Navigation Company, representing the Ministry of Communications, is involved in sea transportation of goods and passengers.

Since 1977, besides stepping up activities in those areas where they traditionally had interests, China-based companies moved into other investment areas, including property, stock-broking, foreign exchange dealing and manufacturing which they had, for one reason or another, previously refrained from entering. Other areas of Chinese investment in Hong Kong included insurance, shipping, aviation, and entrepot trade. It was estimated that during the period 1979-1983, China invested as much as $4 billion in Hong Kong. This investment was undertaken by 50 Chinese trade representative offices in Hong Kong, and more than 300 projects were involved. China surpassed Japan in 1993 to become the foremost investor in Hong Kong in terms of cumulative investment. It was estimated that assets owned by Chinese enterprises and government agencies in Hong Kong were $6 billion in 1984, which grew to $10 billion in 1989, and doubling to $20 billion in 1992.

Since the late 1980s, China has been investing in Hong Kong's corporates and setting up listed companies in Hong Kong – a strategy that not only yields consistently high returns, but also circumvents China's currency restrictions. There were 1,756 Chinese companies registered in Hong Kong, employing over 53,000 people, of which the largest is China International Trust and Investment Corporation (CITIC) Pacific under Larry Yung. Founded in 1990, CITIC has a market capitalisation of $12.1 billion, a 25% holding of Cathay Pacific, another 20% of China Light and Power (which supplies electricity to Kowloon and the New Territories), and is now constructed a blue chrome-and-glass CITIC Tower on one of the most expensive pieces of real estate in Hong Kong Island.[23]

China's investment strengthens the ties of Hong Kong's position as the gateway to China. As China continued to liberalise its foreign exchange controls, more and more Chinese capital flew to Hong Kong. After its merger with China, capital flow to Hong Kong is like water taking its natural course. It is natural for Chinese enterprises and investors to move their capital to Hong Kong, where property rights are more strictly protected and funds can be used more flexibly.

NOTES

1. Jung-fang Tsai, "From Anti foreignism to Popular Nationalism: Hong Kong between China and Britain, 1839-1911" in Ming K. Chan (ed.), *Precarious Balance: Hong Kong between China and Britain 1942-1992* (New York, 1994), p. 11.
2. G.B. Endacott *Government and People of Hong Kong* (Hong Kong, 1984), p. 65.
3. Ibid.
4. James T. H. Tang, "World War to Cold War: Hong Kong's Future and Asia-Chinese Interactions, 1941-55" in Ming K. Chan, (eds.), The Precarious Balance: Hong Kong between China and Britain (New York 1994), pp. 122-23.
5. Y. C. Jao. "The Rise of Hong Kong as a Financial Centre" *Asian Survey* (Berkely) Vol. XIX, No. 7, 1979, pp. 674-685.

6. Y. F. Luk, *Hong Kong's Economic and Financial Future*, (Washington, D.C., 1995), p. 22.
7. Mark Roberti, *The Fall of Hong Kong: China's Triumph and Britain's Betrayal*, (New York, 1994), p. 12.
8. The-pei Yu, "Economic Links Among Hong Kong, PRC with Specific Reference to Trade in Jurgen Domes and – Ming Shaw (eds.) *Hong Kong: A Chines and International Concern* (Boulder, 1988), p. 111.
9. Yun-Wing Sung, *The China- Hong Kong Connection: The Key to China's Open Policy* (Cambridge University Press, 1991) p. 21.
10. Ibid., p. 22.
11. The-pei Yu, n. 8, p. 115.
12. Sung Yun-Wing, "Patterns of Economic Interdependence in the Natural Economic Territory" in Jane Khannna (ed.), *Southern China, Hong Kong and Taiwan: Evolution of Subregional Economy*, (Weshington D.C., 1995), p. 24.
13. *Business India* (New Delhi) 3 June – 13 July, 1997, p. 68.
14. The-pei Yu, n.8, p. 117.
15. Ibid.
16. Sung Yun-Wing, n. 12, pp. 27-28.
17. *The Times of India*, New Delhi, 12 July, 1997.
18. William H. Overhalt, *China: The Economic Super Power*, (London, 1995) pp. 118-19.
19. Piers Jacobs "Hong Kong and the Modernisation of China" *Journal of International Affairs* (London) vol. 39, No. 2, 1986, pp. 76-77.
20. Overholt, n. 18, pp. 123-125.
21. Sung Yun-Wing, n. 12, p. 20.
22. "China play shares" are shares in companies that are registered outside of China but that do a majority of their business in China.
23. *Business India*, n. 13, p. 68.

CHAPTER 4

The Joint Declaration, Basic Law, and 'One Country, Two Systems'

THE PROTRACTED PARLEYS

With economic integration between mainland China and Hong Kong having taken place, the prospect for political integration looked brighter. Following Mao's death and the fall of 'Gang of Four' in 1976, the new Chinese leadership under Deng Xiaoping assigned top priority to China's 'four modernisations' programme, which pushed China into closer relationship with the West, the US in particular. In 1978, Deng Xiaoping's position as China's paramount leader in fact, if not in title, was consolidated. Then, at the Third Plenum of the Eleventh Central Committee in December 1978, the leadership adopted in principle the policy of opening China's doors to the outside world. During this session, Deng put forward three national goals – to modernize the economy, to reunify the country, and to oppose hegemony in Asia.

However, at this stage, the objective of national reunification did not envisage the immediate recovery of Hong Kong. Instead, the Chinese leadership's primary focus was Taiwan. Chinese leaders, including Mao, had long said that Hong Kong and Macao would be recovered after Taiwan's reunification with the mainland. The prospect for re-unification with Taiwan anytime soon was remote. Deng, in fact, hoped to achieve a political settlement with Taiwan by the end of the century. To ensure peaceful re-unification, Chinese leadership conceived of the novelty of 'one country, two systems', which postulated the capitalist system under Chinese sovereignty, practising a socialist polity under the banner of the Communist Party of China.

With regard to Hong Kong, they had a pragmatic approach. Leaving aside the contentious issue of sovereignty over Hong Kong, the Chinese leadership at this stage concentrated on greater economic cooperation and integration between Hong Kong and Guangdong, the adjacent Chinese province contiguous to Hong Kong. This was characteristic of the typical Chinese strategy of taking up the issue of common interest, setting aside vexed questions. At a time when the economy was in ascendancy, politics was of secondary importance to China. This period witnessed greater cooperation and integration between Hong Kong and Guangdong.

The Chinese government's strategy was to take maximum advantage of Hong Kong and encourage the provincial Guangdong government to improve relations with the Hong Kong government. It may be noted that the Chinese government had never officially recognised the Hong Kong government; to do so would have given British rule legitimacy. Behind the scenes, the *Xinhua* News Agency, however, increased contacts with the Hong Kong government and gave broad hints that Governor MacLehose would be welcome to visit China. Then in December 1978, China's vice-minister of foreign trade, Li Quiang, made a brief stopover in Hong Kong on his return from an overseas visit. As a courtesy, the Governor invited Li for a lunch. Li told MacLehose that Hong Kong had a major role to play in China's modernisation programme, and said the Chinese government would like to invite him to visit China. This was followed by a formal letter.[1]

The invitation was a breakthrough, a clear sign that China wanted Hong Kong to play a catalytic role in the country's modernisation. MacLehose felt the visit offered an excellent opportunity to resolve the question of New Territories lease, which was to expire on July 1, 1997. The New Territories constitutes 90% of Hong Kong's territory. In fact, the uncertainty about the future of the Colony had created considerable anxiety and apprehension in the hearts and minds of the people, especially investors and entrepreneurs. During the course of his visit to Beijing in March-April 1979, MacLehose had an opportunity to meet Deng Xiaoping. MacLehose broached the idea whether Hong Kong government could extend the commercial leases beyond 1997 so as to instill confidence and trust among entrepreneurs and investors without compromising the question of Chinese sovereignty over Hong Kong. The basic idea was to probe if China could tolerate British administration in Hong Kong under Chinese sovereignty. Deng Xiaoping, without responding to the proposal of MacLehose, only reiterated China's well-known position with regard to Taiwan and Hong Kong and said investors in Hong Kong "could put their hearts at ease."[2]

Deng's reply was vague and ambiguous. Naturally, therefore, it could not reassure investors in Hong Kong and the crisis of confidence persisted. It, however, opened the channel of communication and highlighted the gravity of the issue. What exacerbated the situation was that unless uncertainties about the future of Hong Kong were cleared, the Colony would not be able to raise capital abroad for projects, as repayment of international commercial loans entail a minimum of 10 to 15 years of time. There was also a downturn in the world economy, and the peaking of a cycle in Hong Kong's property market, a decline in Heng Seng index from 1,400 to 700, a weakening of Hong Kong dollar, capital flights, near disappearance of local investment, and huge lines of panicky people trying get visas at Western embassies.[3]

It was against this backdrop of crisis of confidence that the tempo for a negotiated settlement of the Hong Kong issue gained momentum towards early 1980s. Although the visit of British Prime Minister

Margaret Thatcher to Beijing and Hong Kong in September 1982 was the most significant event of the year, steps had already been taken by opening parleys between China and Britain. Incidentally, Mrs Thatcher was the first British Prime Minister in office who visited China in 1982. Before her historic visit, Humphrey Atkins, the then British deputy foreign secretary, gave notice to Chinese Premier Zhao Ziyang during a visit to Beijing in January 1982 that if nothing was done, come July 1, 1997, British rule would cease in Hong Kong. In the meantime, Zhao said Britain and China should do nothing to jeopardise the stability and prosperity of Hong Kong. Atkins told a press conference in Hong Kong that China had stressed the importance of Hong Kong's free port and its status as a financial and trading centre. The search for a solution, he said, would have to be a step-by-step process.

In June, reports about China's position on Hong Kong started to come out from Beijing. Statements attributed to Deng Xiaoping claimed that China would recover sovereignty over Hong Kong in 1997. The local stock market plummeted, focusing attention on the uncertainty over Hong Kong's future as a capitalist enclave. At the same time, unrealistic hopes grew that Thatcher would achieve substantive progress during her talks in Beijing on the 1997 question. In her talks with Deng Xiaoping and other Chinese leaders, Thatcher tried very hard to exchange sovereignty over Hong Kong in return for continued British administration in the territory to retain the trust and confidence of businessmen and investors. However, it was quite clear from the Chinese leader's remark that they would not compromise on sovereignty and that they would intend to recover sovereignty over the whole of Hong Kong – the Island as well as the New Territories – in 1997 and no later. The fundamental position underlying the Chinese position was that the people of Hong Kong were Chinese and not British. The Chinese refused to budge an inch on the question of both sovereignty and administration.[4] The Chinese side argued that to divide sovereignty was to destroy it. The following evening, Thatcher said in a BBC TV interview that the three treaties concerning Hong Kong were valid in international law, but could be 'varied'. She also added that those who did not honour one treaty would not honour another. By the time she arrived in Hong Kong, her stance on the treaties had hardened.

The British press described Thatcher's trip as a failure, and blamed the Foreign Office for advising her wrongly. Others, however, argued that the iron lady herself was responsible for the ill-chosen words on the treaties, pointing out that Foreign Office aides had been stressing the dangers of stirring Chinese nationalistic feeling on the question of sovereignty and treaties. Moreover, the Foreign Office was said to have a difficult time explaining to Thatcher that while the majority of Hong Kong's five million people preferred a status quo for the economy, it did not mean they were pro-British. The Foreign Office line was reinforced by a poll commissioned by a middle-class lobby called the *Hong Kong Observers*. The survey conducted in May-June 1982 showed that 95% considered the continuation of status quo to be an acceptable solution. The unpopularity of Hong Kong being returned to China as a solution was obvious: this topped the least 'preferred' and unacceptable categories.

No fewer than 22% of those polled, most of them in the 15-34 age group, would "try every means to leave" if Hong Kong reverted to China. Asked what they thought were the most important aspects of the status quo, 86% said they valued freedom of choice. Hong Kong's comfortable living environment also drew a favourable response (86%), as did freedom of speech (83%), and the freedom to make money (82%).[5]

Chinese leaders were convinced that China must claim Hong Kong, while rejecting any British claims to sovereignty and administration over Hong Kong. China acted with great speed after 140 years to make its position clear, and during 1983-84, forcefully indicated that the question of sovereignty was 'non-negotiable' –

as was the question of administration. Pei Monong, the Chinese spokesman on Hong Kong matters, ruled out any role for Britain after 1997. The metaphor of a 'three-legged-stool' (Britain, China, and Hong Kong) was finally rejected, and the Chinese categorically rejected any new treaty involving Britain. Self-government for Hong Kong was ruled out, neither was it possible nor feasible. The Chinese could cut the lifeline of Hong Kong simply by stopping supply of potable water and food supply, not to speak of sending the People's Liberation Army (PLA). However, there was an emphasis on the related principle of *Gangren Zigang*, which refers to the entrusting of Hong Kong people in the local administration of the territory. The people, however, would be presumed to be patriots.

After the initial talks between Thatcher and the Chinese leaders, the two sides agreed to hold discussions on solving the question of Hong Kong through diplomatic channels. In the following six months, consultations made no progress because the British position remained unchanged regarding its sovereignty over Hong Kong. In March 1983, Thatcher wrote a letter to the Chinese Premier in which she guaranteed that she would suggest to the British Parliament that it return sovereignty over Hong Kong to China. Because the British side made some promises regarding sovereignty over Hong Kong, the possibility existed that negotiations might progress. As a result, in the following month, the Chinese Premier wrote to inform her that the Chinese government would agree to hold negotiations as soon as possible.[6]

In July 1983, the delegations from the Chinese and British governments began to hold formal negotiations. At the start of the negotiations, the British side tried to give its recognition of China's sovereignty over Hong Kong in exchange of its continued administration of Hong Kong after 1997. This was totally rejected by the Chinese side. As a result, the negotiations made no progress until the fourth round. In September 1983, at a meeting with visiting former British Prime Minister Edward Heath, Deng Xiaoping said negotiations would get nowhere if Britain simply tried to exchange its continued administration with token sovereignty. He persuaded the British side to change its attitude to avoid a situation in which China would be constrained to unilaterally announce its policies pertaining to the solution of the Hong Kong question. In October 1983, a letter from the British Prime Minister stated that both sides should hold discussions on permanent arrangements for Hong Kong on the basis of China's proposal.[7] In the fifth and sixth rounds of talks, the British side affirmed it would not insist on British administration of Hong Kong nor seek joint control in any form. The British also recognised that China's plan was established on the pre-condition that after 1997, Hong Kong's sovereignty and right of control should return to China. Up to then, major obstacles had been cleared.

From the seventh round of talks, negotiations turned on the Chinese government's basic policies and principles for solving the question of Hong Kong's future. Though the British side had clearly promised not to put forward any suggestion contrary to China's principle pertaining to sovereignty, it continued to put forward through documents submitted for discussion many proposals which could maintain Britain's maximum influence in Hong Kong after 1997. These proposals envisaged separating Hong Kong from the leadership of China's central people's government and proposed to turn Hong Kong into an independent or semi-independent political entity. The Chinese side always adhered to the principle on sovereignty, expressed strong opposition, and declined the British suggestions.

After the 12th round of talks in April 1984, both sides shifted to discussions regarding the transfer of political power in the transitional period. The establishment of a joint organisation in Hong Kong was one of the most difficult questions encountered during the negotiations. The views of both sides diverged greatly on this question. In April and July of the same year, Geoffrey Howe, British Secretary of State for Foreign and Commonwealth Affairs, visited China on invitation. High-level discussions exerted great influence on the progress of the negotiations. After repeated negotiations, both sides finally agreed to set up a Sino-British Joint Liaison Group. This group was only a liaison organisation, not an executive one. Its responsibility included consultations to implement the Sino-British Joint Declaration; discussions on matters regarding the smooth transfer of political power; and exchange of views and consultations on mutually agreed matters. The Sino-British joint Liaison Group became operational on July 1, 1988, and its tenure ended on January 1, 2000.

In the last three rounds of talks, both sides discussed specific question relating to nationality, civil aviation, and land. These were either politically or technically complicated matters. Repeated consultations on the wording of the agreement were held. On September 18, 1984, China and Britain reached an agreement on all questions, and the Joint Declaration was formally initialed on September 26. The Joint Declaration was debated and endorsed by the Standing Committee of the National People's Congress in Beijing on November 14, and by the House of Commons on December 5. It was signed between the Chinese Premier Zhao Ziyang and Prime Minister Margaret Thatcher on December 19, 1984. The two governments exchanged ratification instruments on May 27, 1985, and the Declaration became effective. In autumn that year, both countries' permanent representatives to the United Nations together submitted the Joint Declaration to UN under-secretary-general in charge of legal affairs. This action completed all necessary legal procedures to register the declaration in the United Nations; it is now an internationally recognised legal document.

THE JOINT DECLARATION

During the protracted diplomatic parleys, Deng Xiaoping had instructed the Chinese team that the agreement with Britain should not be too long or too detailed. He said that China's policies could be included in an annexure to the main agreement; however, under no circumstance could the agreement be a treaty. This would raise the question of whether the new treaty was replacing the ones from the 19th century, which China had never recognised. Moreover, Beijing could not agree to include future policies towards a part of its own territory in a formal treaty with a foreign country. Ji Pengfei, the head of the Hong Kong and Macao Affairs Office, wanted this accord to be joint communiqué, similar to the Shanghai Communiqué under which China and United States established relations without resolving points of contention. Each side would simply state its position. The British side accepted that the accord would be called a Joint Declaration and that each side would spell out its own policies.[8]

Although the British side also maintained that it did not matter whether the accord was called a joint agreement or joint declaration, legal experts pointed out subtle differences between the two. Harvey Stockwin, for example, wrote "in English, an agreement is a diplomatic format below that of a joint communiqué." A legal source ranked a Joint Declaration or a Joint Statement as being just above a memorandum of understanding in the international order of diplomacy. It is often used when nations wish to keep their options open, and to reach an agreement devoid of moral sanction. Several sources maintained that Joint Declarations are not normally considered legally binding, Joint Declarations are often used as statements of intent couched in high-sounding principles. China and India, for example, have their joint declaration of 'five principles of peaceful co-existence', but these thoughts did not prevent both nations going to war over a border dispute in 1962.[9] Deng explained that the Joint Declaration – embodying the formula of 'one country, two systems' – was a product of 'Dialectical Marxism and Historical Materialism'. The more circumspect Thatcher called it, 'an ingenious idea'.[10]

The Sino-British Joint Declaration was an unprecedented event in world history. The Joint Declaration enabled China to move a step ahead to realise its long-standing goal of national re-unification, avenging the humiliation it had suffered in the Opium War during the days of 'gunboat diplomacy'. It also afforded Britain an opportunity to make a graceful exit from its last colonial outpost. It was indeed a feat of diplomatic and political craftsmanship and legal dexterity. Although the Joint Declaration was a fait accompli, nevertheless it set at rest speculations and conjectures about the future political and economic set-up of the tiny capitalist enclave beyond the apocalyptic year 1997, and ensured a modicum of stability in the territory.

The Joint Declaration is significant in the sense that while post-World War history had been characterised as a battle between competitive and conflicting ideologies of liberal democracy and communism, which of course has mellowed down in recent years, it provided a political contrivance finding conciliation between two divergent political and economic systems. Perhaps, never before in history had such a unique arrangement ever been contemplated anywhere in the world. Nations have been divided and people segregated under the strait-jacket of ideology. The Berlin Wall, now a relic of history, divided East and West Germany, the 38 Parallel divided North and South Korea, and so was the case of the two Vietnams prior to their re-unification in 1976. It was against this backdrop that the Joint Declaration held the promise of a convergence of two divergent economic and political systems, as Hong Kong entered into its uncharted waters.

The Joint Declaration was pleasantly free of historical recriminations, and its first part merely restates the case that "the question of Hong Kong is leftover from the past.[11] Earlier, the

Chinese authorities had condemned British rule as 'colonialist' and had alluded to the 'humiliations' of the Chinese people. Expressions used earlier read like 'One day the blood debt owed by Imperialism to China would be repaid'. This language, so popular previously, was studiously avoided in the Joint Declaration. Historical references in it were factual statements setting out the respective positions of the two governments. The British stand – based on the legality of the treaties – was reaffirmed, while the well-known Chinese hostility to the Unequal Treaties was articulated.

The Joint Declaration spelt out the basic policy of the Chinese government in the baldest terms. In order to ensure a high degree of autonomy, it stipulated that as per the provision of Article 31 of the Constitution of the People's Republic of China, the Special Administration Region would enjoy a high degree of autonomy. The Joint Declaration also committed that the laws in force in Hong Kong would remain basically unchanged.[12] As regards the structure of the Hong Kong Special Administrative Region (HKSAR), the Joint Declaration mentioned that the nomenclature of the executive apparatus would be broadly composed of local inhabitants. The chief executive would be appointed by the central government on the basis of the results of elections or consultation to be held locally. Principal officials would be nominated by the chief executive of HKSAR for appointment by the Central People's government. Chinese and foreign nationals previously working in the public and police services in the government departments of Hong Kong might remain in employment. British and other foreign nationals might also be employed to serve as advisors or hold certain public posts in government departments of HKSAR.

A closer analysis of this provision amply demonstrates that the Chinese simply replaced the earlier patronage system of 'administrative absorption of politics', whereby the social elites were handpicked by the British government and appointed in the name of the British government. Now, they are chosen by the Chinese government. Meanwhile, the social elites in Hong Kong, barring a few exceptions, have also shifted their loyalty to the Chinese government. Officials who were branded with the earlier regime left the jobs, and a few in subordinate posts followed suit subsequently. The Joint Declaration guaranteed the right to property and freedom of person, speech, press, assembly, association, travel, movement, strike, academic research, religious belief, etc. Hong Kong has been known as a free society. It had the freest press in the world. It appears that now the press in Hong Kong has resorted to self-censorship. Many of the world's prestigious news magazines like *The Asia Week*, *Far Eastern Review*, etc. – which were located in Hong Kong – have ceased their publications.

Hong Kong had also been a leading world centre for research on China. In fact, when China remained closed to the outside world, scholars working on China carried out their research from Hong Kong. The University of Hong Kong had played host to a galaxy of distinguished Sinologists over the years. Such facilities are now a thing of the past. The Joint Declaration committed that during the transitional period between the date of entry into force of the Joint Declaration and June 30, 1997, the Government of United Kingdom would be responsible for the administration of Hong Kong with the object of maintaining and preserving its economic prosperity and social stability; and that the Government of the People's Republic of China would give its cooperation in this connection.

THE BASIC LAW

The Joint Declaration also resolved that a Basic Law would be enacted and promulgated by the NPC for the government and administration of the HKSAR. In deference to these stipulations of the Joint Declaration, the NPC established a Drafting Committee for the Basic Law of HKSAR in April 1985. In June 1985, the NPC passed the membership list of the Drafting Committee comprising 59 members, among whom 23 were from various sectors in Hong Kong. The Drafting Committee set up a Consultative Committee for the Basic Law with a view to assimilating the opinions of the Hong Kong public at large. The Consultative Committee for the Basic Law was established on December 18, 1985, with a membership of 180, drawing representation from various sectors and strata in Hong Kong.[13] Ultimately, after about five years of deliberations and consultations, the Basic Law was promulgated by the NPC in April 1990. The Basic Law elucidated the modalities of the concept of 'one country, two systems'. It may, however, be noted that Basic Law, per se, did not mention the concept of 'one country, two systems.'

EVOLUTION OF 'ONE COUNTRY, TWO SYSTEMS'

Though it may be far-fetched, the conceptual lineage of 'one country, two systems' as a political contrivance for national re-unification with Taiwan and Macao, besides Hong Kong, can be traced back to Mao Zedong's strategy of the United Front forging alliance between the Chinese Communist Party (CCP) and the Kuo-Min Tang (KMT) for national liberation and his theory of contradictions and the methods to resolve non-antagonistic contradictions. If the strategies and tactics of the United Front were political expediency for national liberation, 'one country, two systems' was yet another extension of the United Front strategy with the concomitant methods of resolving the non-antagonist contradictions for the realisation of China's quest for national re-unification. Deng Xiaoping himself located the conception of the formula to the Third Plenary Session of the Chinese Communist Party's Eleventh Central Committee in 1978 which re-established Mao's dictum of 'seeking truth from facts and urged for the peaceful reunification of China.[14] In fact, Deng's aphorism 'it does not matter whether the cat is black or white, as long as it catches mice', contains a streak of pragmatism which can also be noticed in Mao's slogan of 'seeking truth from facts'. Whatever may be the resemblance, the conclusion of the Chinese Communist Party's Twelfth Congress in September 1982 resolved the outstanding ideological, economic, and leadership issues and the Chinese leadership took up the 1997 transfer of Hong Kong earnestly. The promulgation of the PRC's new Constitution in December 1982 provided the testament of the new thinking of the Chinese leadership on a plethora of issues including the question of national reunification. No wonder, therefore, Article 31 of the new Constitution of China provides: 'The system to be instituted in the special administrative regions shall be prescribed by National People's Congress in the light of special conditions.'

In fact, the incorporation of the article in the Constitution of the PRC was a prelude to the constitutional novelty of 'one country, two systems' and thereafter, the Chinese leadership proposed the idea publicly to wean over compatriots from Taiwan, Hong Kong, and Macao. Deng Xiaoping, the architect of the idea, broached the concept in an interview on June 26, 1983, in Beijing with Dr Winston LY Yang, Professor at Seton Hall University, USA. Of course, Deng's interview with Dr Yang centered around the issue of China's re-unification with Taiwan.[15] In retrospect, Deng's interview with Dr Yang is of considerable significance as far as Hong Kong is concerned, in the sense that while Deng proposed that Taiwan might maintain its own armed forces as long as that did not constitute a threat to the mainland, such an offer was ruled out by Beijing in the case of Hong Kong. Later elaborating on the concept, Deng Xiaoping told a group of prominent Hong Kong personalities – Szue-Yuen Chung, Lydia Dunn, and QW Lee that Hong Kong's current socio-economic systems, its lifestyle, and its position as a free port and an international trade and financial centre would remain unchanged. Reassuring compatriots of China's sincerity of purpose on the issue, he further added: "Some people are still worried whether the policy will change. Is there anyone who can change China's current policies of opening to the outside world and invigorating the domestic economy? If they are changed, the living standards of 80 per cent of the Chinese population would be affected and we would lose the support of 80 per cent of the people."In an obvious reference to Taiwan Deng added, "China not only has the problem of Hong Kong; it also has the problem of Taiwan."[16]

SPECIAL ECONOMIC ZONES (SEZS)

Yet another interesting development synchronizing with the conceptualization of the idea of 'one country, two systems' was the establishment of four SEZs in August 1980 in Zhuhai (near Macau), Shenzhen (near Hong Kong), Shantou and Xiamen (both opposite Taiwan). Later, in April 1988, the Hainan Island was also developed as an SEZ. Flexible and preferential policies have been adopted in these areas to attract foreign funds, advanced technology, equipment, and management expertise. When the SEZs were established, the Chinese government stressed that they should develop a foreign trade- oriented economy. Although the primary objective of the SEZs is to encourage joint ventures and collaboration with foreign firms and to attract investment from abroad in order to give a boost to the open-door policy and economic modernization, their geo-political significance for China's reunification strategy with economically prosperous and advanced capital enclaves can hardly be overemphasized. The SEZs, spearhead of China's modernisation drive, were widely seen as a litmus test for the open door economic policies pursued by the Chinese leadership. In a way, they are like futuristic and miniature versions of the HKSAR under the nomenclature of 'one county, two systems', but of course on a restricted scale. The SEZs still implement the socialist system and adhere to socialist orientation for development. In economic activities, the market mechanism is brought into full play under the guidance of the state plan for economic development.

Regulation through the market is more flexible and wider in scope than in other domestic areas.[17] Nevertheless, considering the close proximity of the Shenzhen SEZ to Hong Kong, it assumed crucial significance in the context of Hong Kong's reunification with the mainland. In fact, over the years both Hong Kong and Shenzhen have become integrated and assimilated to a large extent. For some Hong Kong entrepreneurs, SEZ investment was a kind of 1997 insurance, a way of snuggling up to Beijing in preparation for an eventual 'change of management' in their home territory.

BASIC LAW: THE EDIFICE OF 'ONE COUNTRY, TWO SYSTEMS'

The Basic Law of the HKSAR has all the attributes of an ideal liberal democratic polity and laissez faire economy, however, under the shadow of an overarching government under the Communist Party swearing socialist ideology and the Chinese army. The *sine qua non* of the Basic Law is that it promises to give a high degree of autonomy to Hong Kong ensuring the continuity of the existing political, social, and economic system and way of life. As a natural corollary, it also guarantees ownership of private property and mentions that socialism will not be imposed on HKSAR. The Basic Law bestows defence and foreign affairs, the touchstones of sovereignty, with the PRC. As a symbolic mark of its autonomous status, it provides that HKSAR may use a regional flag and a regional emblem, apart from displaying the national flag and national emblem of PRC.

However, a careful study of the detailed provisions of the Basic Law suggest that the high degree of autonomy is cosmetic, while the centralising tendencies are well entrenched. On the face of it, the words used in the Basic Law are liberal; they are, however, to be read in conjunction with the socialist policy and the constitution of the PRC. Because the Basic Law not only draws its sustenance from the constitution of the PRC and the National People's Congress (NPC), it is also dependent upon these institutions in its actual operational aspect. Most of the provisions of the Basic Law have strings attached to them.

ECONOMY

A closer look at the Basic Law indicates that a high degree of autonomy in content and substance goes to the domain of economy – the mainstay of Hong Kong's stability and prosperity. Some striking features in this regard that merit attention are as follows. An important provision that allows autonomy in HKSAR is that the Basic Law permits continuation of the Hong Kong dollar as legal tender and its free convertibility. It also provides foreign exchange control. The Law also gives due recognition to the free port status of Hong Kong and legalises free trade. As regards the free port system, it says that with the exception of foreign war ships, access for which requires the special permission of the PRC central government, other ships enjoy access to the ports of the HKSAR.

So far as external trade is concerned, the Basic Law allows some degree of freedom which impinges on the area of external affairs, a prerogative of the PRC central government. A significant provision in this context is the stipulation that HKSAR, using the name 'Hong Kong China' may participate in international organisations and international trade agreements, including preferential trade arrangement such as the General Agreement on Tariffs and Trade (GATT) and arrangements regarding international trade in textiles. Yet another important article in the Basic Law is the provision that the revenue derived by HKSAR shall be exclusively at its own disposal. All these liberal provisions and attractive concessions clearly indicate Beijing's adroitness in maintaining stability and prosperity in Hong Kong. It is only Article 5 of the Basic Law that stipulates "The socialist system and policies shall not be practised in the Hong Kong Special Administrative Region, and the previous capitalist system and way of life shall remain unchanged for 50 years." No other article mentions about 50 years.While Beijing promised to keep the 'goose that lays the golden egg' in good humour, developments in recent years in post hand-over period probed otherwise.

ALL-POWERFUL CHIEF EXECUTIVE AND TITULAR LEGISLATIVE COUNCIL

So far as political arrangements are concerned, the political complexion of HKSAR has undergone a cosmetic structural change consequent upon the transfer of sovereignty over Hong Kong and the operationalisation of the Basic Law, the constitution of the Hong Kong Special Administrative Region. Under the Basic Law, the Governor is replaced by the Chief Executive, who is the head of the Hong Kong Special Administrative Region. The Basic Law stipulates that the Chief Executive shall be a Chinese citizen of not less than 40 years of age who is a permanent resident of Hong Kong with no right of abode in any foreign country and has ordinarily resided in Hong Kong for a continuous period of not less than 20 years. The Chief Executive is to be elected by a broadly representative Election Committee and appointed by the Chinese Central People's Government. The electoral college, what the Basic Law calls the Electoral Committee, composed of 800 members drawn from sectors such as industry, commerce, finance, social service, religious communities, besides legislative councilors, members of district organisations, Hong Kong deputies to the National People's Congress (NPC) and Hong Kong members of the National Committee of the Chinese People's Political Consultative Conference. The composition of the Electoral Committee is seemingly broad-based and is suggestive of functional representations advocated by the Guild Socialists.

As regards the appointment of the first executive of HKSAR, the Basic Law mentioned that the first Chief Executive shall be selected in accordance with the "Decision of the National People's Congress on the method for the formation of the first Legislative Council of the Hong Kong Special Administrative Region."

Accordingly, the National Peoples' Congress on April 4, 1990, took a decision to set up a Preparatory Committee for the Hong Kong Special Administrative Region. It was stipulated that the Preparatory Committee "shall be responsible for preparing the establishment of the region and shall prescribe the specific method for forming the first government and the first Legislative Council in accordance with this decision. In January 1996, the Preparatory Committee was appointed with Qian Qichen, China's Foreign Minister, Lu Ping (China's Director of the Hong Kong and Macao Affairs Office) as Secretary-General and Vice-Chairman. There were 150 members, 56 from China and 94 from Hong Kong. Of this 94, an overwhelming number were form the business sector.[18] The Preparatory Committee established a 400-member selection committee for the appointment of Chief Executive of HKSAR. Other objective of the Preparatory Committee was to select members of the Provisional Legislative Council.

On December 11, 1996, China appointed Tung Chee-Hwa, a 57-year-old, Shanghai-born shipping magnate as Hong Kong's Chief Executive designate. Thereafter, it handpicked an electoral college of 400 chosen citizens to 'elect' the new Provisional Legislative Council. This new body consisting of several pro-Beijing sympathisers, held its sittings in Shenzhen to draft new laws. The Provisional Legislative Council was formally inaugurated in Hong Kong on July 1, 1997. The first task before the Provisional Legislative Council was to ratify the laws which had been passed in Shenzhen.

Under the Basic Law, the Chief Executive is entrusted with sweeping powers covering the whole gamut of the governmental apparatus. The pre-eminent position and powers of the Chief Executive are very aptly summed by the Joseph YS Cheng, an acknowledged authority on Hong Kong. According to Cheng, 'the political system outlined in Chapter IV of the Basic Law presents an 'executive dominant' system in which the Chief executive will have powers similar to those of the present British Governor.'[19] As the Legislative Council of HKSAR, and the appointment as well as dismissal of the Chief Executive and principal officials have to be approved by the Central People's Government, the autonomy of HKSAR is affected. Until 1991, when the first direct elections were held for a minority of seats (18 out of 60) to the Legislative Council, Hong Kong's constitutional structure remained much as it was in the 19th century. The Governor appointed members to the Executive Council, his top policy advisory body and only with the final election in September 1995, the practice of appointing members to Legislative Council stopped.

Traditionally, appointees to the Executive Council, the Legislative Council and the Hong Kong government's extensive advisory structure, largely represented business and professional viewpoints. It could be said that Hong Kong has been, and is still to a large extent, ruled by an oligarchy, which is euphemistically called 'executive led' style of government by those who wish to preserve the system. This style of government is one where civil servants set policies, with the legislature approving expenditure and passing laws. The Basic Law essentially sought to preserve the 'executive-led' style of government during the drafting process. Thus, even with an increasingly representative legislature elected representatives would not be able to form the government.

As regards legislature, the Basic Law stipulates that the Legislative Council of the HKSAR shall be elected. The strategy for forming the Legislative Council shall be specified in the light of the actual situations in HKSAR and in accordance with the principle of gradual and orderly progress. The ultimate aim shall be the selection of all members of the Legislative Council through general election.

A Provisional Legislative Council was first mooted through the Preliminary Working Committee (PWC) appointed by Beijing shortly after it declared that the political reforms introduced by Chris Patten were against the Basic Law. In August 1994, as noted earlier, the Standing Committee of the NPC passed a resolution that the three-tier system of representative government including the elected Legislative Council would come to an end on June 30, 1997, and the Preparatory Committee would proceed to establish the HKSAR government and the first Legislative Council. Accordingly, on March 25, 1996, the plenary of preparatory committee passed the decision to set up a 60- member provisional Legislative Council.

The Chinese government decided to set up the Provisional Legislative Council through a process of election by a selection committee of 400 members set up by the preparatory committee. The tasks of the Provisional Legislative Council included passing, amending and repealing laws of the HKSAR, approving taxation and public expenditure, debating on the Chief Executive's policy address and endorsing the nomination of the Chief Justice on the Court of Final Appeal. It was also envisaged that the laws passed by the provisional legislature would come into effect on that date. As regards the tenure of the provisional Legislative Council, it was provided that it would operate until the first Legislative Council of the HKSAR was set up, not later than 30 June 1998.

JUDICIARY AND BILL OF RIGHTS

The importance of a judicial system and the rule of law in the set-up of HKSAR under the 'one country, two systems' formula is too obvious to be emphasized. The connotation of a judiciary under a socialist regime like the PRC is distinguished from the Anglo-Saxon tradition of jurisprudence to which Hong Kong is long accustomed. While a socialist regime adheres to a committed judiciary, the rule of law is the guiding gospel of a liberal democratic polity. No wonder, therefore, the need for independent judiciary and a comprehensive Bill of Rights gained momentum in Hong Kong during the pro-democracy movement in June 1989. The Hong Kong government came out with a draft proposal to introduce a comprehensive Bill of Rights for the protection and promotion of basic human rights in Hong Kong. The Bill of Rights was passed in 1991. The Chinese government frowned upon the idea and threatened that the move would jeopardize the spirit of the Joint Declaration.

China's National People's Congress repealed the Bill of Rights claiming that it was not in consonance with the Basic Law. After July 1, it was claimed that freedom of expression is 'guaranteed' if it did not affect national security. Old colonial restrictions on public assembly were brought back. Since 1993, citizens of Hong Kong are required to notify the police before holding a public demonstration. Under the new law, they have to wait for a police permit. The Basic Law also takes away from the Court of Final Appeal both jurisdiction and interpretation of all matters dealing with the interaction between the central and local government. These are some of the lurking fears in the hearts and minds of a section of the Hong Kong population who have been demanding for greater democracy and strengthening of the rule of law.

It is in this context that it is worthwhile to mention that Hong Kong is a signatory to two human rights treatises adopted by the United Nations, viz. the International Covenant on Civil and Political Rights (ICCPR), and the International Covenant on Economic, Social and Cultural Rights (ICESCR). The Covenant set out the basic human rights and fundamental freedoms, and imposed an obligation on all states which became parties to them to implement those rights by all appropriate means. It came into force in 1976. In the same year, the British government ratified the Covenant in respect of the United Kingdom and its dependent territories, including Hong Kong. In 1984, the British and the Chinese government agreed that the Covenant would continue to be applied to Hong Kong after 1997. The Sino-British Joint Declaration stated that the provision of the International Covenant on Economic, Social and Cultural Rights as applied to Hong Kong shall remain in force. This provision is reflected in Article 39 of the Basic law.[20]

SOME EARLY TRENDS

Although the reversion of Hong Kong to China was welcomed by China, Beijing expressed fears two-and-a-half months before Hong Kong's merger with the mainland when a speech by Jiang Zemin appeared on the front page of the *People's Daily*, in which he called for a strengthening of patriotic education to help make China more powerful. The speech was made to senior party officials in October 1996; but it was published just ahead of the Hong Kong handover, as simmering disputes between China and the Philippines over an island in the East China Sea flared up. "The Chinese people have never yielded to invaders, and they have a glorious tradition of ardently loving freedom, seeking progress, and guarding national dignity and state sovereignty," Mr Jiang said.[21]

Fidel Ramos, the then President of the Philippines, the south-east Asian country closest to Hong Kong, responded that China's rise "as an economic colossus with increasing military capabilities aroused a number of security concerns. Among them was whether Beijing would 'decide' to pursue hegemony and carve out a sphere of influence of its own." Mr Ramos said that Beijing's claims to sovereignty over the Spratly Islands and a vast surrounding area of the South China Sea stretching deep into the maritime heart of Southeast Asia was "the litmus test of whether China – as a great power – intends to play by international rules or make its own."[22] China has such disputes with Japan, Taiwan, South and North Korea, the Philippines, Vietnam, Malaysia, and Brunei. Most of the land territory involved is in the form of small, mainly uninhabited islands, atolls, and reefs. But such beach heads have become increasingly important to all claimants because they are the key to control valuable resources, including fisheries, oil and gas, in large areas of surrounding water and sea-bed.

Reports appeared on the eve of Hong Kong's reversion to Chinese sovereignty that the former British colony might lose its most desirable status to do business. Hong Kong was forecast to crash from being ranked the most desirable place in the world to do business to the 14th place, a study by the Economic Intelligence Unit (EIU) said in May 1997. In its first study into global business environment ranking, which looks at how attractive a country is to invest and do business, the EIU said that China's resumption of sovereignty over the booming territory of Hong Kong would be accompanied by a 'significant' risk. The report also predicted that Beijing would fail to fully honour its commitment to Hong Kong, causing its ranking to slide. In its second quarter global outlook report, the EIU predicted that Hong Kong, placed first for its optimal business environment in a comparison of 1992-1996 data, would see the sharpest drop of all 58 locations measured, to the 14th place in 1997-2001.[23] The study ruled out a disaster scenario following the handover of power to Beijing. However, it warned, "there is a significant risk that China will not fully honour its promise, repeatedly stated and enshrined in a number of documents, to keep Hong Kong stable and prosperous." Elements underpinning Hong Kong's free market, such as low taxes, guaranteed property rights, and a liberal trade and exchange regime, would remain after the handover, the EIU study said.

The Basic Law stipulates that Hong Kong will have a high degree of economic autonomy after 1997, but there were constant doubts both in and outside Hong Kong as to whether China would honour its promises. For example, Milton Freidman was quoted saying that China covets the US $43 billion worth of foreign exchange reserves held by the Hong Kong Monetary Authority. Freidman also predicted that the Hong Kong dollar would be scrapped. He was quoted as having said that it is inconceivable that a country like China would allow there to be two separate currencies with a variable rate of exchange between them.[24] Nevertheless, most people in Hong Kong in the run-up to the handover believed the autonomy bestowed on them would last at least on matters related to economic activities, and at least in the near future. Any alternative would be disastrous. For example, if the substitution of the Hong Kong dollar by an inconvertible Renmenbi is anticipated, all physical and financial assets in Hong Kong, dominated in Hong Kong dollar, would sharply deprecate, and there would immediately be an exodus of Hong Kong dollar to shelter in foreign currencies. The fact that this had not happened suggested that the market was still confident that the major economic provisions in the Basic Law would remain intact.

NOTES

1. Mark Roberti, *The fall of Hong Kong: China's Triumph and Britain's Betrayal* (New York, 1994), pp. 17-18.
2. Tsang Tak-Sing, "A Practical History" in *Far Eastern Economic Review*, Special 1997 issue (Hong Kong), p. 20.
3. William H. Overhalt, "Hong Kong and China: A New Relationship", *Current History* (Philadelphia) Vol. 84, No. 503, p. 256.
4. Margaret Thatcher, *The Downing Street Years* (London, 1993) pp. 259-262.
5. *Asia Year Book 1983,* (Hong Kong, 1983) pp. 145-146.
6. *The Origins and Current Circumstances of the Hong Kong Question*, (Beijing, 1994), p. 6.
7. Ibid., p. 7
8. Roberti, n. 1, pp. 84-85.
9. Harvey Stockwin, *South Morning Post* (Hong Kong) 5 August, 1984.
10. Robert Cottrell, *The End of Hong Kong: The Secret Diplomacy of Imperial Retreat*, (London 1993), p. 174.
11. Peter Harris, "Hong Kong Confronts 1997: An Assessment of the Sino-British Agreement", *Pacific Affairs* Vol. 59, No. 1, Spring 1986, p. 49.
12. For the text of the Joint Declaration please see Annexure II.
13. *Reference Paper for the Basic Law Hong Kong Special Administration Region of People's Republic of China* (Hong Kong: Secretariat of the Consultative Committee for the Basic Law February 1987), p. 1.
14. *Beijing Review*, Vol. 27, No. 44, October 1984, p. 16.
15. *Beijing Review*, Vol. 26, No. 32, 8 August 1983, p. 5.
16. *Beijing Review*, Vol. 27, No. 30, 23 July 1984, p. 16.

17. Ram Dev Bharadwaj 'China's Economic Reform: The Role and Significance of SEZs,' *Strategic Analysis* (New Delhi), Vol. XV, No. 11, February, 1993, p. 1097.
18. Margaret Ng. *Note on Preparatory Committee* (Hong Kong', 1996).
19. Joseph Y. S. Cheng. "The Basic Law: Message from Hong Kong People" in Richard Y. C. Wong and Joseph Y. S. Chang ed., *The Other Hong Kong Report 1990* (Hong Kong, 1990), p. 51.
20. *Commentary on the Draft Hong Kong Bill of Rights Ordinance 1990* (Hong Kong: The Government Printer, March 1990), p. 1.
21. *Asian Age*, May 15, 1997.
22. Ibid.
23. *The Tribune*, May 19, 1997.
24. *Far Eastern Economic Review*, February 23, 1997, p. 55.

CHAPTER 5

Political Participation and Democratisation

One major issue that created considerable irritation between Britain and the People's Republic of China in the run-up to the reversion of China's sovereignty over Hong Kong – which was fraught with further tension in Hong Kong pertained to the attempts by Chris Patten, Hong Kong's last British Governor, to introduce and implement democratic reforms in Hong Kong in October 1992. While Chris Patten defended and justified his constitutional package and maintained that his package was in consonance with the Basic Law of the Hong Kong Special Administrative Region and the Sino-British Joint Declaration, Beijing criticised the move and said it was breach of the Joint Declaration, and threatened to abolish the elected Legislative Council, immediately after resumption of sovereignty over the territory. Later, Beijing appointed its own nominated Legislature, which replaced the earlier elected Council.

Although there is no dearth of literature on Hong Kong's democracy movement, most of them are written by scholars who do not approach the problem of democracy in Hong Kong in a historical and socio-economic perspective. Notwithstanding the fact that the basic tenets of democracy remain sacrosanct the world over, every country has its legitimate right to carve out its path to democracy in the light of its historical experience. There is no 'one size fits all' or a prototype of democracy. It is against this backdrop that the narrative of democracy in Hong Kong should be understood in proper perspective. To do so, it is imperative to delineate briefly the nature and character of political economy of Hong Kong and then analyse Patten's constitutional package, juxtaposing with the Joint Declaration and the Basic Law, so as to determine the extent of digression and deviation from the Joint Declaration and the Basic Law and finally the practicability, desirability, and the compatibility of implementing a democratic package which China did not approve.

POLITICAL ECONOMY OF HONG KONG

Ever since the Union Jack was hoisted in the island territory, which was described as a 'fever-stricken rock' and a barren island' to its rise as the El Dorado of the East, the story of Hong Kong has been a story of rags to riches. Productivity and profit have been the guiding gospel of its dynamic people. Hong Kong, from its very inception, had been primarily an economic entity. Its political identity had been incidental and secondary. According to Larry Diamond and Ramon H Myers, "As the Hong Kong territory expanded under new treaties between England and imperial China, a definitive pattern of colonial rule evolved. British authorities brooked no political opposition and permitted no electoral process, but they gave Chinese inhabitants the freedom to live their lives and their family and lineage affairs. Even after the Second World War, the British refused to an electoral process for creating a legislative body to propose and approve laws and monitor the Colony's budget.[1] In Hong Kong, government became an imperative necessity to facilitate trade and commerce. The role and responsibility of the government was limited and restricted to the maintenance of law and order, enforcement of laws and contracts and providing military and naval protection for the promotion of trade and commerce. It was indeed a typical case of Adam Smith's laissez-faire economy, although in later years the role and activities of the colonial government gradually increased touching other spheres of social life. Officials of the Hong Kong government, such as former financial secretary Sir Philip Hadden Cave, however, opined that laissez-faire was inadequate and passive. He preferred to call Hong Kong government's attitude towards economic affairs 'positive non-interventionism'. According to him, positive non-interventionism means, "taking the view that in the great majority of circumstances, it is futile and damaging to the growth of the economy for attempts to be made to plan the allocation of resources available to the private sector and to frustrate the operation of market forces, which in an open economy are difficult enough to predict, let alone to control."[2]

The policy and attitude of the British government with regard to Hong Kong in the formative years of the Colony is discussed in greater detail in Chapter II and they need not be repeated here. The main thrust of the government in Hong Kong was to avoid the exuberance of democracy and the pitfalls of adversarial politics. As such, the policy of the British government and of the colonial administration in Hong Kong was geared to ensure social harmony and political stability so as to create a congenial and conducive atmosphere for trade, commerce, and entrepreneurial pursuit. From the beginning, therefore, the idea and objective of the British government and the colonial administration in Hong Kong was to develop a government through discussion and consultation. This policy has been described by Ambrose Yeo-Chi King as 'administrative absorption of politics' – an arrangement whereby leaders of the Chinese populace were co-opted into the government administrative machinery.[3] This political support accorded to the colonial government by this elite thus produced legitimacy for a polity that worked without the mandate of the people.[4] The elite were drawn from the higher echelons of society, mostly from trade and industry. They were Westernised and Anglicised ethnic Chinese who worked as a connect between the colonial administration and the ethnic Chinese populace. The executive, legislative, and representative institutions which developed in Hong Kong clearly reflected the administrative absorption of politics. In this political arrangement, the executive retained an upper hand and were accountable to the British Parliament through the Secretary of State.

Be that as it may, there was no major attempt – except the attempt made by Sir Mark Young after the Second World War – to introduce representative institutions in the territory until 1980. It may be mentioned that the colonial government had set up a Sanitary Board, with local government functions concerned with the maintenance of public health as early as 1883. The Sanitary Board acquired unofficial members in 1886, two of whom were first elected in 1888. The Sanitary Board later developed into Urban Council, and as such its constitutional importance can hardly be over-emphasised. A major constitutional development after the Urban Council election in 1972 was the decision to constitute District Boards.

The decision of the Hong Kong government in 1981 to introduce District Boards as advisory representative bodies and make it partly elective was in line with the government's commitment to involve and associate people at the grassroots level in the activities of the government, having a bearing on the welfare of the people. In a different nomenclature, District Boards were already in existence in the New Territories, but they were not elective. The decision to hold elections for the District Board was perhaps prompted by the realisation on the part of the British government and the colonial administration in Hong Kong that it would be no longer possible to hold on to the Colony beyond 1997.

It may be mentioned in this context that the then Governor of Hong Kong, Sir Murry Maclehose had visited Beijing in 1979 and held wide-ranging discussions with Deng Xiaoping with regard to the future of Hong Kong. The governor got a clear message from

Deng that the Chinese would not only recover sovereignty over Hong Kong, but also Beijing would have its own administration in the territory. This ruled out any possibility of British administration in Hong Kong under Chinese sovereignty. Thus, the decision to set up District Boards and introduce election for this purpose was suggestive of Britain's desire to make an honourable exit from its last major colonial outpost. The Hong Kong government in June 1980 published the *Green Paper—A Pattern of District Administration in Hong Kong*. The main objective of the proposed District Boards was "to achieve better coordination and a more responsive administration at the district level." In pursuance of the underlying objectives of the *White Paper*, necessary legislations were enacted for the formation of District Boards and for their elections.

As regards the composition of the District Board, it was stipulated that in addition to the appointed official and unofficial members, some members were to be directly elected by the eligible voters of the constituency. The government also explicitly mentioned in the *White Paper* that as far as possible, a majority of the members of the District Board should be directly elected. The appointed official members included the District Commissioners and the representatives of government departments. The appointed unofficial members were to be the members of the public selected and appointed by the government to serve on District Boards, and in case of New Territories, chairman of Rural Committees. The size of each Board was to be 25 to 30 members. The functions of the District Board included civic matters like environmental hygiene, recreational, and cultural activities etc. The functions were more or less in the nature of those performed by residents' welfare associations in a residential colony.

Elections for the District Board were held in the New Territories in April 1982 and for Kowloon and Hong Kong later in September. The government made an all-out effort to enthuse the voters to take part in the electoral processes. However, in spite of the government's well-orchestrated propaganda, only 3,45,000 voters (constituting 38% registered voters) actually exercised their franchise.[5] Yet one more interesting highlight of the election was that none of the candidates raised the issue pertaining to the future of Hong Kong. Presumably, the platform of District Boards was perhaps inappropriate to raise such an issue. Nevertheless, the importance of the first District Board could hardly be overemphasized. While it was yet one more instance of 'administrative absorption of politics,' it also exposed the people of Hong Kong – who are perceived to be apolitical – to the dynamics and complexities of electoral politics in a limited scale.

Although first District Board election did not produce desired result of political participation, Hong Kong government was resolute to go ahead with further development of a representative government in the territory. It is plausible that the British government wanted to develop 'self-rule' in the Colony before finally handing over the territory to a Communist regime. It may also be noted here in this connection that as early as November 20, 1982, Mr Liao Chengzhi, former Vice-Chairman of the National People's Council and head of the Hong Kong and Macao office, told a delegation of Hong Kong factory owners that Beijing would recover sovereignty over Hong Kong by 1997 at the latest and the territory would be administered by Hong Kong people. Later in January 1983, he told a visiting group of Hong Kong New Territory village leaders that "China is working on a draft formula which was yet to be presented to Britain. The format of Hong Kong people administering Hong Kong (*Gangren Zhigang*) can only be implemented after it was presented and recorded by the National People's Council (NPC).[6] The pledge of Hong Kong people administering Hong Kong was later incorporated in the Sino-British Joint Declaration signed in December 1984. The Joint Declaration, as noted earlier, stipulated that the proposed HKSAR would have 'a high degree of autonomy' with a fully 'elected legislature' after 1997. It, however, did not define the mode of election. It only mentioned that the system to be instituted in the HKSAR shall be prescribed by laws enacted by the National People's Congress in the light of the specific conditions.

Thus by 1984, there were two parallel developments taking place in China and Hong Kong. While on the one hand, the negotiation with regard to transfer of sovereignty over Hong Kong was finalised, paving the path for the Sino-British Joint Declaration, on the other hand, Hong Kong government initiated concrete steps for further development of representative institutions in the territory. The British government, in their wisdom, might have felt that since the Chinese authorities were offering the concept of Hong Kong people ruling Hong Kong, it was imperative to introduce and develop representative institutions in Hong Kong. Since the transfer of sovereignty over Hong Kong also entailed handing over the people of Hong Kong – who were used to democratic values and milieus – to a Communist regime, the British government felt it was their moral responsibility to develop representative institutions in Hong Kong before their departure. As the Joint Declaration initiated in September 1984 had to be ratified by the British Parliament, the British government considered it prudent to develop representative institutions so as to ensure ratification of the Joint Declaration by the British Parliament.

It was in this background that in July 1984, the Hong Kong government published the *Green Paper - The Further Development of Representative Government in Hong Kong*. The Paper proposed addition of 12 elected members to the Legco in 1985, six to be immediately elected by an electoral college comprising all members of the District Board, the Urban Council, and the Regional Council, and six directly elected by the functional constituencies consisting of member of the professions and commercial and industrial organisations. It was further proposed that the number of members chosen by the Electoral College and the functional constituencies should be doubled in 1988 and further increased in subsequent years.[7]

The idea of introducing direct elections to the Legislative Council (Legco) sometime in the near future was mentioned, but this possibility was immediately deprecated on the ground that direct elections would run the risk of swift introduction of adversarial politics and the development of political parties, which would make it more difficult to reach decisions pragmatically on the basis of a general consensus, and so would undermine Hong Kong's stability and prosperity. Hong Kong government's official view on the *Green Paper* was articulated by Governor Sir Edward Youde in his address to a special meeting of the Legco on July 18, 1984. He said, "In drawing up our progress, we have had regard to the special circumstances of Hong Kong, and the need to maintain our good relationship with our mainland neighbour. We have also done our utmost in framing the proposal to enable continuity between the system in force both before and after 1997."[8] The proposal greatly annoyed Beijing, and the Chinese authorities believed they had been worked out by the British with the aim of having pro-British people administer Hong Kong after 1997.[9]

The *Green Paper* was followed up by the Hong Kong government with a *White Paper* in November 1984. In many respects, the *White Paper* constituted an advance on the *Green Paper.* In the first place, the *White Paper* proposed that the Electoral College would return 12 unofficial members to the Legislative Council in 1985 elections instead of six members originally mentioned in the *Green Paper*. As regards functional constituencies, the *White Paper* proposed that instead of informal systems of selecting unofficial members of the Council, there should be a formal representative for the election of one or more representative from each functional constituency to serve on the Council. It was also proposed that these arrangements should be introduced progressively, with six unofficial members to be elected by functional constituencies in 1985 and 12 of them in 1988.

As regards appointed unofficial members, the *White Paper* recommended significant reduction in the number of appointed unofficial members in order to accommodate the increase in the number of elected unofficial members. The Hong Kong government, therefore, decided to increase the overall size of the Council to 56 and reduce the number of appointed unofficial members to 22 in 1985. *The White Paper* also proposed to reduce the number of official members to 10 in 1985. All these steps were aimed at making the legislature more representative. The executive, however, still retained its supremacy vis-à-vis the legislature. Regarding direct elections scheduled for 1985, as suggested in the *Green Paper*, the *White Paper* claimed that there was little evidence of support for any move towards direct election. Instead, the *White Paper* suggested a cautious approach with a gradual start by introducing a very small number of directly elected members in 1988.[10] Although the Chinese government did not exert any direct pressure on the British government or the Hong Kong government to restrain them from introducing direct election, the Chinese displeasure and annoyance compelled the British government and the Hong Kong government to slow down the process of direct election to Legco. The first-ever indirect elections to the Legco were held in September 1985, and the 24 newly-elected members took their seats for the first time in October 1985.

Thus from 1982 to 1985, concern for the territory and the challenge posed by the development of representative government contributed to the organisation and development of many political groups and grassroots pressure groups. Their development was further facilitated by the District Board elections and Legco elections of 1985. Middle-class political groups were prompted to develop their organisations at grassroots level and to establish close ties with the grassroots pressure groups. At the same time, they became concerned with the local social issues and took part in the related campaign for citizen's rights. This process contributed to the expansion of almost all political groups and provided the basis for a territory-wide movement for democracy.[11]

The introduction of electoral politics and the prospect of democracy thus polarised the apolitical people of Hong Kong. While the younger generation intelligentsia and the middle class opted for democracy, the conservative business community opposed the move for democracy and direct election. Beijing opposed and criticised the attempts made by the British government and the colonial administration in Hong Kong to introduce democratisation in Hong Kong. The fact that the British government and the Hong Kong government buckled under pressure to rescind the commitment to hold direct elections to Legco in 1988 could be gauged from the *White Paper* on the "Further Development of Representative Government in Hong Kong" brought out in February 1988. The *White Paper* strongly pleaded against holding elections to Legco. Claiming that public opinion was against hasty introduction of direct election, the report mentioned that those who argued against direct election were of the opinion that introduction of direct election in 1988 was too soon because it could endanger stability and continuity. The government, instead, decided to go for direct election in 1991.[12]

The tumultuous Tiananmen Square incident of June 1989, however, triggered the alarm bell for the democracy movement in Hong Kong, which had slowed down earlier. If the epicenter was in Tiananmen Square, the tremor was felt no less strongly in Hong Kong. Events in Beijing galvanized one million Hong Kong citizens to march on behalf of democracy on May 21, and May 28, one-and-a-half million people took out a procession in the streets of Hong Kong. There was erosion of public faith and confidence in the efficacy of the Sino-British Joint Declaration and the Basic Law. The erosion of confidence was reflected in the exodus of people and resources from Hong Kong. The Heng Seng index also fell sharply. Pressure built up in Hong Kong and in British Parliament and the press to beef up democratic institutions in Hong Kong. A high powered delegation from British Parliament visited Hong Kong from April 17 to 22, and presented its report to the British Parliament on June 28. The Foreign Affairs Committee recommended that the Hong Kong government must seize the initiative so as to establish in Hong Kong in advance of 1997 the institutions and systems best designed to guarantee Hong Kong's future autonomy and stability within the terms of the Joint Declaration. As regards introducing direct election to Legco, the Committee recommended that full direct election should be introduced before 1997, and that at the preceding election in 1991, 50% of the members of Legco should be directly elected as the first stage of this process.[13] In Hong Kong, the colonial government amended its earlier decision that only 10 out of 60 seats in Legco would be directly elected by universal suffrage in 1991. On May 24, 1989, members of the Executive and Legislative Council (Omelco) expressed their strong desire to speed up and enlarge the scope of pre-1997 constitutional reform. The 'Omelco Consensus' model aimed at having one kind of the Legco directly elected in 1991, increasing to one-half by 1995. It also proposed direct elections for the entire Legco by 2003.

In Hong Kong, China's crackdown on student protest gave a tremendous boost not just to the demand for self-government as a safeguard against Chinese interference, but also to the more 'subversive' corollary that Hong Kong's only real protection was the democratisation of China itself. Hong Kong's most active democrats, including Martun Lee and teacher's union leader Szeto Wah, formed a new group at this time, the Hong Kong Alliance in Support of the Patriotic Democratic Movement in China. Beijing's leaders quickly dubbed the alliance subversive in its aims.[14]

The conservative big business elites who were the members of the Basic Law Consultative Committee and the Basic Law Drafting Committee, however, relaxed their opposition to directly elected components in both the pre- and post-1997 legislature. Although they did not endorse the Omelco model, they came out with their own model of 4:4:2 in October 1989. This referred to the proportional distribution of directly elected seats (40%), functional constituency seats (40%), and electoral college-originated seats (20%) for the Legco from 1995 to 2000.[15]

BASIC LAW AND THE COMPOSITION OF LEGCO

Meanwhile, on April 4, 1990, the National People's Congress (NCP) promulgated the Basic Law of HKSR. Deng Xiaoping held it as a 'creative masterpiece' with historical and international significance for the whole mankind. As regards the composition of HKSR legislature, Article 67 of the Basic Law provides that it shall be composed of Chinese citizens who are permanent citizens of the region with no right of abode in any foreign country. However, permanent residents of the region who are not of Chinese nationality or who have the right of abode in foreign countries may also be elected members of the Legco provided that the proportion of such member did not exceed 20% of the total membership of the Council.

Article 68 of the Basic Law stipulates that the Legco of HKSR shall be constituted by election. The method for forming the Legco shall be specified in the light of the actual situation in HKSR and in accordance with the principal of gradual and orderly progress. The ultimate aim was the election of all the members of the Legco eventually. As regards the composition of first Legco, the NCP in its third session held on April 4, 1990, decided that the first Legco shall be composed of 60 members, with 20 members returned by the geographical constituencies through direct election, 10 members returned by an election committee, and 30 members returned by functional constituencies. The NCP also decided that if the Hong Kong Legco before the establishment of HKSR was in conformity with relevant provisions of this decision and the Basic Law, those of its members who uphold the Basic Law and pledge allegiance to HKSR and those who meet the requirements stipulated in the Basic Law, upon confirmation by the preparatory committee might become members of the first Legco.

The underlying idea behind allowing the members of last Hong Kong Legco, before the transition to Chinese sovereignty to continue with the first Legco of HKSR under Chinese sovereignty was to have change with continuity and to avoid a vacuum in the transitional period. This was described by the Chinese authorities as the 'through train' emphasizing convergence with the letter and spirit of the Basic Law. An article in *Ta Kung Pao* compared Hong Kong to a running train, the Basic Law having laid down a new track on which it would run. The conclusion was that "unless the train heads for the beginning of the new track now, it might go off the rails and overturn."[16]

THE 1991 ELECTION

In contacts between the British and Chinese government in early spring of 1990, it was eventually agreed that there would be a steady increase in the number of directly elected members of Legco from 18 in 1991 to at least 20 in 1995, and more in subsequent years. The British government made it clear that it would prefer pace, and would continue to press for it.[17] The British government announced its decision to hold election to Legco in 1991 immediately after the promulgation of the Basic Law by the NCP. The announcement was received with mixed reaction in Hong Kong. Martin Lee, the leader of Democracy Movement denounced the secret agreement between Britain and China as "a shameful act of surrender."[18] What he particularly bemoaned was that the people of Hong Kong were not consulted in the finalisation of the drafting of the Basic Law, although some pro-Beijing elites were associated with the Basic Law Drafting Committee.

The announcement to hold elections to Legco was taken both as a challenge and an opportunity by all concerned, the democrats and the conservative business elite. It was indeed a prestige issue for both. The election was a new and different kind of an experience for the people of Hong Kong. The Joint Declaration and the Basic Law had already aroused political consciousness among the people who had a taste of electioneering earlier at the District Board election, Urban Council election and indirect election to the functional constituency of Legco. Although Beijing was opposed to formation of political parties in Hong Kong, once elections were declared, it actively extended support to groups/parties owing allegiance to it. The *Liberal Democratic Federation of Hong Kong* (LDF), supported by the conservative big business elites, was inaugurated on November 6, 1990. The pro-democracy circle's two new political parties, the *United Democrats of Hong Kong* (HKUD), and the *Hong Kong Democratic Foundation* (HKDF) were formally established on April 23 and June 24, 1990 respectively. The historical first direct elections for the Legco held on September 15, 1991, yielded a landslide victory for democratic activists, who captured 16 of the 18 contested seats and 65% of the popular votes. The voter turnout was record at 7,50,000 of 39.15% of the 1.91 million registered voters. A total of 54 candidates for 18 seats in nine electoral districts with 354 polling stations throughout the whole territory.[19] In spite of low percentage of voting, the direct election to Legco and its result can hardly be overemphasized. First of all, it conveyed to Beijing that the people of Hong Kong wanted democracy and a democratic way of life. Secondly, an elected legislature subjected the executive to greater scrutiny and accountability. In fact, it signalled the shape of political changes which were bound to occur in the territory. The democratic election also posed a threat to the hitherto practice of 'administrative absorption of politics.'

PATTEN'S PACKAGE

When Chris Patten unveiled his constitutional reform proposal in his policy address to Legco on October 7, 1992, it gave a further impetus to the tempo of democracy movement in Hong Kong. A major component of Patten's Package was to increase the number of directly elected members of Legco from 18 to 20 and he also promised to increase the number at subsequent elections with ultimate aim of achieving a Council composed entirely of directly-elected members. Patten also proposed to reduce the voting age from 21 to 18 and give each elector a single vote for a singly elected representative in a single seat constituency. His package also created nine more functional constituencies and dispensed with all forms of corporate voting. The corporate voting was replaced with individual voting. Taken together, these measures were aimed at expanding the franchise in the functional constituencies by more than five times.[20]

In his policy address, Patten also promised to increase government spending to provide better education, health and welfare service, public housing, and environmental protection, and to maintain law and order. Patten's proposal created such an outrage in China that *Xinhua* news agency accused him of being 'imprudent'. The Chinese government criticised that the package contravened the Sino-British Joint Declaration, the principle of convergence with the Basic Law, and agreement and understanding already reached between the two sides, both in its content and in the way it was produced.[21]

The Chinese side further alleged that without prior consultations with the Chinese authorities, the British government suddenly and unilaterally made public a constitutional package in gross violation of the above-mentioned provisions of the Joint Declaration. However, Patten claimed in his policy address that in their meeting in New York in the last week of September 1992, the Secretary of State for Foreign and Commonwealth Affairs made the case to the Chinese Foreign Minister for an expansion in the number of members of the 1995 Legco to be chosen by direct election. The Chinese position was that such a move would be incompatible with the Basic Law and he said that the Basic Law could not be changed before 1997.

Some political observers in Hong Kong attributed China's obstinate attitude towards Patten's reforms to Beijing's 'conspiracy theory'. Chinese leaders regarded Patten's democratisation proposals as a carefully planned strategy devised by Western capitalist societies – the so called 'anti-China chorus' – to exert pressure on China, using Hong Kong as a potential bridgehead. In this vein, Lu Ping Director of China's Hong Kong and Macao Affairs Office argued that there had been lengthy consultations with the British before an agreement was reached and the Basic Law approved by China's National People's Congress. The sudden change in British policy was nothing more than 'setting a trap' for China. "The crux of the matter was not whether one wanted democracy or not, but whether one needed to keep one's word."[22]

It was against this backdrop of mutual suspicion and distrust, both sides made attempts to break the stalemate. When a compromise seemed elusive, the Hong Kong government on March 12, 1993, formally gazette the draft legislation on the Legco. This action of the Governor was criticised by Beijing. Chinese Premier Li Peng while addressing the first session of the Eighth National People's Congress on March 15, 1993, said that the action of British Governor was in essence designed to create disorder and impede the smooth transfer of power.[23] Speaking at a press conference in Beijing, Lu Ping warned that China would start preparations for setting up a 'new kitchen' – its own legislative structure for Hong Kong after 1997 in accordance with the Basic Law – since the doors for talks between China and Britain had been shut by Chris Patten. Lu further added that China always stood for the development of democracy in Hong Kong, but the process of democratisation had to be 'gradual, or step by step' as it was for the sake of safeguarding the long-term prosperity and stability of Hong Kong".[24] Patten's constitutional reforms proposal polarised the polity and society in Hong Kong. The middle-class intelligentsia and the pro-democracy camp were led by Martin Lee. On the other side of the fence were the conservative big business elite who accorded a high premium to stability and prosperity than democracy.

1995 ELECTION TO LEGCO

As envisaged under Patten's constitutional reform, election to the 60 members' Legco was held on September 17, 1995. The election had already created considerable media attention not only in Hong Kong, but the world over. In spite of Beijing's threat that the elected legislature would be scrapped immediately after the reversion of Chinese sovereignty, 35.8% of registered voters voted in the election. Although Beijing had publicly criticised the election, it encouraged the Democratic *Alliance for the Betterment of Hong Kong*, a party formed from traditional pro-Beijing groupings such as unions, guilds, and neighbourhood organisations to fight the election.

The *Democratic Party* and its allies scored a resounding victory in the election. Of the 25 seats it contested, Martin Lee's *Democratic Party* itself secured 19 seats. Lee himself had a cakewalk, securing 80% of the votes in his constituency, the highest for any candidate. Commenting on the result, Lee said, "Hong Kong people voted with their hearts and minds for freedom and genuine democracy. The elections are a mandate for democratic government in Hong Kong and real constitutional, legal, and human rights reforms to ensure basic freedom after 1997."[25] Other supporters of Lee included the *Association for Democracy* and *People's Livelihood* (ADPL), a grassroots party with social welfare concerns, plus prominent independents like Emily Lau. The pro-China camp led by the *Democratic Alliance for Betterment of Hong Kong* (DAB) won seven seats. The DAB had campaigned as the party best able to defend Hong Kong's interests, because of its ability to work with Beijing. The DAB chairman Tsang Tou-sing, one of China's blue-eyed politicians, lost by a big margin. Sandwiched between the two camps was the pro-business Liberal Party which won two seats. Independents and other together won remaining 20 seats.

The moment the result was declared, China reiterated its earlier position. A spokesman for *Xinhua* News Agency was quoted as suggesting that the elections had been unfair. "To be fair, they had to be orderly, and no one has to explain", he said. "The result showed that the hope for a smooth transition and love of the motherland and Hong Kong remain the main trend in Hong Kong." The Chinese government also made it clear that the three-tier political structure, (Legislative Council, Municipal Council, and District Boards) formed under Patten's package would stop functioning in mid-1997 when China resumed exercise of sovereignty over Hong Kong.[26]

MARTIN LEE

The resounding success of the Democratic Party in the election catapulted the leader of the *Democratic Party* Martin Lee to prominence not only in Hong Kong, but also internationally. In a society where politics had so far been regarded as taboo, Lee was quite successful not only in enthusing the apolitical denizens of Hong Kong, but also in bringing together motley democratic elements in the Colony against the formidable opposition of Beijing and the conservative forces in the colony. Although international media gave due reportage on the election is Hong Kong, coverage on Martin Lee, the chief architect of democratic victory, was subdued. The media in Hong Kong from where some of the most prestigious newspapers and magazines are published resorted to self-censorship for obvious reasons.

As a child, Lee aspired to become a diplomat. Ironically, however, Hong Kong (where he was born in 1938) was not destined to become an independent state. Lee's father was originally a domicile of Guangdong, a Chinese province adjacent to Hong Kong. He could have obtained the status of British nationality by virtue of being born in a British territory, but his father insisted otherwise. Incidentally Lee's father was a very good friend of Zhou Enlai who later became

Chinese Premier under Mao Zedong. In spite of their ideological difference, they continued to be friends and agreed to disagree and finally parted company. Lee's father could have also fled to Taiwan when *Kuo-min-tang* (KMT) led by Chiang-Kai Shek established the Republic of China, but the rampant corruption endemic in the nationalist government was too much for him to withstand. He, therefore, decided to settle in Hong Kong. Martin Lee graduated from Hong Kong University in 1960, and in 1965 went to London to study Law. He came back to Hong Kong to start his career and established himself as one of the most successful lawyers in the Colony. In his spare time, he had been active in the social and political life of Hong Kong. Although he could not become a diplomat, events in Hong Kong during the transitional years pitchforked him to the role of an astute politician negotiating with both Beijing and London for a best deal for Hong Kong.

When negotiation between China and Britain started in 1982 after Ms Thatcher's visit to the Chinese capital, Beijing leadership tried to garner Lee's support in their efforts to forge a united front strategy to win over Hong Kong's intelligentsia. Since Lee commanded a good deal of respectability among Hong Kong citizenry, particularly teachers, students, lawyers, and liberal trade union workers, Beijing though it wise to rope him in. *Xinhua*, Beijing's unofficial embassy in Hong Kong, was given instructions accordingly. No wonder, therefore, when the historic Joint Declaration with regard to the transfer of sovereignty was signed between London and Beijing in the Chinese capital in December, 1984, Lee had the honour of witnessing the event along with few other invitees from Hong Kong. Later in July 1985, the Beijing leadership in their united front exercise appointed Martin Lee to the Basic Law Drafting Committee (BLDC).

Lee was elected to the Legco in September 1985 representing the lawyer's constituency in the system of functional representation when indirect elections were held for the first time to the Council. His election to the council gave him the platform to speak for Hong Kong more authoritatively and firmly. His membership of the legislature gave him greater leverage to plead with Beijing firmly during the parleys in the meetings of the Drafting Committee. The Drafting Committee was, however, dominated by members from the mainland and pro-Beijing elements from Hong Kong with the only exception of Szeto Wah, a like-minded liberal democrat representing the teaching community from Hong Kong. In the Drafting Committee, Lee and Wah together strongly pleaded for Hong Kong's cause and argued for greater autonomy, the rights and freedom of its inhabitants and for an independent judiciary.

Things, however, always do not move in a linear path and both Lee and Wah had a very excruciating experience in the Drafting Committee so much so that both declared that they would not serve as long as the Deng-Li-Yang clique remained in power, referring to senior leader Deng Xiapeng, Premier Li Peng and head of the State Yeng Shangkun. In November 1989, National People's Congress of China declared that Lee and Szeto had engaged in activities inconsistent with the status of Drafting Committee members and suspended them.[27] Martin Lee, however continued his fight for democracy and formed Hong Kong's first political party *The United Democrats* in 1990. The result of the 1995 election was yet another feather in his cap. However, what worried Lee most was not reversion of Hong Kong's sovereignty and administration to China, but the fear that this tiny capitalist enclave may perhaps lose its democratic values such as freedom of expression, legal, judicial, and human rights which have so successfully nourished this capitalist enclave for years ever since its inception.

Lee, therefore, would have liked the political system to be transparent and responsive to the ethos and social milieu of Hong Kong. He was particularly haunted by the nightmare of the Tiananmen Square incident of June 1989 which gravely affected the climate of confidence in Hong Kong. He was skeptical that Hong Kong may not be the same again after July 1, 1997. In 2008, Martin Lee decided to quit politics, but he continued his fight for democracy in Hong Kong. All these years, however, he remained in political hibernation, only to be shot into limelight when he was arrested by the Hong Kong authorities along with 14 other pro-democracy activists in mid-April 2020.

DEMOCRACY AND DEVELOPMENT: THE HONG KONG PARADIGM

The debate on democracy in Hong Kong had triggered a moot question: whether faster democratisation in Hong Kong would promote or retard growth and development in that island city, other than making the Colony's legislature more representative and broad-based? The causal connection between democracy and development is of critical importance in case of Hong Kong. This is because this thriving island territory had a long-standing tradition of laissez faire market economy, and because of it, the delinquencies of electoral politics of liberal democracy were more of an aberration than the rule.

China's major concern was that if Hong Kong was allowed to go ahead with rapid democratisation, the territory would be used as base of subversion of the Communist system, and the compulsions of electoral politics may seriously destabilise Hong Kong's economy and society at large. China's concern was not without substance in the light of Hong Kong's role during the pro-democracy movement in the mainland in June 1989. Initially an entrepot, Hong Kong in the present-day world had emerged as the world's third largest financial centre, besides being a leading manufacturing and trading centre.

It is against this backdrop of the consensus politics of Hong Kong, which had given stability and prosperity, that there had been a plea not to disturb the social harmony in Hong Kong. Adherents of such viewpoints advocate a sort of right-wing authoritarian capitalism which can be obtained either through the rule of a dominant party or through charismatic leadership. Such an approach is advanced by most of the high profile pro-Beijing businessmen of Hong Kong like Mr TA Ann, a leading industrialist; Sir YK Pao, the shipping tycoon; and David Li of the Bank of East Asia.[28] Mention may also be made of Mr Harilela, the doyen of the Indian community and a leading businessman in Hong Kong.

Echoing the sentiment expressed by Leo Kuan Yew, the most charismatic leader of Singapore and one of the world's most brilliant economic policy makers that the exuberance of democracy leads to indiscipline and disorderly conduct which are inimical to development, Phillip Tose, chairman of the Peregrine Investments, a Hong Kong Merchant Bank, was of the view that what Hong Kong needed was not political democracy but economic democracy.

Comparing cases of Asia like India and Philippines, which have rich natural resources, with the newly industrialised countries of Asia such as Singapore, Taiwan, South Korea, and Hong Kong, Tose was of the view that the high economic growth of the newly industrialised countries was due to the authoritarian regimes that had created the right environment for business to thrive.[29] Interestingly, Tose was of the firm view that the failure of countries like India and Philippines to achieve prosperity was attributable to the democratic polity that existed in both the countries. The common thread running through all these alternative approaches to the question of democracy in Hong Kong was that electoral politics of the parliamentary variety would politicise the people of Hong Kong which, in turn, would unleash disruptive and destabilising forces. So, the major thrust of their emphasis was on maintaining the stability and prosperity of Hong Kong as a pre-requisite for maintaining the economic growth of the city.

CONCLUSION

The pro-democracy movement in Hong Kong, and China's attempts to muzzle it through various means (including the latest measure of National Security Law discussed in the subsequent chapters) has certainly eroded the tenets of the 'one country, two systems', as pledged under the Sino-British Joint Declaration and the Basic Law, and in turn the efficacy of Hong Kong as an international business hub and financial centre. Hong Kong – the eighth largest exporter of goods in the world – is the world's fourth largest stock exchange. Its banking system is seamlessly connected with the world, and its currency is pegged with the US dollar. All these are at stake if stability in Hong Kong continues to be affected. Already, ever since the reversion of Hong Kong to mainland China, some corporate houses have relocated themselves to other places – including Singapore, Australia, and Canada – and more may follow in the course of time. Taiwan has already started appealing to students from Hong Kong for admission in its universities and colleges.

POLARISATION OF SOCIETY AND POLITY

The pro-democracy movement in Hong Kong has polarised Hong Kong society and polity. Broadly, we can divide the citizens of Hong Kong into three categories – those Anglicised, who co-opted themselves with the British and benefited from them in service or business; the immigrant Chinese who share deep loyalty to the motherland; and finally the younger generation, those born during or after Hong Kong's handover to China. In fact, these younger generation people are spearheading the pro-democracy movement in Hong Kong. Yet students from mainland China who are studying in the universities and colleges of Hong Kong are loyal to China and they are looked at with suspicion by their peers in Hong Kong. The pro-democracy movement has broken the political apathy or insularity of Hong Kong people. The unprecedented turnout in the District Board elections and the resounding victory of pro-democracy parties have clearly signalled the advent of electoral politics which Hong Kong has shunned all these years. Now onwards, the demand for direct election to Legco for all seats will increase. Since the elected members of the District Board also have a voting share for the election to the Legco, the number of democratic candidates will increase. But as per the revised electoral law, an aspiring member for Legco has to obtain the prior approval of China.

NOTES

1. Larry Diamond and Ramon H. Myers, "Introduction: Elections and Democracy in Greater China", *China Quarterly,* No. 126, June, 2000, p. 379.
2. Philip Hadden Cave, "Introduction: The Making of some Aspects of Public Policy in Hong Kong" in David Lethbridge (ed). *The Business Environment in Hong Kong* (Hong Kong, 1980), p. 12.
3. Ambrose Yeo-Chi King, "Administrative Absorption of Politics in Hong Kong: Emphasis on the Grassroots level", *Asian Survey* (Berkeley), vol. 15, no. 5, 1975, pp. 422-439.
4. Lee Ming-Kwan, "Politicians" in Richard Wong and Yoseph Cheng (ed.), *The Other Kong Report 1990*, (Hong Kong, 1990), pp. 22-23.
5. Lo Shiu-hing, "Decolonisation in Hong Kong", *Asian Survey* (Berkeley), vol. XXVIII, no. 6, 1988, p. 615.
6. H.K. Lamb, *A Date with Fate* (Hong Kong, 1985), p. 193.
7. *Green Paper: The Further Development of Representative Government in Hong Kong*, (Hong Kong Government Printers, July 1984), p. 9.
8. Norman Miners, "Move Towards Representative Government 1984-1988", in Kathleen Cheek-Milby, and Miron Mushkat (ed.) *Hong Kong: The Challenges of Transition*, (Hong Kong, 1989), p. 21.
9. *South China Morning Post* (Hong Kong) September 16, 1984.
10. *White Paper: The Further Development of Representative Government in Hong Kong*, (Hong Kong Government Printers, 1984), pp. 5-7.
11. Joseph Y.S. Cheng, "The Democracy Movement in Hong Kong" *International Affairs* (London) vol. 65, No. 4, 1989, p. 446.
12. *White Paper: The Further Development of Representative Government: The Way Forward*, (Hong Kong Government Printers, 1988), pp. 8-9.

13. House of Common Foreign Affairs Committee, Second Report, (London, 1989), pp. 14-15.
14. Suzanne Pepper, "Elections, Political Change and Basic Law Government: The Hong Kong System in Search of a Political Form", *China Quarterly*, No. 126, June, 2000, p. 423.
15. Ming K. Chan, "Decolonization without Democracy: Pluralistic Politics" in Edward Freidman (ed.), *The Politics of Democratization East Asia Experience* (New York, 1994), p. 168.
16. Mark Rowswell, *Beijing Update on Hong Kong, Canada and Hong Kong Update* (Ontario), no. 4, Spring, 1991, p. 5.
17. Alastair Goodlad, "Hong Kong Legacy, Britains's Legacy, China Inheritance" *World Today* (London), vol. June 1994, p. 112.
18. Mark Roberti, *The Fall of Hong Kong: China Triumph and Britain Betrayal* (New York, 1994), p. 288.
19. *Hong Kong Standard*, 16 September, 1991.
20. Christopher Patten, *Our Next Five Years: The Agenda for Hong Kong* (Legislative Council Hong Kong, 1992), pp. 36-39.
21. Ministry of Foreign Affairs of the People's Republic of China "Fact About a Few Important Aspects of Sino-British Talks on 1994-95 Electoral Arrangements in Hong Kong," (Hong Kong: Joint Publishing Company, 1994).
22. *South China Morning Post* (Hong Kong), 23 December, 1992.
23. *China Daily* (Hong Kong), 16 March, 1993.
24. *China Daily* (Hong Kong), 18 March, 1993.
25. *Asia Week* (Hong Kong), 29 September, 1995, p. 39.
26. Summary of World Broadcast (SWB), FE/24/3f/1, 20 September, 1995.
27. Roberti, n. 18, pp. 286-88.
28. George L. Hicks, "Hong Kong After the Sino-British Agreement: The Illusion of Stability" in Jurgen Domes and Yu-Ming Shaw (eds.), *Hong Kong A Chinese and International Concern* (Boulder, 1988), p. 237.
29. Coonoor Kriplini: "The 1992 Debate on Democracy in Hong Kong" *China Report* (New Delhi), Vol. 29, No. 2, 1993, p. 174.

CHAPTER 6

The Nationality Issue and Hong Kong Indians

The transfer of sovereignty over Hong Kong was not only the transfer of territory; it also involved handing over a strata of its population, especially the non-ethnic Chinese to the Chinese government – a Communist regime. Hong Kong from the beginning has been a cosmopolitan city. Its position as a free port, manufacturing, trading, and financial centre attracted people from far and wide looking for greener pastures. Most of them came to Hong Kong with practically nothing, but rose to the pinnacle of fame and fortune by sheer perseverance and hard work under the benign British administration.

Although a majority of Hong Kong's population are ethnic Chinese, a section of it are non-ethnic Chinese, such as Eurasians, Portuguese, and South Asians from India, Pakistan, and Bangladesh. According to some earlier estimate, there were about 4,518 Indians (excluding about 17,500 having Indian passports), 2,255 Portuguese, 2,127 Pakistanis, and 2,685 people from other nationalities.[1] Barbara-Sue White, who has done a pioneering work on Hong Kong Indians opines that in Hong Kong parlance, an Indian is a person or the descendant of a person from anywhere in the Indian sub-continent. Indians were established in Hong Kong for more than a 100 years before the Partition of India in 1947. Sindh, a predominantly Hindu province in the north-western part of erstwhile India, became part of the new Muslim Pakistan. Many Hindu Sindhis departed, heading for Bombay, and then for other points including Hong Kong, which saw a large influx in the 1950s and 1960s.[2] Commenting on their primordial affiliation, she observes that the success of Indian businessmen in Hong Kong has enabled them to uphold their religious and ethical norms, which dictate responsibility and generosity to their own groups as well as to the broader community. "While separated from life on the Indian sub-continent, they have simultaneously been detached from the numerically dominant Chinese and the politically powerful British in Hong Kong, forming instead a sub-culture of their own," she elucidates in her seminal work.

The website of the Consulate-General of India in Hong Kong mentions that the Indian community in Hong Kong is estimated to be nearly 38,000 (including Indian nationals and people of Indian origin) and approximately 3,200 who hold Indian passports.[3] While numerically their number is not impressive, historically they had played a very significant role in the economy of Hong Kong. However, as the handover year 1997 approached, uncertainty and anxiety gripped their hearts and minds. The rich and wealthy Indians having passports of other countries explored to migrate to those countries; some with extra money tried to get their children married with partners abroad. A major grey area of the Sino-British Joint Declaration and the Basic Law pertained to the future nationality status of non-ethnic Chinese. The Joint Declaration envisaged the governance structure under the political edifice of 'one country, two systems', but was silent on citizenship.[4] International law contains some rules on the effects of moving frontiers on the nationality of the population. Generally speaking, the population loses the nationality of the state that cedes a certain territory and acquires the nationality of the state that assumes the exercise of sovereignty over the territory.

The acquisition of the new nationality is a legal obligation of the successor state, because otherwise, the population living in the territory that changes sovereignty becomes stateless.

The regulation in the Joint Declaration and especially in the two memoranda and the British Hong Kong Act 1985 in relation to nationality is worth noting. The British Hong Kong Act of 1985 stated that as from July 1, 1997, "Her majesty shall no longer have sovereignty or jurisdiction over any part of Hong Kong. It contained a schedule relating to specific matters such as nationality, which were considered as "consequential on or connected with" the ending of sovereignty of jurisdiction over Hong Kong. Although the British government in February 1997 decided to grant full British citizenship with right to abode in Britain to the holders of British passports, the ethnic Indians had to live under considerable anxiety and tension for years together. Moreover, granting of British citizenship to holders of British passports did not solve the problems of ethnic Indians altogether, because they had settled down there for business and trade purposes and adopted the territory as their home. It is imperative therefore to discuss the problems in detail.

CONTRIBUTION OF HONG KONG INDIANS

The Indian community's link with Hong Kong can be traced back to the days of the erstwhile British East India Company when a British naval force landed in Hong Kong in January 1841 and hoisted the Union Jack at Possession Point, about 2,700 Indian troops and four Indian merchants were witness to the historic occasion. In fact, the Treaty of Nanking makes a specific mention of Indians. It was in India that the Colony raised its first military force. The Hong Kong Regiment recruited Pathans, Punjabis, and Bengalis in 1890.

The colonial government recruited personnel in the police and the administration to man services such as health, education, and communication. It was much cheaper and quicker to recruit such people from India, which was then a part of the British Empire. According to Kewal Ram Sital, who was the chairman of the Council of Hong Kong Indian Associations, out of 3,475 Indians living in Hong Kong in 1931, almost 1,800 were employed in the administration.[4] It may be a little-known fact that the founders of Hong Kong's oldest trading firm Jardine & Matheson had worked in Calcutta in the East India Company before moving out to Hong Kong. William Jardine was a surgeon in one of the East India Company's ships before settling down to trade on his own account. James Matheson worked in a counting house of his uncle's firm and had gone to China almost by chance because his uncle was angry with him for having failed to deliver a letter to one of the firm's captains and had threatened to send him home. Jardine and Matheson together built up a highly successful firm which is still today one of the few largest business conglomerates in Hong Kong.[5]

Paul Catchik Chater, a Christian Armenian from Calcutta, also made significant contribution to the growth and development of Hong Kong. Paul Chater arrived in Hong Kong in 1864 at the age of 18. Starting as a bank clerk, he soon had a finger in every kind of profitable pie – wharfing, electricity, rope-making, trams, ferries, banking, hotels, and land. His Hong Kong and Kowloon Wharf and Godown Company became Hong Kong's chief dock operators, and his most brilliant real estate acquisition was the Praya Reclamation Scheme in Central Hong Kong, which created a slab of the most valuable building land on earth. An Anglophile and enthusiastic royalist, Chater indulged in all the right activities. He became almost unbelievably rich and built himself a vast and awful place in Hong Kong's posh Mid-Levels. Among the Indian business community, the Parsees were perhaps the earliest to settle down and start business. They came along with the British from Canton in the mid-1800s. Supremely Occidental, Parsees were loved by the British for their club etiquette, their Western attitudes, their philanthropy, and fondness for things imperial. In 1880, Dorabjee Naorojee began the Star Ferry Service between Hong Kong and Kowloon that was the precursor to today's Star Ferry.

Hormusjee Mody, successful opium merchant and stock broker, donated HK $180,000 to help set up the University of Hong Kong. Mody, along with Paul Chater, established the Hong Kong Stock Exchange. Mody's portrait adorns the Senate Hall of Hong Kong, and a road in Kowloon has been named after him. He also established the Seaman's Institute at Wanchai, and made donations to the Imperial Cancer Research Fund and the National Society for the Prevention of Cruelty to Children.[6]

During Japanese occupation, among those who were tortured were two leading members of the Indian community, Ruttonjee and his son. The Japanese had tried to get the former to become president of the Indian Independence League, but he refused steadfastly to collaborate. Ruttonjee's philanthropic activities are still remembered in the territory. The Ruttonjee Sanitarium and Freni Memorial Convalescent Home are a standing testimony to his contributions. The Parsees could not hold ground from the 1970s. Over the years, their number has dwindled. Among the earliest Indian settlers of the Parsees, the name of Hatma Ebrahim is fondly remembered in the Indian community. He was the great grandson of Ebrahim Noordin, an Indian migrant who had started the first cross-border ferry linking Hong Kong with Kowloon in 1842. Abdoolally Ebrahim is a private limited company that trades in pulses (imported from China and Myanmar), kitchenware (from Guangdong and Shanghai to Europe), and cotton yarn from India and Pakistan to China.[7]

The Sindhis who constitute the majority of Indian population arrived in Hong Kong in the post-war years. The 1950s had witnessed the influx of Indians in Hong Kong in the wake of partition of the sub-continent. During the early years of Hong Kong's rise, quite a few Indians made their mark in the corporate sector of Hong Kong's economy. Indians were members of the Board of Directors of leading corporations such as Hong Kong and Kowloon Wharfs and Godown Company, Hong Kong Land Investment Company, and Hong Kong Land Reclamation Company. The first bank to be opened in Hong Kong in 1845 was the branch of an Indian Bank, the Oriental Bank of Calcutta. In the provisional committee set up in 1864 to establish the Hong Kong and Shanghai Banking Corporation, three of its members were Indians.[8]

Risking an uncertain future, the Indian community contributed to the development and prosperity of Hong Kong, under the benign British rule. When the Chinese started to manufacture, the Indians found the export market for the manufactured goods. The Indian merchants explored and opened markets in the Middle East, the Gulf, the West, and East Africa. Among persons of Indian origin who have carved out a niche for themselves in the social, economic, and political life of Hong Kong, the name of Hari N Harilela stands foremost. A self-made man who had a very humble origin, the rise of Harilela reads like the proverbial rags-to-riches story. If Hong Kong has risen from the obscurity of a 'barren island' to one of the leading financial centres of the world, so also Harilela had risen from penury to the status of a 'Sindhi Onassis', heading a multi-million dollar business empire, which includes luxury hotels and real estate in the United States, Canada, and South East Asia, besides Hong Kong. If Hong Kong has weathered many storms, Harilela too had seen the ups and downs in his personal life. In fact, Harilela is the personification of the spirit of Hong Kong, the spirit that includes drive, dynamism, resilience, and adaptability.

Born in 1822 to a Sindhi gem merchant Lilaram who had brought his family to Guangzhou and then after his trade failed in the wake of the Great Depression to Hong Kong, Harilela had started his business in a very humble way, selling everything from newspapers to eggs to eke out a living. Harilela faced the Depression with fortitude and courage. When he got the job of a manager in an export-import farm, he felt secured. However, for a man bustling with drive and dynamism, the job of a manager circumscribed his innate spirit of enterprise. He gave up the job and started his own silk trade with his accumulated savings. The outbreak of the Second World War, however, seriously affected his business.

After a temporary setback, when the war was over, his silk business picked up and he diversified to textiles and tailoring. The tailoring business turned out to be the veritable golden goose. The outbreak of the Korean War in the 1950s created a huge demand for stitched clothes for British and American soldiers who flew through Hong Kong during the war. By 1960, Harilela's *Custom Tailors* was a household name in Hong Kong. It emerged as the largest tailoring network in Hong Kong. Harilela played a very important role in Hong Kong under China. The Chinese government had nominated him as an advisor in Hong Kong affairs.[9]

After Harilela, it is Kewal Ram Sital whose name is reckoned with among the prominent Hong Kong Indians. Sital was born in Hyderabad in the province of Sindh in Pakistan where his parents had a small clothing store. After partition in 1947, he moved to Mumbai and then in 1952 to Hong Kong at the call of his brother. He came to Hong Kong at the most opportune time when Hong Kong began to develop its manufacturing industries and this made it all the more attractive as a business hub. *Sital's Style* Asia with a well-established import-export farm had an office in New York and a strong commercial base in West Africa and the countries of the Middle East.[10] Although Indians constitute less than two per cent of the population in Hong Kong, the 400 or so Indian trading firms, according to an earlier estimate, accounted for an estimated 10% of Hong Kong's annual US $75.8 billion in exports.[11] Most of the Indian businessmen in Hong Kong are engaged in trade and commerce, procuring finished goods such as garments, toys, watches, etc. from Hong Kong and other neighbouring countries and exporting them to places as far away as Africa, Europe, and Latin America.

It was unfortunate, however, that in spite of their significant contributions to the progress and prosperity of Hong Kong under British rule, the British government initially denied them the right of abode in the United Kingdom. In the run-up to the Sino-British Joint Declaration, the British quietly tinkered with the British Nationality Act. Under the amended British Nationality Act of 1981, the Gibraltarians were granted the right to register as full British citizens. In 1983, under yet another amendment to the Act, the Falkland islanders were given full British citizenship with retrospective effect. While both these groups were granted the right of abode in Britain, British nationals elsewhere were stripped of the same right. The hardest hit were the British citizens of the Colony, especially Hong Kong Indians. They were classified as British Dependent Territory Citizens (BDTCs). However, this status ceased to exist with effect with from July 1, 1997, consequent upon the reversion of sovereignty over Hong Kong. The British government replaced the BDTC passports with British National Overseas (BNO) passports. The BNO passports, however, did not grant the holder the right of abode in the United Kingdom; it only extended British consular protection to its holders. It was more of a travel document than a passport.

The British authorities gave trivial arguments while denying full British citizenship to ethnic Indians. The first argument was that granting of British citizenship would undermine the Sino-British agreement, because the memoranda associated with the agreement stipulated that China would give Chinese nationality to non-ethnic Chinese. The second argument was that though it was the responsibility of the British government to provide nationality to BDTCs of Indian origin, Beijing would object to such a move. This argument was not tenable in the light of available facts, as the Chinese government had made it clear that they regarded the nationality of non-ethnic Chinese BDTCs as the responsibility of the British government.

The Chinese authorities were on record to have said that the ethnic minorities were welcome to stay in Hong Kong after 1997, and that their resolve to remain there would be considerably strengthened if they were given the right of abode in Britain. The newspaper *Wen Wei Po*, which is supposed to reflect the views of Beijing, carried an editorial urging the case of both the non-Chinese and the servicemen. Leaders of the Hong Kong Indian community asked Mr Li Qixin, the then Vice-Director of *Xinhua* News Agency, whether acquiescence by the British government in the Indian community's demand for full British citizenship would be read by the Chinese authorities as lack of confidence in the Sino-British Agreement, Li was unequivocal in his reply. He said there was absolutely no question of such an interpretation being put forth and that, in fact, the Chinese authorities would be happy if the Hong Kong ethnic minorities were offered British citizenship.[12] The third argument was that singling out the ethnic Indians for special treatment might be resented by the majority Chinese community. If the views expressed in the Hong Kong Legislative Council were any indication, this argument was untenable.

The nationality provisions of Hong Kong Act, 1985, were debated in the Hong Kong Legislative Council on December 4, 1985. Many members supported the demand of ethnic Indians for full British citizenship. Out of the seven speakers who covered the position of non-Chinese BDT citizenship, five were ethnic Chinese, and all five spoke in favour of more satisfactory arrangements for the minorities. Participating in the debate, Allen Lee, an important member of the Legislative Council, said.

> "I have talked to quite a few BDTC passport-holders. I can safely say that they have no objection to the minorities obtaining British citizenship or retaining their BDTC status.

In fact, they wish the minorities the best of luck. In my view, this is a British responsibility. Failing to take up this responsibility is unthinkable. I hope that members of the British Parliament consider this carefully."

Endorsing the forceful appeal of Allen Lee, Stephen Cheong said:

"Please take heed of the request of the small number (less than 10,000) of British subjects of Hong Kong who are not ethnic Chinese. The uniqueness of their case must be equal with, if not higher than, the case of the Gibraltarians or Falklanders, for it is the British government that decided to return Hong Kong to China."[13]

The Omelco met on April 25, 1986, to deliberate the British Nationality Order providing for the BNO status to Hong Kong residents after 1997. Registering the anguish of the Council over denial of full British citizenship to the minorities, the motion said: "We are disappointed that the British government did not accept our request for ethnic minorities to be granted full British citizenship, despite the fact this has been an issue on which the community at large has spoken with one voice. Britain has a moral responsibility to this small group, and we urge our friends in British Parliament to continue to press their legitimate claim."[14]

ACQUIRING CHINESE CITIZENSHIP?

The fourth argument was that the Hong Kong Indians should be encouraged to apply for Chinese nationality. This amounted to shirking of the British responsibility. The Chinese had said they would consider giving Chinese citizenship to Hong Kong Indians or individuals among those on application. However, this was not an undertaking, but an assurance. Article 7 of the Chinese Nationality

Law provides for acquisition of Chinese nationality by aliens or stateless persons. But this is only a conditional or discretionary right, therefore nobody knew whether or not Hong Kong Indians would be granted Chinese citizenship until the first supplication was made after 1997. Besides, China has an ethnic or racial nationality policy. One could not expect the Chinese to change their long-standing nationality policy to accommodate ethnic Indians, among quite a lot of others who would also like to be helped. This issue of acquiring Chinese nationality was only a theoretical issue which had no traction, given the sensitive and delicate nature of relationship between the two countries.

China's track record of honouring minority rights is far from satisfactory, at least in light of the inept handling of Tibet and the Muslim minority in China's north-western province of Xinjiang, bordering the troubled Tajikistan. The question arises that if the Chinese could not protect the socio-cultural rights of Tibetans during the Cultural Revolution in spite of constitutional stipulation, what is the guarantee that Beijing would honour the political and economic rights of an aggressive trading community such as the Hong Kong Indians, who would be competing with an equally aggressive Chinese community.

Early in 1993, the Chinese government indicated that the ethnic Indians could, if they so wished, apply for Chinese nationality after 1997. Lu Ping, the director of China's Hong Kong and Macao Affairs Office, told a representative of the Indian business community that they had an option of applying for naturalisation as a Chinese citizen. Lu's comment on the future of ethnic Indians and other non-Chinese in Hong Kong after 1997 came as a surprise to many who thought China did not allow foreigners to be naturalised as Chinese. But what Lu said was that Indians could apply for Chinese citizenship, however there was no guarantee that the applications would be approved.[15] In April 1996, one of the Chinese officials with responsibility for Hong Kong affairs was quoted as saying that while the Chinese government sympathised with the plight of ethnic minorities, subsidiary legislation would be required to enable the minorities to secure Chinese nationality. It also remained murky on how persons other than Chinese nationals would be assured of their right of abode in Hong Kong after 1997.[16]

POSITION OF INDIAN GOVERNMENT

The Government of India consistently maintained that the British government had the basic responsibility towards BDTC and BNO passport-holders, and that it should take necessary steps to safeguard the status of these persons as British citizens. In an oral reply, the Minister of External Affairs told Rajya Sabha on May 12, 1985, that with regard to the 15,000 Indians carrying Indian passports, however, there was no problem as they were the responsibility of the Government of India.[17]

THE JOINT DECLARATION, BASIC LAW, AND ETHNIC MINORITIES

The complexity of the problems of Hong Kong Indians was not, however, as simplistic as it was made out. What further exacerbated the plight of Hong Kong Indians during the period of transition prior to the transfer of sovereignty was their nebulous position in the Sino-British Joint Declaration and the Basic Law. It may be noted that although the Joint Declaration covered broadly all aspects of the future governance of Hong Kong Special Administrative Region (HKSAR), both the signatories to it could not reach an agreement with regard to the sensitive nationality issue of ethnic minorities in Hong Kong. This issue was covered in the Memorandum exchanged between Britain and the Peoples' Republic of China. The Chinese unilaterally asserted that all Hong Kong Chinese compatriots, whether they were holders of the 'British Dependent Territories Citizen's passports' or not, were Chinese nationals. The Memorandum did not refer to other minorities such as

Hong Kong Indians, Pakistanis, Eurasians, Malaysians, or Portuguese. The British were merely able to promise that all British subjects in Hong Kong would be able to travel on British Passports after July 1, 1997, however, without right of abode in Britain.

The Basic Law also failed to clearly define the future nationality of minorities. It, however, gave the right of residence to them. Clause 4 of Article 24 of the Basic Law stated that persons not of Chinese nationality but who have ordinarily resided in Hong Kong for a continuous period of no less than seven years and have taken Hong Kong as their place of permanent residence before or after the establishment of HKSAR shall have the status of permanent residents of Hong Kong. The ethnic minorities point out that the identity cards issued by the Hong Kong Government have three small stars to indicate Chinese origin, while the racial minorities are coded separately from the ethnic Chinese.[18]

They also apprehended that they might be overlooked in any future administrative set up in Hong Kong. Due to their small number, they contend that they cannot muster enough votes to have any representative elected to the representative bodies. Their fear of discrimination stemmed from a clause in the Basic Law which debarred them from holding any responsible position in the future governmental set-up. Their worry was that in future they may be subjected to still more discrimination which would affect their vocation. Their fears and anxieties are not a figment of imagination but based on hard realities of life. In Uganda, ethnic Indians were driven out and their properties confiscated. The way ethnic Indians were treated in Fiji was a nightmare to Hong Kong Indians, who are apolitical in spite of the volatile nature of Hong Kong's contemporary political spectrum. Considering the sensitive and delicate relationship between India and China, their anxiety and apprehension seemed quite natural.

It was against this backdrop that various Indian organisations in Hong Kong huddled together under the Council of Hong Kong

Indian Associations to campaign for full British citizenship with right of abode in the United Kingdom. Leading the campaign were the Hong Kong two prominent Indian businessmen, Hari Harilela and Kewalram Sital, president and chairman respectively of the Council. Harilela, Sital, and other members of the Council repeatedly flew to London, separately and collectively, to lobby members of British Parliament. They met members of the Conservative and opposition Labour parties, as well as other influential leaders of the community. They also lobbied for the support of the powerful Indian community in Britain for their cause.

Both Harilela and Sital made over a half-a-dozen lobbying visits to Britain on behalf of the community at their own expense. Though the visits initially did not produce the desired results, they at least managed to highlight the plight of the minorities in Hong Kong. Even the indomitable Margaret Thatcher herself addressed a letter to the Council of Hong Kong Indian Associations through Sital. In the letter dated May 7, 1986, she sought to allay the fears of the ethnic minorities, even as she refused to restore full British nationality rights.[19] Encouraged by this response from the British Prime Minister, the Council members continued to lobby their case with senior British ministers, and members of British Parliament.

Members of both the Houses of British Parliament had evinced keen interest with regard to their moral obligation towards the ethnic minorities of Hong Kong, including the Indians. Such was the pressure on the government from the Parliament that Baroness Young, the then Foreign Office Minister in the House of Lords, on February 19, 1985, clearly committed British government to undertake amendments in line with the prevailing views in Hong Kong and in both the Houses.[20] Lord Glen Arthur also conceded that every speaker in the House of Lords debate on January 20, 1986, supported the minorities' wishes, along with the other recommendations.[21] All but two of the 18 members who spoke in the Commons debate on the nationality provisions of the

Hong Kong Act on January 16, 1986, supported the recommendations of Hong Kong Legislative Council, which included among others granting full British Citizenship rights to ethnic Indians holding BDTC passports. Members of the House of Commons belonging to different parties were highly critical of the government's refusal to recognize the just claims of the ethnic minorities for an effective citizenship. As expected, given the size of the government's majority in the Commons, the order had a smooth passage in the House. However, soothing the concern and anxiety of the ethnic minorities as expressed by the Members of the House, the then Minister of State of the Home Office Mr Waddington said, "In the unlikely event of any British nationals being forced to leave Hong Kong and having nowhere to go, we have made it clear that we would expect the government of the day to consider sympathetically whether to admit such people on a case by basis in the light of particular circumstances."[22]

It was against this background that in the House of Lords, Lord Cledwyn moved a motion seeking a blocking amendment to the draft of the Nationality Order, thus, forcing the government to make concessions to Hong Kong ethnic minorities. The concern and anxiety expressed by the members who participated in the debate on May 16, 1986, was so overwhelming that Lord Glen Arthur, then the Home Office Minister, had to give a categorical statement. "We should consider it an obligation for any future government to treat with very considerable and particular sympathy the case for admission to the UK of any individual British nationals under pressure to leave Hong Kong."[23]

It was for the first time that the word 'obligation', in this context, was used by any government minister. Following this strong commitment from the government on the floor of the House, Lord Cledwyn withdrew the motion proposed by him. This undertaking from Lord Glen Arthur raised cautious optimism in the minds of Hong Kong Indian community leaders. The Foreign Affairs Committee of the House of Commons which visited Hong Kong in April 1989, in their report submitted in June that year held that the Committee did not believe that assurances given by the government were sufficient. The Committee also recommended that "the British government has an obligation to provide proper citizenship (i.e. British citizenship) to this group of people which it has cooperated in consigning them otherwise to a second-class citizenship.[24]

The nationality package offering full British citizenship to 50,000 BDTC passport-holders of Hong Kong passed by the British Parliament in the second reading of the Bill on April 19, 1990, came as an anti-climax to the Indian community after protracted lobbying in Hong Kong and London. Mr Peter Shore shared the views of those who expressed the unsatisfactory position of non-ethnic Chinese and impressed upon the need for stronger guarantees for their future, otherwise they would be citizenless after 1997, he added. Mr Nigel Forman who described the Bill as sensible and timely supported the cause of Asian people for full British citizenship. He said Asians had solid family lives, they believed in the value of education, and tended to be self-sufficient high-achievers. "In short they are exactly the sort of people who should be welcomed to United Kingdom, if they ever felt the need," he added. Mr Andrew Faulds, who argued for the restoration of full British citizenship to all British nationals in Hong Kong said that the scheme's most damaging flaw was its disregard for non-ethnic minorities who have no nationality other than the British and who would become stateless after 1997. "In all justice, special consideration should have been given to that category in a loading of points. Better still, those people should be given special dispensation to gain full and proper British citizenship," he further said.

Mr Norman Tebbit, who defied the party whip and led the Tory revolt against the Bill, said, "If we were not to see social upheavals from religious, cultural, and ethnic differences, we have more than enough to do to integrate existing communities into British society without adding to that burden or exacerbating existing problems". He, however, expressed his concern about the fate of Asians of Indian descent who were likely to become stateless and possibly refugees. He pleaded with the Foreign Secretary to intervene most strongly on their behalf with the Government of India. While the Labour Party criticised the bill, the party strongly argued in favour of full British citizenship for ethnic Indians and other vulnerable groups in Hong Kong. Mr Roy Hattsersley said that if the Labour Party came to power, they would offer citizenship to non-ethnic Chinese among other groups. Mr Gerald Kaufman and Mr Max Madden also supported the cause of ethnic minorities in Hong Kong, including the Indian Community.

Mr Paddy Ashdown of the Liberal Democrat Party who sought to strengthen and improve the Bill in the Committee stage also pleaded for the needs of non-ethnic minorities. Participating in the debate, the Home Secretary Mr Waddington, in reply to Mr Max Madden, reiterated the consistent stand of the government that an undertaking had been given to the non-ethnic Chinese in Hong Kong that if by any chance an individual were to come under severe pressure after 1997, the government would consider his application to come to the United Kingdom.[25] The Bill, which obtained royal assent in July 1990, however, shattered the hope of Hong Kong Indians for their full British Citizenship rights.

GRANTING OF RIGHT OF ABODE

The long-drawn and sustained campaign by ethnic minorities for full British citizenship with right to abode in the United Kingdom ultimately fructified on February 4, 1997, when the British Home Secretary Michael Howard in a written reply in House of Commons committed those ethnic minorities in Hong Kong would be granted full British citizenship. In his reply he said:

> I have carefully reviewed the position of the solely British ethnic minorities in Hong Kong in the light of expression of concern in the House of Parliament here and in Hong Kong that their nationality status will be uncertain after June 30, 1997. It is clear that the assurances they have been given over a number of years have not allayed this concern. Therefore, I intend to make provisions enabling them to apply for registration as British citizens, giving them the right of abode in the United Kingdom after June 30, 1997. I expert that the great majority of them will continue to reside in Hong Kong, where they have the right of abode.[26]

The Conservative government had resisted any measure before the general elections that could seem like letting more immigrants into Britain, but it bowed to strong pressure and lobbying in Parliament. He, however, made a point suggesting that the new British citizens were unlikely to migrate to Britain. The lobbying was led by two Indians from Hong Kong, Ravi Gidoomal and Kavita Daswani. They met with several MPs in London and gave vivid accounts of the legal and emotional implication of living as stateless citizens. The British government stood in danger of losing a vote on the issue, facing opposition from Labor and many of its own members who had expressed strong concern. The result was an unusual triumph of a private member's bill that of Sir Partrick Cormanch, a Conservative – on the granting of citizenship. Earlier, the Lords supported the bill overwhelmingly. It was then returned to the House of Commons for reconsideration. In granting full citizenship right to ethnic minorities, Chris Patten, Hong Kong's last Governor, had played a very meaningful and constructive role. He argued that by leaving these minorities stateless Britain would damage its credibility in its civil rights negotiations with China. He said that to leave Hong Kong's non-Chinese ethnic minorities stateless would be an "exceptionally unfortunate way for Britain to bring the curtain down on the last of the great colonial dependencies.[27]

INDIA-HONG KONG RELATIONS IN THE POST-HANDOVER PERIOD

There was no major change in India-Hong Kong relations in the post-handover period. Rather, the uncertainty about the future of Hong Kong Indians was stabilised suggesting change with continuity. Kirti Narain in her book *Co-prosperity in Cross-culturalism: Indian in Hong Kong*, attributing to K Sital, writes that not a single Indian family left Hong Kong, though many others did. Indians had come as businessmen to Hong Kong, and as long as the government (British or Chinese) provided business opportunities, they would stay. They accepted the rule of China as a natural substitute to British rule. Raj Sital, the son of K Sital, reiterated the cordial relationship of Indians with the Hong Kong government which has become even friendlier after 1997, as they were very concerned about negative publicity in the international arena. But one 'is not really confident about the future of Hong Kong. As an exporter and businessperson, it would be naïve for us to think that without integrating with China, we would be able to remain in business in Hong Kong.'[28]

Be that as it may, the Commission of India (set up in 1959) was re-designated as Consulate-General of India in October 1996 in the run up to reversion of Chinese sovereignty over Hong Kong. Hong Kong continued to act as a 'gateway' to India for the mainland companies. Hong Kong remains the major re-exporter of items it imports from India to mainland China and vice-versa. Hong Kong and India enjoy a robust bilateral trade between the two. India was Hong Kong's third largest export market destination after China and the US in 2017 and Hong Kong was India's third largest export market after US and UAE. The two-way trade between India and Hong Kong was US$34.11 billion in 2017. India continued to retain its position as the seventh largest trading partner of Hong Kong in 2017. The city-state continues to attract Indian professionals in the service industries, including in banking, finance, information technology, and shipping.

Official exchange of visits between India and Hong Kong has given a fillip in the post-handover period. Donald Tsang, the then Chief Executive of Hong Kong along with the Governor of Guangdong province visited India leading an entourage of business delegation in October 2010. This visit was followed later by the visit of the then Chief Executive CY Leung in February 2016 at the invitation of the Chief Minister of Maharashtra. From the Indian side, Finance Minister late Arun Jaitley visited Hong Kong in September 2015 and met the Chief Executive of Hong Kong and addressed the investors at the India Capital Markets and Institutional Investors Summit. Many Hong Kong-based companies are operating in India. This includes China Light and Power (CLP), Li and Fung, Shangri La Kerry Logistics and Peak Re to name a few.

Hong Kong is a major tourist destination for Indians. With more than half a million Indian tourists visiting Hong Kong every year, the Hong Kong-India tourism has been steadily rising. Direct air links between India and Hong Kong are through Air India, Jet Airways, Spice Jet, Indigo, and Cathay Pacific which connects six cities in India – New Delhi, Chennai, Hyderabad, Bangalore, Mumbai and Kolkatta. Altogether, there are 83 direct flights operating between India and Hong Kong every week. Until January 2017, Hong Kong government used to permit visa on arrival for Indian nationals for 14 days. However with effect from January 23, 2017, the Hong Kong government had made Pre-Arrival Registration a compulsory requirement for all Indian nationals who intend to visit Hong Kong for 14 days.

After the reversion of sovereignty over Hong Kong and Hong Kong becoming a Special Administrative Region of China, a number of bilateral agreements have been signed between India and Hong Kong. Some of important agreements are the Double Taxation

Avoidance Agreement (DTAAA) signed in March 2018, Agreement on Mutual Legal Assistance in Criminal Matters signed in September 2009 and Surrender of Fugitive offenders signed in 1997.

The Reserve Bank of India (RBI) in January 2014 included Hong Kong and Macau in the sensitive list of countries along with Pakistan and China that requires prior approval to set up business-related activities in India. Pakistan, Bangladesh, Sri Lanka, Afghanistan, Iran and China are already in the sensitive list which means entities and residents in theses countries and territories need prior RBI per mission to establish a branch office or liason office or a project office in India. Macau and Hong Kong are two special Administrative Regions controlled by China. Business in these two regions are mostly controlled by the Chinese. They could easily come to India through their firms registered in Hong Kong and Macau. Many foriegn funds which operate in India are controlled from Hong Kong, Singapore and other financial hubs.

REPERCUSSIONS OF THE GALWAN VALLEY INCIDENT

The bloody clash between the Indian Army and the People's Liberation Army (PLA) in the Line of Actual Control (LAC) in India-China border in Ladakh in June 2020 in which India lost 20 of its soldiers and China also suffered severe casualties resonated in India-Hong Kong relations. This incident took place during the time when China imposed its National Security Law on Hong Kong. There were suggestions in India that New Delhi should raise the issue in the United Nations as a riposte to China's raising the issue relating to abrogation of Article 370 which enshrined a special status to the Indian state of Jammu and Kashmir in the United Nations. The argument was that if China could raise the issue which is absolutely a domestic issue, then why not India does a tit for tat to China. What has heightened Chinese anxiety was that in recent times there is a bounty of goodwill for Taiwan, a democratic entity which China regards as a renegade province, in India and elsewhere. Two members of Indian Parliament belonging to the ruling party BJP participated in the virtual inauguration ceremony of Taiwan's President, in spite of India's commitment to India's 'one China policy'. This action of India annoyed Chinese embassy in India.

With regard to Hong Kong, however, India adopted a much-calibrated response. India's ambassador to the United Nations Human Rights Council in Geneva Rajiv Kumar Chander said that given the large Indian community that lives in the Hong Kong Special Administrative Region, India has been keeping "a close watch on recent developments. We have heard several statements expressing concerns on these developments. We hope that the relevant parties will take into account these views and address them properly, sincerely and objectively".[29] The statement was significant as it was for the first time that India raised the issue of Hong Kong and the large-scale protests against China internationally. In the past, India has been sulking to even give visa to pro-democracy activists of Hong Kong and along with Indonesia was the only other member of G-20 which refused even to meet pro-democracy activists to accept a petition in 2019 so as to put pressure on China. To discourage India from raising the Hong Kong issue, the Chinese ambassador in India writing in an English newspaper of India urged, "India and Hong Kong have close economic and trade relations. It serves India's interest to maintain the prosperity and stability in Hong Kong. The national security legislation will better protect the legitimate rights and interests of foreign nationals in Hong Kong, including that of India. We hope Indian friends can uphold fairness and justice, respect and support China's efforts to safeguard national security law in Hong Kong in accordance with law."[30]

NOTES

1. "1997 And Hong Kong Indians", *Council of Hong Kong Indian Associations*, (Hong Kong, 1990), p. 1.

2. Barbara-Sue White, *Turbans and Traders: Hong Kong's Indian Communities* (Hong Kong, 1984: Oxford University Press), p. 1.
3. Consulate-General of India, Hong Kong.
4. Kewal Ram Sital, "The Indian Connection", *Financial Express,* (New Delhi) 27 July 1984.
5. Edgar Holt, *The Opium Wars in China* (London, 1964), pp. 37-38.
6. Sital, n. 1.
7. *Business India*, (New Delhi), 30 June to 13 July, 1997, p. 74.
8. Sital, n. 4.
9. *Economic Times Esquire*, (New Delhi) 25 February, 1994.
10. Geral Balke, *Hong Kong Voice*, (Hong Kong, 1989), p. 85.
11. *Far Eastern Economic Review*, (Hong Kong), 12 April, 1990, p. 44.
12. *1997 and Hong Kong Indians,* Council of Hong Kong Indian Associations, (Hong Kong, 1990), p. 3.
13. Legislative Council Debate (Hong Kong) 4 December, 1985.
14. *A Place under the Sun*, Council of Hong Kong Indian Associations (Hong Kong, 1990), p. 6.
15. Frank Ching, "Hong Kong Stateless Indians Need Chinese Citizenship now" *Far Eastern Economic Review*, 22 April 1993, p. 29.
16. Circulated by Christine Loh, member of Legislative Council, April 1996.
17. *Rajya Sabha Debate*, 2 May 1985.
18. Based on my interview with Hong Kong Indian during my field study to Hong Kong in March-April 1990.
19. I acknowledge with my gratitude to Mr. Kewalram Sital for providing me all the correspondence and other material and giving me an extended interview in Hong Kong in March-April, 1990.
20. UK House of Lords, Parliamentary Debates Vol. 460. Col.505/6
21. Ibid, Vol. 470. Col. 71-73.
22. UK House of Commons, Parliamentary Debates, Vol. 89. Columns. 1268-1272.
23. UK House of Lords, Parliamentary Debates, Vol. 474, Columns 1437-8.
24. Foreign Affairs Committee House of Commons (Second Report, 1989).
25. UK House of Commons Parliamentary Debate. Vol. 170, Col. 1564-1650.
26. Sanjay Suri, "Britain now Backs citizenship for Indians" *India Abroad* (New York) 14 February, 1997, p. 16, quoting House of Commons Debate.
27. *Indian Express* (New Delhi) 5 February, 1997.
28. Kwok Siu-tong and Kirti Narain, *Co-prosperity in Cross-culturalism: Indians in Hong Kong, The Commercial Press*, (Hong Kong, 2003), pp. 122-23.
29. 'Keeping close watch: India calls to address situation in Hong Kong.' *DNA*, July 1, 2020.
30. Sun Weidong, 'Towards national security and peace in Hong Kong', *The Hindu*, 24 July 2020.

CHAPTER 7

Pangs of Transition

While in Hong Kong, Chris Patten went ahead with the election to Legco, in September 1995 Beijing was preparing for the provisional Legco to take over the outgoing elected Legco from July 1, 1997. A provisional Legco was first mooted through the Preliminary Working Committee (PWC) appointed by Beijing shortly after it declared that the political reforms introduced by Governor Chris Patten were against the Basic Law. In August 1994, the Standing Committee of the National People's Congress passed a resolution that the three-tier system of representative government, including the elected Legco, would come to an end on June 30, 1997, and the Preparatory Committee would proceed to establish the HKSR government and the first Legco. Accordingly, on March 25, 1996, the plenary of Preparatory Committee passed the decision to set up a 60-member Provisional Legco.

The Provisional Legco was formed following the appointment of Tung Chee Hwa as the first chief executive of HKSR, and was formally inaugurated on 1st July, 1997, after Hong Kong was transferred to Chinese sovereignty. Participating in this historical occasion of transfer of sovereignty, Chinese President Jiang Zemin reaffirmed that his government would implement the basic principles of 'one country, two systems' and that Hong Kong people would be allowed to govern the territory with a high degree of autonomy.

He further said that there would be a gradual progress towards democracy in Hong Kong and its laws would protect its business and culture of the city state. Hwa echoed the words of Jiang and said elections to Legco would take place sometime in May 1998. When the Chinese authorities reaffirmed their earlier commitment before the world, it aroused a sense of hope and optimism about the future of Hong Kong under the Communist regime. The way the world electronic media were allowed to air their views and comments, and the way people were allowed to speak out their feelings, sentiments, and anxieties, was certainly uncharacteristic of a regimented society. They were more like the attributes of a free society, the way Hong Kong was and would like to be seen as.

Yet one more instance of Chinese and HKSR government's tolerance of dissent and freedom at this stage was evident when they allowed a protest demonstration by the Democratic Party against the Provisional Legco on June 29, 1997, on the eve of transfer of sovereignty, and again when Martin Lee addressed the world over television cameras from the balcony of Legco building on the midnight of June 30, after the historic handover ceremony. In fact, it would have been quite a cultural shock to the protagonists of democracy who had all along been raising the bogey of Communism and totalitarianism, and were paranoid because of the Cultural Revolution and the Tiananmen Square incident. For a moment, it seemed as if they had been raising a false alarm. What was in store for the future unfolded in the later years, belying the pledges and promises enshrined in the Joint Declaration and the Basic Law.

THE UMBRELLA MOVEMENT, 2014

It is of interest to note how the autonomy of HKSR, as enshrined in the Joint Declaration and the Basic Law, is slowly getting eroded over the years since 1997. The Umbrella Movement of 2014 clearly demonstrated the hiatus between the promises and performance of

HKSR under the Communist regime when it came to implementation of various provisions of the Basic Law. Article 45 of the Basic Law provides that the Chief Executive of HKSR shall be selected by election or through consultations held locally, and be appointed by the Central Government. It further says that the method for selecting the Chief Executive shall be specified in the light of the actual situation in HKSR, and in accordance with the principle of gradual and orderly progress. Thus, it is an open-ended provision. On August 31, 2014, China decided that Beijing would tightly control the nomination of candidates for election of the Chief Executive of HKSR, a move that triggered mass protest and resentment in the territory, which came to be known as 'umbrella movement'. The protest movement was called 'umbrella movement' because the protesters used umbrellas as a shield against the use of pepper spray by Hong Kong Police. The Standing Committee of NPC decided that the city's next Chief Executive would be elected by popular vote in 2017, but only after each candidate is approved by a majority of the 1,200-member Election Committee. The state-run news agency *Xinhua* declared 'the nominating committee shall nominate two to three candidates for the office of the Chief Executive in accordance with the democratic procedure."[1]

CARRIE LAM: FIRST ELECTED CHIEF EXECUTIVE

Be that as it may, the direct election to the position of the Chief Executive of the Hong Kong Special Administrative Region was held in March 2017 after the massive pro-democracy protest in 2014. With 777 votes out of the total 1,194 of the Election Committee, Carrie Lam who had served the Hong Kong government as the second most senior functionary, and had resigned from the post to fight the election, was declared elected. She was appointed as the fourth Chief Executive of the territory on July 20, 2017, on the occasion of the 20th anniversary of the handover. Carrie Lam campaigned mainly on her much-touted strength as a capable long-time public administrator, having worked in Hong Kong since she graduated in 1980. She received more than double the votes of John Tsang, her main rival. Tsang was the former Financial Secretary until December 2016, who resigned from the post to fight for the election. He received 365 votes from the Electoral Committee. His support largely came from electors belonging to the pro-democracy camp, many of whom described him as the 'lesser evil'[2]. The next election to the office of the Chief Executive was due in March 2022, and election to the Legislative Council was scheduled for September 2020, which was postponed due to Covid-19, and was held on December 19, 2021. The election of the Chief Executive has been deferred to May 2022.

ABORTED EXTRADITION BILL, JUNE 2019

Ever since Carrie Lam took over the reins of power of the territory, she has been faced with humongous challenges. A major problem that she had to grapple with early in 2019 was the massive people's protest at the move of the government to initiate an extradition bill to enable the Hong Kong government to extradite offenders of the law. The Hong Kong government announced on February 13, 2019, that it had reviewed the existing legal provisions for co-operation with the Hong Kong government and other places on juridical assistance in criminal matters, and was considering amending the Mutual Legal Assistance in Criminal Matters Ordinance and the Fugitive Offenders Ordinance. The proposed changes to the law were titled as the 'Fugitive Offenders and Mutual Legal Assistance in Criminal Matters Legislation (Amendment) Bill 2019'. The changes were justified by the Hong Kong government because of loopholes in the extant system of extradition of suspects in criminal cases to other jurisdictions.

What prompted the Hong Kong government to draft the extradition bill in June 2019 was a murder committed in 2018 in

Taiwan by a Taiwanese, who had moved into Hong Kong and was charged with the offence of money-laundering in Hong Kong, was to be extradited to Taiwan after the expiry of his imprisonment in Hong Kong. As Hong Kong has no extradition treaty, it was not possible to send the convict back to Taiwan for his trial in the Taiwanese court. It was in this backdrop that the Hong Kong government decided to pass the extradition bill to enter into an agreement with other countries, including mainland China, for extradition of offenders of law. It was feared in Hong Kong that the HKSR authorities might invoke the extradition law to extradite offenders, including pro-democracy leaders and activists in Hong Kong to mainland China. The colonial era drafters of Hong Kong's extant law excluded the mainland from extradition because its courts could not be trusted to deliver impartial justice.

The proposed legislation evoked resentment and strong protest in Hong Kong in June 2019. Hundreds of thousands of people took to the streets to annul the proposed extradition law. The movement took a violent turn and there were ugly clashes. Flights too were suspended. China said the protest movement had reached 'near terrorism' after a night of ugly clashes at the city's airport on June 14, where demonstrators set upon and detained two members they suspected of being government sympathisers. US President Donald Trump described the volatile situation as 'tricky', and said China's government had moved troops near the border with Hong Kong.[3] Both the Houses of US Congress passed the Hong Kong Human Rights and Democracy Act.

China warned that it could not tolerate the efforts of protesters to threaten the Central government's authority in Hong Kong, and suggested that it could, if needed, mobilise troops in the PLA garrison there to maintain order. The warning came as China released a new defence strategy that accused the United States of undermining global stability, and identified separatism as China's most immediate security threat. In case of Hong Kong, the Chief Spokesperson for the Ministry of National Defence, Senior Colonel Wu Qian, cited the protest outside the Central government liaison office in Hong Kong, which the protesters painted with graffiti, as an instance of destructive behaviour, straining its relationship with Beijing. He pointed out that Article 14 of the Basic Law – detailing relations between the city and Beijing – allowed PLA to intervene, when requested by the Hong Kong government to maintain order, or assist in case of natural disasters.[4]

INVOCATION OF EMERGENCY LAW, 1922

What further execrated the situation was the Hong Kong Police shooting and wounding of a teenage boy on 4 October, 2019, when violent protests erupted after Carrie Lam invoked a colonial era (1922) emergency power, used more than 50 years ago, to quell the protests. One of the emergency measures was to ban the face mask the protesters were using to avoid being identified. The pro-democracy lawmakers appealed to the Hong Kong High Court seeking an emergency injunction against the ban, arguing that the emergency powers bypassed the legislature and contravened the Basic Law. But the senior judge dismissed their injunction demand. The Hong Kong legislature, on 23 October, formally withdrew the planned legislation that would have allowed extraditions to mainland China.

THE DISTRICT COUNCIL ELECTIONS, NOVEMBER 2019

It was against this backdrop of angst that the District Council Elections were held in November 2019. In the first place, the fact that the elections were held on schedule, in spite of the political turmoil, was a clear message of the independence of the Hong Kong government. It was certainly not manipulated by the Communist regime in Beijing. The elections were free and fair. A record 71% of the 4.13 million citizens who registered to vote had cast their ballots. Pro-democracy candidates captured 389 of 452 elected seats, up from 124, and far more than they had ever won. The government allies held just 56 seats, a remarkable decline from 300 in 2015. The election results were viewed as a referendum. "There has been a very deep awakening of Hong Kong people," said Alan Leong, chairman of the Civic Party, one of the largest pro-democracy parties.[5] The *South China Morning Post* commented, "The tsunami of disaffection among voters was clear across the board, as pan-democrats rode the wave to win in poor and rich neighbourhoods, in both protest and non-protest afflicted districts and town areas, as well as suburbs. Less immediately obvious was whether there was a generational divide in the way people voted, but the ousted re-establishment District Councils suggested that young, first-time voters had been instrumental in dislodging them from their perch."[6] *China Daily* observed, "The record turnout has sent the message that however violent the rioters are, ordinary residents are concerned about their own well-being."

Traditionally, the District Council elections are never taken seriously politically as they are concerned with mundane civic issues such as transport, streetlights, bus-stops etc., but this time around it acquired a political connotation altogether, given the circumstances in which the elections were held. The election result was fraught with serious consequences for the election of the Chief Executive of HKSR in 2022, and for the Legislative Council election scheduled for September 2020, which got postponed on ground of Covid-19. The District Councils are among the most democratic bodies in Hong Kong. Almost all seats are directly elected, unlike the Legislative Council (Legco), where the proportion is just more than half. The territory's Chief Executive is also not chosen directly by voters, but instead selected by a committee tilted in favour of Beijing. The District Councils name about a tenth of the group's 1,200 members; the reconstituted District Council could tilt the balance in favour of the pro-democracy camp. Democracy advocates were already in control about a quarter of the seats, while other previously pro-Beijing sector of the Committee now started to lean towards democracy, most notably accountants and real estate lawyers. Mr Leong, the Civic Party Chairman, called on the Chinese Communist Party to change its policies in Hong Kong. "Unless the CCP is doing something concrete to address the concerns of the Hong Kong people, I think this movement cannot end," he said. Carrie Lam was graceful enough to admit that public dissatisfaction with her government fuelled a landslide win by pro-democracy candidates in the local elections. She admitted that the District Council election results revealed public concerns over deficiencies in government, including unhappiness with the time taken to deal with the unrest.

PROMULGATION OF NATIONAL SECURITY LAW, MAY 2020

It was in this context of the sustained pro-democracy movement in Hong Kong and the failure of the Hong Kong government to stem them that the central government of China promulgated the National Security Law. The approval of the law titled as Establishing and Strengthening the Safeguarding of the National Security for Hong Kong which was submitted earlier to the National People's Congress (NPC) on May 28, 2020, aroused a great deal of concern and anxiety in Hong Kong, and also resonated beyond the city-state. The National Security Law proscribes "actions to split the country, terrorism, and subversion of state power. The legislature of Hong Kong, the Legislative Council, was not consulted on the matter, although the deputies representing Hong Kong were present in the NPC meeting. The law also aims at preventing foreign political organisations from operation in Hong Kong.[7] China defended and justified the promulgation and implementation of the law. In an article in a leading English daily of India, the Chinese ambassador in New Delhi wrote that the national security law "marks a major turning point from unrest to peace and order, and a farewell to the history of unguarded national security in Hong Kong." He further wrote that since the turbulence over the amendment bill in 2019, with the support from foreign and external forces, the anti-China forces have openly instigated 'Hong Kong independence' separatist acts and serious violent incidents, which highlight big national security loopholes in the city. The city's GDP registered a negative growth for the first time in a decade, and the unemployment rate hit a record high in nearly 10 years. In the article, he also articulated that "the legislation will guarantee the sustained implementation of 'one country, two systems'. One country is the pre-condition and basis for two systems. Only when One Country is safe and secure, can Two Systems be safeguarded. The ambassador further observed that some western politicians use the national security legislation as an excuse to interfere in China's internal affairs.[8]

There is widespread concern that the National Security Law is fraught with eroding the autonomy and freedom pledged under the Sino-British Joint Declaration and the Basic Law of Hong Kong Special Administrative Region (HKSR). The USA and UK, the two major stakeholders in Hong Kong's stability and prosperity severely criticised China for trying to impose the dreaded law on Hong Kong. President Donald Trump threatened to order the removal of special status accorded to Hong Kong since the city was no longer sufficiently autonomous to enjoy the privilege. The UN human rights experts viewed that the new security law for Hong Kong "infringes upon certain fundamental rights", and voiced concerns that it could be used to prosecute political activists in the former British colony. In a rare joint letter signed by UN human rights experts in September 2020 which was submitted to the Chinese government, the human rights experts said that the provisions of the national security law appear to undermine the independence of HK's judges, and lawyers and the right to freedom of expression.[9]

What exacerbated the atmospherics in Hong Kong was the decision of Hong Kong government on July 30, 2020, to debar 12 pro-democracy candidates to contest elections to the territory's legislature for their opposition to National Security Law imposed by Beijing. Disqualified candidates included pro-democracy activist Joshua Wong, some members of the Civic Party, a moderate, old-guard opposition group, and others who won an unofficial primary vote held by the opposition camp earlier in July. On July 31, the day after debarring pro-democracy leaders, Carrie Lam postponed the LegCo election, scheduled for September 6, 2020, by one year because of the rise of coronavirus cases, which was a setback to democratic opposition. Defending her decision, Lam said she had to invoke an emergency law to make the postponement, and no political considerations were involved. She said the decision was aimed at safeguarding people's health. "We have three million voters going out in one day across Hong Kong. Such a flow of people would cause high risk of infection," she said. Hong Kong had reported more than 3,000 COVID-19 cases since January 2020, far lower than other major cities around the world.[10] But the number of new infections was in triplicate when the decision to postpone the election was taken. Singapore, which had a larger virus outbreak, held an election in July 2020.

The postponement of the election evoked resentment by pro-democracy leaders in Hong Kong, and critical international reaction. In Hong Kong, it was perceived by pro-democracy leaders as a 'cynical move to contain political emergency' and to deny Hong Kong people their right to choose their government. After the National Security Law came into force, the Hong Kong government arrested many pro-democracy leaders under the provisions of the law in August 2020. The most high-profile arrest was that of city's media tycoon and editor of the *Apple Daily* Jimmy Lai. He was arrested on suspicion of collusion with foreign forces. Along with Lai, a young women activist Agnes Chow (23), was also arrested under the National Security

Law on the charges of colluding with foreign forces. Her supporters likened her to Mulan, the legendary heroine who fought to save her family and country. Two dozen pro-democracy activists, including Joshua Wong, were also charged for defiance of the government's orders prohibiting participation in an illegal assembly at the vigil on June 4, 2020, in the territory to commemorate the Tiananmen Square incident of 1989. It was for the first time that the vigil was banned in Hong Kong on grounds of coronavirus restrictions; still, tens of thousands lit candles across the city. The June 4 commemorations are banned in mainland China.

In November 2020, the Standing Committee of the National People's Congress of China passed a resolution empowering the Hong Kong government to directly disqualify elected lawmakers without even approaching the court. According to the resolution, the legislators can be disqualified if they espouse Hong Kong's independence, fail to acknowledge China's sovereignty, or encourage foreign forces to interfere in the city's affairs. Soon after the resolution was passed by the Standing Committee of China's National People's Congress, the Carrie Lam government disqualified four legislators belonging to the democratic opposition camp. They included Alvin Yeang, Dennis Kwok, Kwok Ka-ki and Kenneth Leung. The four had urged foreign governments to sanction China and Hong Kong as China cracked down on dissent. On the same day, the 15 remaining member pro-democracy legislators announced that they would resign in protest against the dismissal of four of their colleagues from the LegCo. Most of them did not attend a regular session of LegCo on November 12, 2020, and some later handed in resignation letters at the Legislative Council's secretariat. China sharply criticised the resignation of the legislators. Its Hong Kong and Macao Office Affairs Office called the mass resignation 'an open challenge' against the authority of the central government and the Basic Law. "If these lawmakers hope to use their resignations to provoke opposition and beg for foreign interference, they have miscalculated, "it said in a statement. Chinese foreign ministry spokesman Wang Wenbin reiterated Beijing's support for Hong Kong government in "fulfilling its duty according to the NPC Standing Committee's decision." Wang said, "No country will turn a blind eye to acts of betrayal of the country by public officials, including members of the Legislative Council, who break their oath of office."

The disqualification of the four members of LegCo evoked strong criticism, particularly by the 'five eyes' intelligence alliance, including Britain and the US. Britain summoned China's ambassador in London, Liu Xiaoming, to express its concerns. Its deputy foreign minister told Parliament that Britain was considering possible sanctions on individuals over China's action. Foreign minister Dominic Raab said the expulsion of the legislators constituted an assault on Hong Kong's freedom as provided in the UK-China Joint Declaration. This campaign to harass, stifle and disqualify democratic opposition tarnishes China's international reputation and undermines Hong Kong's long-term stability. Reacting to the development, then US national security adviser Robert O'Brien said, "Beijing's actions disqualifying pro-democracy legislators from Legislative Council has flagrantly violated its international commitments." It criticised that the Chinese Communist Party had flagrantly violated its international commitments. Earlier, in August 2020, the US imposed sanctions on Hong Kong, which bars Americans from doing business with Hong Kong. The US also imposed sanctions on the Hong Kong chief executive Carrie Lam and ten other top Hong Kong and Chinese officials for their role in curtailing political freedoms in the territory. The sanctions which came on August 7, 2020, more than a month after Beijing imposed national security legislation aim at freezing any US assets of its US officials, and to bar Americans and American and American companies from doing business with them. The US government also decided that goods made in Hong Kong for exports to US to be labelled as made in China after September 2020. Carrie

Lam criticised US action and said Hong Kong and China were two separate WTO members, and Hong Kong would lodge a complaint against the US decision. The Hong Kong government denounced the US sanctions as "shameless and despicable' and 'blatant and barbaric' interference in China's internal affairs.

The passing of the National Security Law also created panic among a section of the populace and eroded of confidence of the people in the autonomy of the territory. Immigration consultancy firms and banks received a number of queries regarding emigration and transferring money abroad. Some even accelerated their decision to buy property overseas. The uncertain future of Hong Kong, impelled some high net worth-individuals – defined as those having more than Hong Kong $10 million (1.29 million) of wealth to diversify their assets into other cities like London, Singapore, and Taiwan.

In a very thought provoking and compelling article which appeared both in *The Times* and *The South China Morning Post*, the British Prime Minister Boris Johnson bemoaned that the imposition of National Security Law by China on Hong Kong would curtail its freedom and dramatically erode its autonomy. He wrote, "If China proceeds, this would be in direct conflict with its obligation under the Joint Declaration, a legally binding treaty registered with the United Nations. Britain would then have no choice but to uphold our profound ties of history and friendship with the people of Hong Kong." He further wrote, "Today, about 350,000 of the territory's people hold British National Overseas passports and another 2.5 million would be eligible to apply for them. At present, these passports allow visa-free access to the United Kingdom for up to six months. If China imposes its national security law, the British government will change our immigration rules and allow any holder of these passports from Hong Kong to come to the UK for a renewable period of 12 months, and be given further immigration rights, including right to work, which would place them on a route to citizenship."[11]

The offer to grant BNO passports to eligible Hong-Kongers flabbergasted Beijing. It accused Britain of 'colonial mentality' after Johnson promised to offer the citizenship rights to bonafide residents of Hong Kong, if the situation so demands. Expressing strong dissatisfaction and opposition to the offer, the Spokesperson of China's foreign ministry Zhao Lijian said, "The UK has recklessly commented on Hong Kong and made groundless accusation to interfere in Hong Kong affairs." Johnson's offer evoked mixed reaction in Hong Kong. While the rich and well-off residents have shown some interest, the younger generation of people who are spearheading the pro-democracy movement in Hong Kong are not so enthused.

NOTES

1. Gabriel Dominquez, "Beijing rejects full Hong Kong democracy", *Deutsche Wells*, 31 August 2014, https://www.dw.com/en/beijing-rejects-full-hong-kong-democracy/a-17891743
2. "Carrie Lam is elected as Hong Kong's new Chief Executive", *Time*, 26 March 2017. https://time.com/4713306/carrie-lam-hong-kong-chief-executive/
3. "China says Hong Kong protests near 'terrorism', *The Hindu*, 14 August 2019, https://www.thehindu.com/news/international/china-says-hong-kong-protests-near-terrorism/article29094572.ece
   Also see Martin Purbricck, "A report of the 2019 Hong Kong Protests", *Asian Affairs*, 2019 volume L.no 1V, 465-487
4. "China says military can be deployed at the request of Hong Kong", *Scroll.in*, July 2019, https://scroll.in/latest/931604/china-hints-military-may-be-deployed-in-hong-kong-to-quell-protests
5. "Hong Kong Election Results Give Democracy Backers Big Win", *New York Times,* November 24, 2019,https://www.nytimes.com/2019/11/24/world/asia/hong-kong-election-results.html
6. *South China Morning Post*, November 25, 2019, https://www.scmp.com/news/hong-kong/politics/article/3039151/hong-kong-elections-tsunami-disaffection-washes-over-city
7. Willy Wo Lap Lam," Beijing Announces Its Intention to Impose a New National Security Law on Hong Kong", *China Brief*, May 26, 2020, https://jamestown.org/program/jamestown-early-warning-brief-beijing-announces-its-intention-to-impose-a-new-national-security-law-on-hong-kong/
8. "Towards national security and place in Hong Kong," *The Hindu*, 24 July 2020.
9. "UN experts decry Hong Kong security law in letter to China", *The Times of India*, September 9, 2020.
10. "Citing pandemic, Hong Kong delays polls", *The Hindu*, August 1, 2020.
11. Boris Johnson, "For Hong Kongrs fearing for their way of life, Britain will provide an alternative", *South China Morning Post*, June 3, 2020.

CHAPTER 8

Congential Irreconliability

The Hong Kong handover on the midnight of June 30, 1997, was a major event of the contemporary world. It was indeed a triumph of diplomacy when Britain handed over the covetous territory almost after 150 years of tutelage to the People's Republic of China. When the British took possession of the island of Hong Kong, it was in the words of British Foreign Secretary Lord Palmerston, 'a barren island', and when Britain handed it over to China, it was one of the fastest growing economies of the world, the third largest financial centre of the world after New York and London, having a GDP of US$ 23,200. Hong Kong had enjoyed an average real GDP growth of 6.5 each year during the past 10 years prior to its reversion to Communist China. The tiny capitalist enclave has the distinction of the world's third largest airport in terms of international passenger throughput; and second busiest in terms of cargo throughput stock market in the world in terms of capitalisation.

After a century-and-a-half of humiliation and ignominy of the 'Opium War' followed by unequal treaties, the Chinese people could restore their national pride on equal terms from a position of strength. The imperial esteem of China was inflicted a humiliating jolt on August 29, 1842, when the hapless Chinese commissioner Chi-Ying was dictated to sign on the dotted lines of the Treaty of Nanking on board the British ship *HMS Cornwallis*. The wheel of history turned its full circle on July 1, 1997, when the ship *Royal Britannica* retreated from the shores of Hong Kong after taking with it the last British Governor Chris Patten and other British dignitaries, bidding adieu to the last major colonial outpost of Britain.

Although a high degree of autonomy has been guaranteed for the Hong Kong Special Administrative Region, doubts were raised with regard to its implementation in letter and spirit. Since the Standing Committee of the National People's Congress has the power to interpret the Basic Law, critics point out that the so-called high degree of autonomy is vague and subject to interpretation by the National People's Congress, the rubber stamp Parliament of the Communist regime. The term 'autonomy' does not mean that the Hong Kong Special Administrative Region, being vested with executive, legislative, and independent judicial powers, including that of the final adjudication, will have the competence of final decisions in all legislative matters. This proviso also applies to the laws prevailing in force in Hong Kong, which will be reserved except those which are contrary to the Basic Law. If they are in contrast to the Basic Law, the Standing Committee of the NPC can annul them.

Further, Article 23 of the Basic Law directs the HKSAR to enact laws on its own to 'prohibit any act of treason, secession, sedition, subversion against the Central People's Government, or theft of state secrets, to prohibit foreign political organisations or bodies from conducting political activities in the region, and to prohibit organisations or bodies of the Hong Kong Special Administrative Region from establishing ties with foreign political organisations or bodies. Subversion is an alien concept to the present Hong Kong legal system. There is concern that the HK Special Administrative Region will be required to prohibit whatever China considers to be subversion. Under Chinese criminal law, subversion is a crime of counter-revolution committed with the goal of overthrowing the political power of dictatorship of the proletariat and the socialist system. There had been some suggestion in Hong Kong, therefore, that Article 23 should be amended to delete a stipulation requiring the Special Administrative Region to enact laws on its own to prohibit subversion against the Central People's Government.[1]

FRAGILITY OF HONG KONG'S RESILIENCE

Although Hong Kong, in the past ever since its inception, had weathered many a storm and displayed a remarkable resilience to bounce back, the developments in the territory in the past 25-odd years have raised serious questions with regard to its future stability and prosperity. The root cause of this is the congenital irreconcilability of two divergent political systems – China, a regimented Communist regime; and Hong Kong, a classical laissez fare economy with the ethos of a liberal democracy. True, Hong Kong has survived under the shadow of a protracted civil war in Mainland China, the rise and birth of Communist China in 1949, the adverse effects of the Second World War and its economic consequences, and the power struggle during the tumultuous Cultural Revolution (1967-69), but the developments ever since the Tiananmen Square incidents of 1989, the promulgation of the National Security Law in May 2020, and China's estrangement because of its belligerence with a number of countries (including the 'Five Eyes' industrialised nations) have greatly dented its much vaunted pride of resilience and adaptability. The Sino-US spat and the trade war between the world's two top economies amidst Covid-19 resonated in Hong Kong, where the USA is a major stakeholder. Hong Kong has been caught in some sort of an ideological cold war between the 'Washington Consensus' and the 'Beijing Consensus'.

CHINA'S FEAR: HONG KONG A BASE TO UNDERMINE CHINA

Beijing alleges that the Western democracies use Hong Kong as a base to undermine China. Its concerns may be true, as there may not be any denial of China's grouse. But it is also a fact that Hong Kong, as an enclave of democracy, will continue to be an anathema to the Communist Party of China, particularly in the context of a suppressed desire for democracy and freedom in the Mainland. A large segment of the Hong Kong populace, born after the birth of Communist China, lack a primordial affiliation to the Mainland, and even the aged and elderly who migrated from the Mainland and settled in Hong Kong grew up in the milieu of a liberal democracy. Even if Hong Kong did not have the electoral democracy of the Western variant, it had a rule of law, a robust and vibrant media, and the culture and values of a liberal democracy.

In fact, a study conducted by the University of Hong Kong in 2011 found that the number of respondents who viewed themselves as Hong-Kongers was more than the number who viewed themselves as Chinese, and that bonds of identity with the Mainland had weakened since British relinquished sovereignty in 1997. The findings of the survey infuriated Beijing. Media controlled by the Chinese Communist Party directed a torrent of abuses at Robert Chung, the director of Hong Kong University's Public Opinion Program and his work. "Chung's survey has evil political aims," the *Wen Wei Po* newspaper opined. The paper criticised Chung as a "slave of black political funding" and accused him of seeking to "divide Hong Kong people from their compatriots." Chung dismissed the allegations as 'Cultural Revolution style smear campaign."[2]

It was in this backdrop that in February 2021, the Hong Kong government unveiled controversial guidelines for schools in the territory that include teaching students as young as six about colluding with foreign forces and subversion as part of a new national security curriculum. The Education Bureau's guidelines show that Beijing's plans for Hong Kong go beyond quashing dissent, and aim for social overhaul. 'National security is of great importance', prescribes the guidelines and urges teachers "should clearly point out that safeguarding national security is the responsibility of all nationals, and that as far as national security is concerned, there is no room for debate or compromise."[3]

ENVIRONMENTAL TURBULENCE

Maintaining autonomy in business and trade in Hong Kong after the handover has also been a concern. An echo system, both internally and externally determined, has been the driver of Hong Kong's growth and development. There is now a challenge to its echo system, which has all the potential to disrupt Hong Kong's growth and development. In assessing Hong Kong's resilience to cope with the challenges both from within and outside, it is useful to apply the conceptual framework of 'environmental turbulence', a term coined by Emery and Trist in 1965. The concept was applied in the case of Hong Kong by Miron Mushkat in a paper published in 1989, after the conclusion of the Sino-British Joint Declaration in 1985. The authors used the term to capture the essence of an emerging societal condition characterised by a high degree of complexity and rapid change, and to differentiate it from the more simple and stable environmental patterns.

Applying the analogy to Hong Kong in 1989, Mushkat wrote, "It might be argued that the coming re-unification with the Mainland is likely to constitute a far greater menace than anything experienced before. Thus, the fact that environmental dislocation was brought under control on previous occasions is not entirely relevant if one assumes that future turbulence could be of a different order altogether. The enormous uncertainty which engulfed Hong Kong during various phases of the Sino-British negotiations may be indicative of the potent negative forces which external stimuli can unleash (it is true that the territory has since more or less regained its momentum, but the disturbance was relatively short-lived, and the ultimate point of no return was never actually reached).[4]

He further observed that "sharp escalation in the level of environmental stress is not the only potentially disruptive development looming on the Hong Kong horizon, the territory's much vaunted adaptive capacity could also diminish as a result of a build-up of intense external and internal pressures. There is no reason to posit that the mechanism on which Hong Kong has thus far relied successfully to absorb environmental shocks are not vulnerable to corrosion and breakdowns. A confluence of externally and internally induced crises might conceivably, past performance notwithstanding, damage them beyond repair. The almost mythical belief that the territory is destined to thrive, irrespective of the circumstances, is unfortunately a myth."[5]

What Mushkat wrote in 1989 proved correct in Hong Kong in the run-up to the transfer of Hong Kong to Chinese rule on July 1, 1997. There was a flight of capital and exodus of people. Two major British corporate entities – Hong Kong Bank and Jardine – had to relocate their corporate domicile overseas ahead of the handover of sovereignty. Canada, which was a major destination of Hong Kong immigrants, witnessed a significant rise. The immigration figures for 1990 revealed that the number of Hong Kong immigrants who landed in Canada rose over previous years from 23,281 in 1988 to 28,949 in 1990.[6] The spike in the population exodus from Hong Kong reflected the erosion of people's confidence in the future stability and prosperity of the island territory.

THE SECOND GOVERNMENT

Some people describe the economic reform in China as having produced a 'bird-cage economy' – that is, a controlled economy with some room for market forces. Sceptics on Hong Kong's future under Chinese sovereignty say Hong Kong will only have a 'bird-cage' autonomy with a top-down approach and macro management. There is a perception that the Hong Kong government is now remotely controlled by what is euphemistically described in the island as the 'second government'. The 'second government' includes state entities such as the Ministry of Foreign Affairs, *Xinhua* (New China News Agency), and the People's Liberation Army (PLA), besides the Hong Kong and Macau Affairs Office. It is questionable whether the 'second government' has in fact become the first government.[7]

CAN SHENZHEN REPLACE HONG KONG?

There are also developments to suggest that Beijing is now developing Shenzhen to supplement, if not supplant, Hong Kong. In mid-October 2020, President Xi Jinping unveiled some economic reform measures, while speaking at Shenzhen on the occasion of the 40th anniversary of establishment of Special Economic Zone there. He called it a "comprehensive reform pilot project to promote socialism with Chinese characteristics." He urged upon the city of 13 million to expand and accelerate the all-round opening up of policies, with institutional guarantees, such as rules and norms. In his address, Xi said that Beijing had allowed Shenzhen to "explore a more flexible policy, system, and a more scientific management system in terms of domestic and foreign trade, investment and financing, finance and taxation, financial innovation as well as personnel exit and entry." Stressing the importance of Shenzhen as a model, Xi stressed that "reform must never stop, and there is no end to opening up the economy. Shenzhen must push forward reforms and 'open door policies' from even a higher vantage point."

While Shenzhen has been touted as China's Silicon Valley, this is the first time that the budding metropolis has been exhorted by Xi Jinping to excel in the financial sector and services such as accounting, design, and the legal arena. Even though Shenzhen's GDP surpassed that of Hong Kong, the latter continues to be China's only international financial centre with a close business connection with most of the Western countries, and the city is regarded as the dragon head of the region. Scholars argue as long as Beijing maintains rigid control over capital-account movements and refuses to abide by internationally accepted practices of the rule of law, it is unlikely that Shenzhen can rival Hong Kong as a global financial hub.[8]

In a report authored by the Institute Defence and Security Research of Taiwan in Januray 2022, it was speculated that if Hong Kong's chief executive Carrie Lam is re-elected in the election scheduled for March 2022, which is now postponed to May 2022, it is likely that the territoty would become more like nearby Shenzhen, which is directly under Beijing's control. The idea of "Southern Shenzhen" was first raised by investment banker Alex Shiu, who cited aerbitrary arresta and monitoring of individuals as becoming the norm in Hong Kong as it is in China, opined Shin Chien-yu, author of the report.[9]

CAN 'ONE COUNTRY, TWO SYSTEMS' BE REPLICATED IN TAIWAN?

Political developments in Hong Kong and China's iron fist attempts to suppress and stifle the democratic aspirations of the people have raised doubts about the efficacy of 'one country, two systems' in Hong Kong, and the prospect of its replication in Taiwan, where the Democratic Progressive Party (DPP) is growing strong, and even the opposition KMT – sensing the people's sentiment in Taiwan – has started distancing itself from Mainland China. China does not care much about the economic well-being of Hong Kong; it has already started mentoring Shenzhen as an alternative financial hub. China is rather more worried that if the pro-democracy movement is allowed to grow there in Hong Kong, in the long run, it will have a contagion effect on China, arousing fresh bouts of democratic aspiration there. It, thus, wants to demonstrate that 'enough is enough', no dissent can be tolerated in the Communist regime.

The decline of Hong Kong has already set in, and its resilience is being put to test.

Taiwan had been caught in a number of dilemmas since the Hong Kong negotiation between Beijing and London began in 1982. In the first place, because of nationalistic reasons, Taiwan could not oppose Hong Kong's return to Chinese sovereignty, but at the same time it could not accept its relegation to Chinese Communist rule. Secondly, Taiwan considers itself a continuation of the Chinese government that operated on the Mainland until the Communist insurrection drove it to Taiwan in 1949. It still holds the original copies of the three 19th century Sino-British treaties regarding Hong Kong, Kowloon, and the New Territories.[10]

While China's position with regard to Taiwan is that "re-unification is inevitable and China would never tolerate Taiwan's independence," DPP maintains that it cannot accept becoming a part of China under 'one country, two systems'. From 2008 to 2016, the KMT party (which is inclined and amenable towards Mainland China) was in power in Taiwan. The KMT President Ma Yingjeou's position with regard to China had been 'No unification, no independence, and no use of force.'

The DPP is anathema to China because it does not subscribe to 'unification' with the Mainland, but rather proclaims 'independence', and this makes a huge difference. President Tsai Ing-wen has said "Taiwan is an independent state called Republic of China (its official name) and does not want to be a part of the People's Republic of China." What is worrying for China is not only the victory of DPP in the election and its increasing popularity, but also its capacity to co-opt and absorb KMT to its fold and make basic changes in governance structure through referendum, which is fraught with far-reaching consequences detrimental to KMT and China indirectly. For example, when Chen Shui-bian and Annette Hsiu-lien Lu of the DPP were elected President and

Vice-President, ending the KMT's more than 50-year rule in 2000, heralding the first transfer of government in Taiwan, in a very smart move President Chen Shui-bian appointed a former chief of General Staff and former Defence Minister Gen Tang Fei, a KMT veteran, as Prime Minister and a cabinet, of which the majority of ministers were from the KMT.

BRITISH LEGACY

No study of Hong Kong is, however, complete without making some assessment of the British contributions. Generally, a very charitable view is taken in terms of British contributions in Hong Kong for the rule of law, the civil service, and an enabling business environment. There are also scholars who make a more objective and dispassionate assessment about the British legacy.[11] One major criticism is that the British did not develop representative institutions, and they did so half-heartedly in a piecemeal manner in the twilight years of their rule. Beijing criticised Hong Kong's last Governor Chris Patten for trying to fast-track the representative institutions, breaching the Joint Declaration and the Basic Law.

It would be factually incorrect to say that the British did not introduce democratic reforms. It has been amply demonstrated in the book that there were calibrated attempts of succeeding British Governors to give representation to the local Chinese populace without inviting adversarial and competitive electoral politics. More than electoral politics, the rule of law, providing a level playing field, a vibrant and independent media, and finally 'cosmopolitanism' are some of the enduring legacies of the British tutelage of the Colony, albeit with the caveat of George Bernard Shaw, "an Englishman does everything on principles – he fights on patriotic principles, he robs on business principles, and he enslaves on imperial principles."

Hong Kong will not remain the same cosmopolitan city. China will continue to be haunted by the vestiges of democracy in Hong

Kong; the erosion of confidence in the novelty of 'one country, two systems' has also dampened the prospect of unification of the Mainland with its estranged sibling Taiwan. The pro-democracy movement will dissipate in times to come and Hong Kong will be another Shenzhen, stripped off its cosmopolitan elan. Hong Kong is not a city alone, it is a way of life, a way of doing business, a melting pot of multi-culturalism, a confluence of the Orient and the Occident.

NOTES

1. Christen Loh, *Hong Kong: A High Degree of Autonomy and the Basic Law*, (Hong Kong, 1995), p. 31.
2. "Beijing angry over survey which says Hong Kongers feel less Chinese", *The Hindustan Times,* January 14, 2012.
3. "HK to teach kids as young as six about subversion", *The First Post* February 6, 2021, https://www.firstpost.com/world/hong-kong-to-teach-children-as-young-as-six-about-subversion-foreign-interference-9275791.html
4. Miron Mushkat, "Environmental Turbulence and the Economic Prospects of Hong Kong", *Hong Kong : The Challenge of Transformation*, University of Hong Kong, 1989, p. 298.
5. Ibid, p. 299.
6. Diana Lary, "Immigration Patterns, 1990-91", *Canada and Hong Kong Update*, No. 4, Spring 1991, p. 7.
7. Martin Purbrick, "A Report of the 2019 Hong Kong Protests", *Asian Affairs,* Volume L, No. IV, 2019.
8. Willy Wo-Lap Lam, "Beijing Raises Shenzhen status at the expense of Hong Kong", *China Brief*, 23 October 2020.
9. "HK's future tied to Lam's re-election," *Taipei Times*, January 27, 2022.
10 James C. Hsiung, "The Hong Kong Settlement: Effects on Taiwan and Prospects foe Peking's Reunification Bid", *Asian Affairs: An American Review*, Volume 12, No. 2, 1985, p. 51.
11. Ming K. Chan, "The Legacy of the British Administration of Hong Kong: A View from Hong Kong', *China Quarterly*, No. 151, September 1997.

CHAPTER 9

POSTSCRIPT China overhauls Hong Kong's Electoral System

After postponing the election to the Legislative Council, Beijing unveiled the electoral reforms proposal for Hong Kong Special Administrative Region. In early March 2021, Zhang Yesui, a spokesperson for the National People's Congress (NPC) said that the NPC had the constitutional power to "improve" Hong Kong's system and a draft decision would be discussed in the annual parliamentary session.[1] Zhang said the changes would include increasing the size of the election committee to select the chief executive of Hong Kong Special Administrative Region from 1200 to 1500 and the city's legislature from 70 to 90. He further said that developments in the territory showed the electoral system "needs to be improved to implement the principle of patriots governing Hong Kong." Carrie Lam, the chief executive officer of the city fully welcomed the proposed changes saying that, "there are loopholes in the electoral systems, there are also flaws in the systems in Hong Kong." The USA criticised the move. The State Department spokesperson Ned Price denounced them saying, "These are direct attacks on Hong Kong's autonomy, Hong Kong's freedoms, and the democratic processes, limiting participation, reducing democratic representation, and stifling political debate in order to defy the clear will of the people of Hong Kong and to deny their own voice in their own government and governance."

The National People's Congress passed the proposed changes on 11 March 2021. The NPC said that the move was to ensure that "the electoral system should conform to the policy of 'one country, two systems', meet the realities if HKSAR and serve to ensure that Hong Kong is administered by people who love the country and love Hong Kong." The idea to ensure the administration of Hong Kong people with patriots as the main body" was described by Beijing as response to the 2019 pro-democracy protests that roiled the city and called for universal suffrage. Under the extant system, half of the 70 member Legislative Council members were directly elected and rest were nominated. With the electoral reform, the number of Legislative Council member was increased to 90, with the additional members also to be nominated, thereby reducing the number of elected representatives. The expanded Election Committee is now composed of 1,500 members, up from 1200, with the new members being nominated by Beijing to include Hong Kong members of the National People's Congress, and the Chinese People's Political Consultative Conference (the political advisory body or the upper house. The Election Committee, is responsible for electing the chief executive and will also choose some of the members of the Legislative Council.[2]

CRITERION OF PATRIOTISM

The selection of "patriots" is ensured by the setting up of a new candidate qualification review committee which the NPC said "shall be responsible for reviewing and confirming the qualification of the candidates for the Election Committee members, the Chief Executive and the LegCo members." Responding to the criticism that pushing the idea of "patriots governing Hong Kong" tends to shrink the democratic space, Tegina Ip, a leading law maker and the founder of pro-Beijing *New People's Party*, said that who is a patriot has been defined by Deng Xioping earlier in 1980s. In his work, a patriot is someone who respects own people, genuinely supports Hong Kong's reunification with China, and would not do anything to hurt the interests of Hong Kong.[3] Mr Song Ru'an, Deputy Commissioner of China's Ministry of Foreign Affairs in Hong Kong elucidating on patriotism earlier in April 2021 said, "When we talk about patriotism, we are not talking about the abstraction of loving a cultural or historical China, but rather loving the currently existing People's Republic of China under the leadership of the Chinese Communist Party." He added, "Patriots should respect the Chinese Communist Party."

LEGCO ELECTION, DECEMBER 2021

After promulgating the National Security Law and overhauling the electoral system, election to the Legislative Council was held on 19th December 2021. As expected candidates loyal to China's Communist Party won a landslide victory after pro-democracy activists were imprisoned and authorities were empowered to exclude those considered inappropriate for the office. Most of the law makers were Hong Kong's leader Carrie Lam said that she was "satisfied" with the election despite 30.2% voter turnout- the lowest since the British handed over the territory to China in 1997. She said that the number of registered voters reached 92.5%, a record high compared to 2012 and 2016 elections, when around 70% of voters had registered. "For registered voters, deciding whether they to exercise their voting rights in a particular election is entirely a matter for themselves", she said. She argued that 1.35 million votes cast also endorsed the support of the voters for the improved electoral system. The opposition camp criticised the elections, with the largest pro-democracy party, the *Democratic Party*, fielding no candidates for the first time since 1997 handover. Beijing attributed the low turnout to the pandemic, the disruption and sabotage of anti-China elements in Hong Kong and external forces. Some of the overseas pro-democracy activists, including London based Nathan Law, urged a boycott of the votes, saying the elections were undemocratic. Under the new election law, incitement to boycott the voting or to cast invalid votes could be punished by up to three years in jail and a 200,000 Hong Kong dollar ($26,500) fine.

NOTES

1. Greg Torode, "China Parliament seeks to shake up Hong Kong politics, put 'patriots' in China-official." *Reuters,* March 4, 2021, https://www.reuters.com/article/china-parliament-hongkong-idINKCN2AW28F
2. Ananth Krishnan, "China overhauls Hong Kong's poll system", *The Hindu*, March 11, 2021, https://www.thehindu.com/news/international/chinese-lawmakers-set-to-tighten-control-on-hong-kong/article34042532.ece
3. Ananth Krishnan, "Radical change is need in the mindset and governance of Hong Kong,". *The Hindu* December 2021, https://www.thehindu.com/news/international/radical-change-is-needed-in-the-mindset-and-governance-of-hong-kong-says-pro-beijing-lawmaker-regina-ip/article37980271.ece

ANNEXURE 1

Treaty of Nanking (Nanjing), August 29, 1842[1]

ARTICLE I: There shall henceforward be peace and friendship between Her Majesty, the Queen of the United Kingdom of Great Britain and Northern Ireland; and His Majesty, the Emperor of China; and between their respective subjects, who shall enjoy full security and protection for their persons and property within the dominions of the other.

ARTICLE II: His Majesty, the Emperor of China, agrees that British subjects, with their families and establishment, shall be allowed to reside for the purpose of carrying on their mercantile pursuits, without molestation or restraint at the cities and towns of Canton, Amoy, Foochow-fu, Ningpo, and Shanghai; and Her Majesty, the Queen of the United Kingdom, will appoint Superintendents or Consular Officers, to reside at each of the above-named cities or towns, to be the medium of communication between the Chinese authorities and the said merchants, and to see that the just duties and

1 Source: *The Maritime Customs, Treaties, Conventions, etc., Between China and Foreign States,* Second (Edition), Shanghai 1917, vol. 1, 351-56

other dues of the Chinese government, as hereafter provided for, are duly discharged by Her Britannic Majesty's subjects.

ARTICLE III: It, being obviously necessary and desirable, that British subjects should have some port whereat they may careen and refit their ships, when required, and keep stores for that purpose, His Majesty, the Emperor of China, cedes to Her Majesty, the Queen of UK, the island of Hong Kong, to be possessed in perpetuity by Her Britannic Majesty, Her heirs and successors, and to be governed by such laws and regulations as Her Majesty shall see fit to direct.

ARTICLE IV: The Emperor of China agrees to pay the sum of six million dollars as the value of opium, which delivered up at Canton in the month of March 1839, as a ransom for the lives of Her Britannic Majesty's Superintendent and Subjects, who had been imprisoned and threatened with death by the Chinese high officers.

ARTICLE V: The Government of China having compelled the British merchants trading at Canton to deal exclusively with certain Chinese merchants called Hong Kong Merchants (or Cohong) who had been licensed by the Chinese Government for that purpose, the Emperor of China agrees to abolish that practice in future at all ports where British merchants may reside, and to permit them to carry on their mercantile transactions with whatever persons they please, and His Imperial Majesty further agrees to pay to the British Government the sum of three million dollars, on account of debts due to British subjects by some of the said Hong merchants (or Cohong), who have become insolvent, and who owe very large sums of money to the subjects of Her Britannic Majesty.

ARTICLE VI: The Government of Her Britannic Majesty having been obliged to send out an expedition to demand and obtain redress for the violent and unjust proceedings of the Chinese high authorities towards Her Britannic Majesty's officers and subjects, the Emperor of China agrees to pay the sum of twelve million dollars on account of the expenses incurred, and Her Britannic Majesty's Plenipotentiary voluntarily agrees, on behalf of Her Majesty, to deduct from the said amount of twelve million dollars, any sums which may have been received by Her Majesty's combined forces as ransom for the cities and towns in China, subsequent to the 1st day of August 1841.

ARTICLE VII: It is agreed that the total amount of 21 million dollars, described in the three preceding articles, shall be paid as follows:

Six million immediately.

Six million in 1843. That is: Three million on or before the 30th of the month of June, and three million on or before the 31st of December.

Five million in 1844. That is: Two million-and-a-half on or before the 30th of the month of June, and three million-and-a-half on or before the 31st of December.

Four million in 1845. That is: Two millions on or before the 30th of the month of June, and two million on or before the 31st of December; and it is further stipulated, that interest at the rate of 5% per annum, shall be paid by the Government of China on any portions of the above sums that are not punctually discharged at the periods fixed.

ARTICLE VIII: The Emperor of China agrees to release unconditionally all subjects of Her Britannic Majesty (whether natives of the Empire or India) who may be in confinement at this moment, in any part of the Chinese Empire.

ARTICLE IX: The Emperor of China agrees to publish and promulgate, under His imperial sign Manula Arid Seal, a full and entire amnesty and act of indemnity, to all subjects of China on account of their having resided under, or having had dealings and intercourse with, or having entered the service of Her Britannic Majesty, or of Her Majesty's officers, and His Imperial Majesty further engages to release all Chinese subjects who may be at this moment in confinement for similar reasons.

ARTICLE X: His majesty, the Emperor of China, agrees to establish at all the ports which are by the 2nd article of this treaty to be thrown open for the resort of British merchants, a fair and regular tariff of export and import customs and other dues, which tariff shall be publicly notified and promulgated for general information, and the Emperor further engages, that when British merchants shall have once paid at any of the said ports the regulated customs and dues agreeable to the tariff, to be hereafter fixed, such in the merchandise may be conveyed by Chinese merchants, to any province or city in the interior of the Empire of China on paying a further amount as transit duties which shall not exceed (blank) per cent, on the tariff value of such goods.

ARTICLE XI: It is agreed that Her Britannic Majesty's Chief High Officer in China shall correspond with the Chinese High Officers, both at the capital and in the Provinces, under the term 'Communication'..... The Subordinate British Officers and Chinese High Officers in the Province under the terms 'Statement'... on the part of the former, and on the part of the latter, 'Declaration'... and the Subordinates of both Countries on a footing of perfect equality. Merchants and others not holding official situations and, therefore, not included in the above, on both sides, to use term 'Representation'.... in all Papers addressed to, or intended for the notice of the respective governments.

ARTICLE XII: On the assent of the Emperor of China to this treaty being received and the discharge of the first installment of money,

Her Britannic Majesty's forces will retire from Nanking and the Grand Canal, and will no longer molest or stop the trade of China. The military post at Chinhai will also be withdrawn, but the islands of Koolangsoo and that of Chusan will continue to be held by Her Majesty's forces until the money payments, and the arrangements for opening the ports to British Merchants be completed.

ARTICLE XIII: The ratification of this treaty by Her Majesty, the Queen of Great Britain, etc., and His Majesty, the Emperor of China, shall be exchanged as soon as the great distance which separates England from China will admit; but in the meantime, counterpart copies of it, signed and sealed by the Plenipotentiaries on behalf of their respective sovereigns, shall be mutually delivered, and all its provisions and arrangements shall take effect.

Done at Nanking, and Signed and Sealed by the Plenipotentiaries on board Her Britannic Majesty's ship Cornwallis, this twenty-ninth day of August, 1842, corresponding with the Chinese date, twenty-fourth day of the seventh month in the twenty-second year of Taou Kwang.

ANNEXURE II

Joint Declaration[2]

Of the Government of the People's Republic of China and The Government of the United Kingdom of Great Britain and Northern Ireland On the Question of Hong Kong

The Government of the People's Republic of China and the Government of the United Kingdom of Great Britain and Northern Ireland have reviewed with satisfaction the friendly relations existing between the two Governments and peoples in recent years and agreed that a proper negotiated settlement of the question of Hong Kong, which is left over from the past, is conducive to the maintenance of the prosperity and stability of Hong Kong and to the further strengthening and development of the relations between the two countries on a new basis. To this end, they have after talks between the delegation of the two Governments, agreed to declare as follows:

1. The Government of the People's Republic of China declares that to recover the Hong Kong area (including Hong Kong Island, Kowloon, and the New Territories, hereinafter referred to as Hong

2 Source: Jurgen Domes and Yu-ming Shaw eds., *Hong Kong: A Chinese and International Concern*, (Boulder, 1988) pp. 246-266

Kong) is the common aspiration of the entire Chinese people, and that it has decided to resume the exercise of sovereignty over Hong Kong with effect from July 1, 1997.

2. The Government of the United Kingdom declares that it will restore Hong Kong to the People's Republic of China with effect from July 1, 1997.
3. The Government of the People's Republic of China declares that basic policies of the People's Republic of China regarding Hong Kong are as follows:
   (i) Upholding national unity and territorial integrity and taking account of the history of Hong Kong and its realities, the people's Republic of China has decided to establish in accordance with the provisions of Article 31 of the Constitution of the People's Republic of China, a Hong Kong Special Administrative Region upon resuming the exercise of sovereignty over Hong Kong.
   (ii) The Hong Kong Special Administrative Region will be directly under the authority of the Central People's Government of the People's Republic of China. The Hong Kong Special Administrative Region will enjoy a high degree of autonomy, except in foreign and defence affairs which are the responsibilities of the Central People's Government.
   (iii) The Hong Kong Special Administrative Region will be vested with executive legislative and independent judicial power, including that of final adjudication. The laws current in force in Hong Kong will remain basically unchanged.
   (iv) The Government of the Hong Kong Special Administrative Region will be composed of local inhabitants. The chief executive will be appointed by the Central People's Government on the basis of the result of elections or

consultations to be held locally. Principal officials will be nominated by the chief executive of the Hong Kong Special Administrative Region for appointment by the Central People's Government. Chinese and foreign nationals previously working in the public and police services in the government departments of Hong Kong may remain in employment. British and other foreign national may also be employed to serve as advisers or hold certain posts in government departments of the Hong Kong Special Administrative Region.

(v) The current social and economic system in Hong Kong will remain unchanged and so will the lifestyle. Rights and freedoms, including those of the persons, of speech of the press, of assembly, of association, of academic research and of religious belief will be ensured by law in the Hong Kong Special Administrative Region. Private property, ownership of enterprises, legitimate right of inheritance and foreign investment will be protected by law.

(vi) The Hong Kong Special Administrative Region will retain the status of a free port and a separate customs territory.

(vii) The Hong Kong Special Administrative Region will retain the status of an international financial centre, and its markets for foreign exchange, gold, securities and future will continue. There will be free flow of capital. The Hong Kong dollar will continue to circulate and remain freely convertible.

(viii) The Hong Kong Special Administrative Region will have independent finances. The Central People's Government will not levy taxes on the Hong Kong Special Administrative Region.

(ix) The Hong Kong Special Administrative Region may establish mutually beneficial economic relations with the

United Kingdom and other countries, whose economic interests in Hong Kong will be given due regard.

(x) Using the name of 'Hong Kong, China', The Hong Kong Special Administrative Region may, on its own, maintain and develop economic and cultural relations and conclude relevant agreements with states, region and relevant international organisations.

The Government of the Hong Kong Special Administrative Region may on its own issue travel documents for entry into and exit from Hong Kong.

(xi) The maintenance of public order in the Hong Kong Special Administrative Region will be the responsibility of the Government of the Hong Kong Special Administrative Region.

(xii) The above stated basic policies of the People's Republic of China regarding Hong Kong and the elaboration of them in Annex I to this Joint Declaration will be stipulated in a Basic Law of the Hong Kong Special Administrative Region of the People's Republic of China, by the National People's Congress of the People's Republic of China, and they will remain unchanged for 50 years.

4. The Government of the People's Republic of China and the Government of the United Kingdom declare that, during the transitional period between the date of the entry into force of this Joint Declaration and June 30, 1997, the Government of the United Kingdom will be responsible for the administration of Hong Kong with the object of maintaining and preserving its economic prosperity and stability; and that the Government of the People's Republic of China will give its cooperation in this connection.

5. The Government of the People's Republic of China and the Government of the United Kingdom declare that, in order to ensure a smooth transfer of government in 1997. And with a view to the effective implementation of this Joint Declaration, a Sino-British Joint Liaison Group will be set up when this Joint Declaration enters into force: and that it will be established and will function in accordance with the provisions of Annex II to this Joint Declaration.
6. The Government of the People's Republic of China and the Government of the United Kingdom declare that land leases in Hong Kong and other related matters will be dealt with in accordance with the provisions of Annex III to this Joint Declaration.
7. The Government of the People's Republic of China and the Government of the United Kingdom agree to implement the preceding declarations and the Annexes to this Joint Declaration.
8. This Joint Declaration is subject to ratification and shall enter into force on the date of the exchange of instruments of ratification, which shall take place in Beijing before June 30, 1985. This Joint Declaration and its Annexes shall be equally binding.

Done in duplicate at Beijing in 1984 in the Chinese and English languages, both texts being equally authentic.

(Signed)
For the
Government of the
People's Republic of China

(Signed)
For the
Government of the United
Kingdom of Great Britain
and Northern Ireland

ANNEX I

Elaboration by the Government of The People's Republic of China of Its Basic Policies Regarding Hong Kong

The Government of the People's Republic of China elaborated the basic policies of the People's Republic of China regarding Hong Kong as set out in paragraph 3 of the Joint Declaration of the Government of the People's Republic of China and the Government of the United Kingdom of Great Britain and Northern Ireland on the Question of Hong Kong as follows:

I

The Constitution of the People's Republic of China stipulates in Article 31 that "the state may establish special administration regions when necessary. The systems to be instituted in special administrative regions shall be prescribed by law enacted by the National People's Congress in the light of the specific conditions." In accordance with this Article, the People's Republic of China shall, upon the resumption of the exercise of sovereignty over Hong Kong on July 1, 1997, establish the Hong Kong Special Administrative Region of the People's Republic of China (hereinafter referred to as the Basic Law) in in accordance with the Constitution of the People's Republic of China, stipulating that after the establishment of the Hong Kong Special Administrative Region, the socialist system and socialist policies shall not be practised in the Hong Kong Special Administrative Region and that Hong Kong's previous capitalist system and lifestyle shall remain unchanged for 50 years.

The Hong Kong Special Administrative Region shall be directly under the authority of the Central People's Government of the People's Republic of China and shall enjoy a high degree of autonomy. Except for foreign and defence affairs, which are the responsibilities of the Central People's Government, the Hong Kong Special Administrative Region shall be vested with executive, legislative, and independent judicial power, including that of final adjudication. The Central People's Government shall authorise the Hong Kong Special Administrative Region to conduct on its own those external affairs specified in Section XI of this Annex.

The government and legislative of the Hong Kong Special Administrative Region shall be composed of local inhabitants. The chief executive of the Hong Kong Special Administrative Region shall be selected by election or through consultations held locally and be appointed by the Central People's Government. Principal officials (equivalent to Secretaries shall be nominated by the chief executive of the Hong Kong Special Administrative Region and appointed by the Central People's Government. The legislature of the Hong Kong Special Administrative Region shall be constituted by elections. The executive authorities shall abide by the law and shall be accountable to the legislature.

In addition to Chinese, English may also be used in organs of government and in the courts in the Hong Kong Special Administrative Region.

Apart from displaying the national emblem of the People's Republic of China, the Hong Kong Special Administrative Region may use a regional flag and emblem of its own.

II

After the establishment of the Hong Kong Special Administrative Region, the laws previously in force in Hong Kong (i.e. the common law, rules of equity, ordinances, subordinate legislation, and customary law) shall be maintained, save for any that contravene the Basic Law and subject to any amendment by the Hong Kong Special Administrative Region legislature.

The legislative power of the Hong Kong Special Administrative Region shall be vested in the legislature of the Hong Kong Special Administrative Region. The legislature may on its own authority enact laws in accordance with the provisions of the Basic Law and legal procedures, and report them to the Standing Committee of the National People's Congress for the record. Laws enacted by the legislature which are in accordance with the Basic Law and legal procedure shall be regarded as valid.

The laws of the Hong Kong Special Administrative Region shall be the Basic Law and the laws previously in force in Hong Kong and laws enacted by the Hong Kong Special Administrative Region legislature as above.

III

After the establishment of the Hong Kong Special Administrative Region, the judicial system previously practised in Hong Kong shall be maintained, except for those changes consequent upon the vesting in the courts of the Hong Kong Special Administrative Region of the power of final adjudication.

Judicial power in the Hong Kong Special Administrative Region shall be vested in the courts of the Hong Kong Special Administrative

Region. The courts shall exercise judicial power independently and free from any interference. Members of the judiciary shall be immune from legal action in respect of their judicial functions. The courts shall decide cases in accordance with the laws of the Hong Kong Special Administrative Region and may refer to precedents in other common law jurisdictions:

Judge of the Hong Kong Special Administrative Region courts shall be appointed by the chief executive of the Hong Kong Special Administrative Region acting in accordance with the recommendation of an independent commission composed of local judges, persons from the legal profession and other eminent persons. Judges shall be chosen by reference to their judicial qualities and may be recruited from other common law jurisdictions. A judge may only be removed for inability to discharge the functions of his office, or for misbehaviour by the chief executive of the Hong Kong Special Administrative Region, acting in accordance with the recommendation of a tribunal appointed by the chief judge of the court of final appeal, consisting of not fewer than three local judges. Additionally, the appointment or removal of principal judge (i.e. those of the highest rank) shall be made by the chief executive with the endorsement of the Hong Kong Special Administrative Region legislature and reported to the Standing Committee of the National People's Congress for the record. The system of appointment and removal of judicial officers other than judges shall be maintained.

The power of final judgment of the Hong Kong Special Administrative Region shall be vested in the court of final appeal in the Hong Kong Special Administrative Region, which may as required invite judges from other common law jurisdictions to sit on the court of final appeal.

A prosecuting authority of the Hong Kong Special Administrative Region shall control criminal prosecutions free from any interference.

On the basis of the system previously operating in Hong Kong, the Hong Kong Special Administrative Region Government shall, on its own, make provision for local lawyers and lawyers from outside the Hong Kong Special Administrative Region to work and practice in the Hong Kong Special Administrative Region.

The Central People's Government shall assist or authorise the Hong Kong Special Administrative Region Government to make appropriate arrangement for reciprocal juridical assistance with foreign states.

IV

After the establishment of the Hong Kong Special Administrative Region, public servants previously serving in Hong Kong in all government departments, including the police department, and member of the judiciary may all remain in employment and continue their service with pay, allowances, benefits and conditions of service no less favourable than before. The Hong Kong Special Administrative Region Government shall pay to such persons who retire or complete their contracts, as to those who have retired before July 1, 1997, or to their dependents, all pensions, gratuities, allowance and benefits due to them on terms no less favourable than before, and irrespective of their nationality or place of residence.

The Hong Kong Special Administrative Region Government may employ British and other foreign nationals previously serving in public in Hong Kong, and may recruit British and other foreign nationals holding permanent identity cards of the Hong Kong Special Administrative Region, to serve as public servants at all levels, except as heads of major government departments (corresponding to branches or departments at Secretary level) including the police department, and as deputy heads of some of those departments. The Hong Kong Special Administrative Region Government may also employ British and other foreign nationals as advisers to government departments, and when there is a need, may recruit qualified candidates from outside the Hong Kong Special Administrative Region to professional and technical posts in government departments. The above shall be employed only in their individual capacities and, like other public servants, shall be responsible to the Hong Kong Special Administrative Region Government.

The appointment and promotion of public servants shall be on the basis of qualifications, experience, and ability. Hong Kong's previous system of recruitment, employment, assessment, discipline, training, and management for the public service (including special bodies for appointment, pay and conditions of service) shall, save for any provisions providing privileged treatment for foreign nationals, be maintained.

V

The Hong Kong Special Administrative Region shall deal on its own with financial matters, including disposing of its financial resources and drawing up its budgets and its final accounts. The Hong Kong Special Administrative Region shall report its budgets and final accounts to the Central People's Government for the record.

The Central People's Government shall not levy taxes on the Hong Kong Special Administrative Region. The Hong Kong Special Administrative Region shall use its financial revenues exclusively for its own purpose and they shall not be handed over to the Central People's Government. The Systems by which taxation and public expenditure must be approved by the legislature, and by which there is accountability to the legislature for all public expenditure, and the system for auditing public accounts shall be maintained.

VI

The Hong Kong Special Administrative Region shall maintain the capitalist economic and trade system previously practised in Hong Kong. The Hong Kong Special Administrative Region Government shall decide its economic and trade policies on its own. Rights concerning the ownership of property, including those relating to acquisition, use, disposal, inheritance, and compensation for lawful deprivation (corresponding to the real value of the property concerned, freely convertible and paid without undue delay) shall continue to be protected by law.

The Hong Kong Special Administrative Region shall retain the status of a free port and continue a free trade policy, including the free movement of goods and capital. The Hong Kong Special Administrative Region may, on its own, maintain and develop economic and trade relations with all states and regions.

The Hong Kong Special Administrative Region shall be a separate customs territory. It may participate in relevant international organisations and international trade agreements (including preferential trade arrangements), such as the General Agreement on Tariffs and Trade, and arrangements regarding international trade in textiles. Export quotas, tariff preferences, and other similar arrangements obtained by the Hong Kong Special Administrative Region shall be enjoyed exclusively by the Hong Kong Special Administrative Region. The Hong Kong Special Administrative Region shall have the authority to issue its own certificates of origin for products manufactured locally, in accordance with prevailing rules of origin.

The Hong Kong Special Administrative Region may, as necessary, establish official and semi-official economic and trade mission in foreign countries, reporting the establishment of such a mission to the Central People's Government for the record.

VII

The Hong Kong Special Administrative Region shall retain the status of an international financial centre. The monetary and financial systems previously practised in Hong Kong, including the system of regulation and supervision of deposit-taking institutions and financial markets, shall be maintained.

The Hong Kong Special Administrative Region Government may decide its monetary and financial policies on its own. It shall safeguard the free operation of financial business and the free flow of capital within, into, and out of the Hong Kong Special Administrative Region. No exchange control policy shall be applied in the Hong Kong Special Administrative Region. Markets for foreign exchange, gold, securities and futures shall continue.

The Hong Kong dollar, as the local legal tender, shall continue to circulate and remain freely convertible. The authority to issue Hong Kong currency shall be vested in the Hong Kong Special Administrative Region Government. The Hong Kong Special Administrative Region Government may authorise designated banks to issue or continue to issue Hong Kong currency under statutory authority, after satisfying itself that any issue of currency will be soundly based and that the arrangements for such issue are consistent with the object of maintaining the stability of the currency. Hong Kong currency bearing references inappropriate to the status of Hong Kong as a Special Administrative Region of the People's Republic of China shall be progressively replaced and withdrawn from circulation.

The Exchange Fund shall be managed and controlled by the Hong Kong Special Administrative Region Government, primarily for regulating the exchange value of the Hong Kong dollar.

VIII

The Hong Kong Special Administrative Region shall maintain Hong Kong's previous system of shipping management and shipping, including the system for regulating conditions of seamen. The specific functions and responsibilities of the Hong Kong Special Administrative Region Government in the field of shipping shall be defined by the Hong Kong Special Administrative Region Government on its own.

Private shipping business and shipping-related businesses and private container terminals in Hong Kong may continue to operate freely.

The Hong Kong Special Administrative Region shall be authorised by the Central People's Government to continue to maintain a shipping register and issue related certificates under its own legislation in the name of 'Hong Kong, China'.

With the exception of foreign warships, access for which requires the permission of the Central People's Government, ships shall enjoy access to the ports of the Hong Kong Special Administrative Region in accordance with the laws of the Hong Kong Special Administrative Region.

IX

The Hong Kong Special Administrative Region shall maintain the status of Hong Kong as a centre of international and regional aviation. Airlines incorporated and having their principal place of business in Hong Kong and civil aviation related business may continue to operate. The Hong Kong Special Administrative Region shall continue the previous system of civil aviation management in Hong Kong, and keep its own aircraft register in accordance with provisions laid down by the Central People's Government concerning nationality marks and registration marks of aircraft. The Hong Kong Special Administrative Region shall be responsible on its own for matters of routine business and technical management of civil aviation, including the management of airports, the provision of air traffic services within the flight information region of the Hong Kong Special Administrative Region, and the discharge of other responsibilities allocated under the regional air navigation procedures of the International Civil Aviation Organisation.

The Central People's Government shall, in consultation with the Hong Kong Special Administrative Region Government, make arrangements providing for air services between the Hong Kong

Special Administrative Region and other parts of the People's Republic of China for airlines incorporated and having their principal place of business in the Hong Kong Special Administrative Region and other airlines of the People's Republic of China. All Air Service Agreements providing for air services between other parts of the People's Republic of China and other states and regions will stops at the Hong Kong Special Administrative Region, and air services between the Hong Kong Special Administrative Region and other states and regions with stops at other parts of the People's Republic of China shall be concluded by the Central People's Government. For this purpose, the Central People's Government shall take account of the special conditions and economic interests of the Hong Kong Special Administrative Region and consult the Hong Kong Special Administrative Region Government. Representatives of the Hong Kong Special Administrative Region Government may participate as members of delegation of the Government of the People's Republic of China in air service consultations with foreign governments concerning arrangements for such services.

Acting under specific authorisation from the Central People's Government, the Hong Kong Special Administrative Region Government may:

- renew or amend Air Service Agreements and Arrangements previously in force; in principle, all such agreements and arrangements may be renewed or amended with the rights contained in such previous agreements and arrangements being as far as possible maintained;
- negotiate and conclude new Air Service Agreements providing routes for airlines incorporated and having their principal place of business in the Hong Kong Special Administrative Region and rights for overflights and technical stops; and
- negotiate and conclude provisional arrangements where no

air service agreement with a foreign state or other region is in force.

All scheduled air services to, from, or through the Hong Kong Special Administrative Region which do not operate to, from, or through the Mainland of China shall be regulated by Air Service Agreements or provisional arrangements referred to in this paragraph.

The Central People's Government shall give the Hong Kong Special Administrative Region Government the authority to:

- negotiate and conclude with other authorities all arrangements concerning the implementation of the above air service agreements and provisional arrangements;
- issue licences to airlines incorporate and having their principal place of business in the Hong Kong Special Administrative Region;
- designate such airlines under the above Air Service Agreements and provisional arrangements; and
- issue permits to foreign airlines for services other than those to, from or through the mainland of China.

X

The Hong Kong Special Administrative Region shall maintain the educational system previously practiced in Hong Kong. The Hong Kong Special Administrative Region Government shall, on its own, decide policies in the fields of cultural, education, science and technology, including policies regarding the educational system and its administration, the language of instruction, the allocation of funds, the examination system, the system of academic awards and the recognition of educational and technological qualifications. Institutions of all kinds, including those run by religious and community organisations, may retain their autonomy. They may continue to recruit staff and use teaching materials from outside the Hong Kong Special Administrative Region. Students shall enjoy freedom of choice of education and freedom to pursue their education outside the Hong Kong Special Administrative Region.

XI

Subject to the principle that foreign affairs are the responsibility of the Central People's Government, representatives of the Hong Kong Special Administrative Region Government may participate, as members of delegations of the Government of the People's Republic of China, in negotiations at the diplomatic level directly affecting the Hong Kong Special Administrative Region conducted by the Central People's Government. The Hong Kong Special Administrative Region may on its own, using the name 'Hong Kong China', maintain and develop relations and conclude and implement agreements with states, regions, and relevant international organisations in the appropriate fields, including the economic, trade, financial and monetary, shipping communications, touristic, cultural, and sporting fields. Representatives of the Hong Kong Special Administrative Region Government may participate, as members of delegation of the Government of the People's Republic of China, in international organisations or conferences in appropriate fields limited to states and affecting the Hong Kong Special Administrative Region, or may attend in such other capacity as may be permitted by the Central People's Government and the organisation or conference concerned, and may express their view in the name of 'Hong Kong, China', the Hong Kong Special Administrative Region may, using the name 'Hong Kong, China' participate in international organisations and conferences not limited to states.

The application to the Hong Kong Special Administrative Region of international agreements to which the People's Republic of China is or becomes a party shall be decided by the Central People's Government in accordance with circumstances and needs of the Hong Kong Special Administrative Region, and after seeking the views of the Hong Kong Special Administrative Region Government. International agreements to which the People's Republic of China is not a party but which are implemented in Hong Kong may remain implemented in the Hong Kong Special Administrative Region. The Central People's Government shall, as necessary, authorise or assist the Hong Kong Special Administrative Region Government to make appropriate arrangements for the application to the Hong Kong Special Administrative Region of other relevant international agreements. The Central People's Government shall take the necessary steps to ensure that the Hong Kong Special Administrative Region shall continue to retain its status in an appropriate capacity in those international organisations of which the People's Republic of China is a member, and in which Hong Kong participates in one capacity or another. The Central People's Government shall, where necessary, facilitate the continued participation of the Hong Kong Special Administrative Region in an appropriate capacity in those international organisations in which Hong Kong is participant in one capacity or another, but of which the People's Republic of China is not a member.

Foreign consular and other official or semi-official missions may be established in the Hong Kong Special Administrative Region with the approval of the Central People's Government. Consular and other official missions established in Hong Kong by states which have established formal diplomatic relations with the People's Republic of China may be maintained. According to the circumstances of each case. Consular and other official missions of states having no formal diplomatic relations with the People's Republic of China may either be maintained or changed to semi-official missions. States not recognised by the People's Republic of China can only establish non-governmental institutions.

The United Kingdom may establish a Consulate-General in the Hong Kong Special Administrative Region.

XII

The maintenance of public order in the Hong Kong Special Administrative Region shall be the responsibility of the Hong Kong Special Administrative Region Government. Military forces sent by the Central People's Government to be stationed in the Hong Kong Special Administrative Region for the purpose of defence shall not interfere in the internal affairs of the Hong Kong Special Administrative Region. Expenditure for these military forces shall be borne by the Central People's Government.

XIII

The Hong Kong Special Administrative Region Government shall protect the rights and freedoms of inhabitants and other persons in the Hong Kong Special Administrative Region according to law. The Hong Kong Special Administrative Region Government shall maintain the rights and freedoms as provided for by the laws previously in force in Hong Kong. Including freedom of the person, of speech, of the press, of assembly, of association, to form and join trade unions, of correspondence, of travel, of movement, of strike, of demonstration, of choice of occupation, of academic research, of belief, inviolability of the home, the freedom to marry and right to raise a family freely.

Every person shall have the right to confidential legal advice, access to the courts, representation in the courts by lawyers of his choice, and to obtain judicial remedies. Every person shall have the right to challenge the actions of the executive in the courts.

Religious organisations and believers may maintain their relations with religious organisations and believers elsewhere, and schools, hospitals and welfare institutions run by religious organisations may be continued. The relationship between religious organisations in the Hong Kong Special Administrative Region and those in other parts of the People's Republic of China shall be based on the principles of non-subordination, non-interference, and mutual respect.

The provisions of the International Covenant on Civil and Political Rights and the International Covenant on Economic, Social and Cultural Rights as applied to Hong Kong shall remain in force.

XIV

The following categories of persons shall have the right of abode in the Hong Kong Special Administrative Region, and, in accordance with the law of the Hong Kong Special Administrative Region, be qualified to obtain permanent identity cards issued by the Hong Kong Special Administrative Region Government, which state their right of abode:

- all Chinese nationals who were born or who have ordinarily resided in Hong Kong before or after the establishment of the Hong Kong Special Administrative Region for a continuous period of 7 years or more, and persons of Chinese nationality born outside Hong Kong of such Chinese nationals:
- all other persons who have ordinarily resided in Hong Kong before or after the establishment of the Hong Kong Special Administrative Region for a continuous period of 7 years or more and who have taken Hong Kong as their place of permanent residence before or after the establishment of the Hong Kong Special Administrative Region, and persons under 21 years of age who were born of such persons in Hong Kong before or after the establishment of the Hong Kong Special Administrative Region.
- any other person who had the right of abode only in Hong Kong before the establishment of the Hong Kong Special Administrative Region.

The Central People's Government shall authorise the Hong Kong Special Administrative Region Government to issue in accordance with the law, passports of the Hong Kong Special Administrative Region of the People's Republic of China to all Chinese nationals who hold permanent identity cards of the Hong Kong Special Administrative Region, and travel documents of the Hong Kong Special Administrative Region of the People's Republic of China to all other persons lawfully residing in the Hong Kong Special Administrative Region. The above passports and documents shall be valid for all states and regions and shall record the holder's right to return to the Hong Kong Special Administrative Region.

For the purpose of travelling to and from the Hong Kong Special Administrative Region, residents of the Hong Kong Special Administrative Region may use travel documents issued by the Hong Kong Special Administrative Region Government, or by other competent authorities of the People's Republic of China or of other states. Holders of permanent identity cards of the Hong Kong Special Administrative Region may have this fact stated in their travel documents as evidence that the holders have the right of abode in the Hong Kong Special Administrative Region.

Entry into the Hong Kong Special Administrative Region of persons from other parts of China shall continue to be regulated in accordance with the present practice.

The Hong Kong Special Administrative Region Government may apply immigration controls on entry, stay in, and depart from the Hong Kong Special Administrative Region by persons from foreign states and regions.

Unless restrained by law, holders of valid travel documents shall be free to leave the Hong Kong Special Administrative Region without special authorisation.

The Central People's Government assist or authorise the Hong Kong Special Administrative Region Government to conclude visa abolition agreements with states or regions.

ANNEX II

Sino-British Joint Liaison Group

1. In further of their common aim and in order to ensure a smooth transfer of government in 1997, the Government of the People's Republic of China and the Government of the United Kingdom have agreed to continue their discussions in a friendly spirit and to develop the cooperative relationship which already exists between the two governments over Hong Kong with a view to the effective implementation of the Joint Declaration.
2. In order to meet the requirements for liaison, consultation, and the exchange of information, the two Governments have agreed to set up a Joint Liaison Group.
3. The functions of the Joint Liaison Group shall be:
   (a) to conduct consultations on the implementation of the Joint Declaration:
   (b) to discuss matters relating to the smooth transfer of government in 1997:
   (c) to exchange information and conduct consultations on such subjects as may be agreed by the two sides.

Matters on which there is disagreement in the Joint Liaison Group shall be referred to the two Governments for solution through consultations.

4. Matters for consideration during the first half of the period between the establishment of the Joint Liaison Group and July 1, 1997, shall include:
   (a) action to be taken by the two Governments to enable the Hong Kong Special Administrative Region to maintain its economic relations as a separate customs territory, and in particular to ensure the maintenance of Hong Kong's participation in the General Agreement on Tariffs and Trade, the Multi-fibre Arrangement and other international arrangements; and
   (b) action to be taken by the two governments to ensure the continued application of international rights and obligations affecting Hong Kong.
5. The two governments have agreed that in the second half of the period between the establishment of the Joint Liaison Group and July 1, 1997, there will be need for closed cooperation, which will therefore be intensified during that period. Matters for consideration during this second period shall include:
   (a) procedures to be adopted for the smooth transition in 1997:
   (b) action to assist the Hong Kong Special Administrative Region to maintain and develop economic and cultural relations and conclude agreements on these matters with states, regions and relevant international organisations.
6. The Joint Liaison Groups shall be an organ for liaison and not an organ of power. It shall play no part in the administration of Hong Kong or the Hong Kong Special Administrative Region. Nor shall it have any supervisory role over that administration. The members and supporting staff of the Joint Liaison Group shall only conduct activities within the scope of the functions of the Joint Liaison Group.
7. Each side shall designate a senior representative, who shall be of Ambassadorial rank and four other members of the group. Each side may send up to 20 supporting staff.

8. The Joint Liaison Group shall be established on the entry into force of the Joint Declaration. From July 1, 1988, the Joint Liaison Group shall have its principal base in Hong Kong. The Joint Liaison Group shall continue its work until January 1, 2000.
9. The Joint Liaison Group shall meet in Beijing, London, and Hong Kong. It shall meet at least appropriate when in the three location in each year. The venue for each meeting shall be agreed between the two sides.
10. Members of the Joint Liaison Group shall enjoy diplomatic privileges and immunities as appropriate when in the three locations. Proceedings of the Joint Liaison Group shall remain confidential unless otherwise agreed between the two sides.
11. The Joint Liaison Group may be agreement between the two sides decide to set up specialist sub-groups to deal with particular subjects requiring expert assistance.
12. Meeting of the Joint Liaison Group and sub-groups may be attended by experts other than the members of the Joint Liaison Group. Each side shall determine the composition of its delegation to particular meetings of the Joint Liaison Group or sub-group in according with the subjects to be discussed and the venue chosen.
13. The working procedure of the Joint Liaison Group shall be discussed and decided upon by the two within the guideline laid down in this Annex.

ANNEX III

Land Leases

The Government of the People's Republic of China and the Government of the United Kingdom have agreed that, with effect from the entry into force of the Joint Declaration, land leases in Hong Kong and other related matters shall be dealt with in accordance with the following provisions:

1. All leases of land granted or decided upon before the entry into force of the Joint Declaration and those granted thereafter in accordance with paragraph 2 or 3 of this Annex, and which extend beyond June 30, 1997, and all rights in relation to such leases shall continue to be recognised and protected under the law of the Hong Kong Special Administrative Region.
2. All leases of land granted by the British Hong Kong Government not containing a right of renewal that expire before June 30, 1997, except short-term tenancies and leases for special purposes, may be extended if the lessee so wishes for a period expiring not later than June 30, 2047, without payment of an additional premium. An annual rent shall be charged from the date of extension equivalent to 3% of the ratable value of the property at that date, adjusted in step with any changes in the ratable value thereafter. In the case of old schedule lots, village lots, small housed and similar rural holdings, where the property was on June 30, 1984,

held by, or, in the case of small houses granted after that date the property is granted to, a person descended through the male line from a person who was in 1898 a resident of an establish village in Hong Kong, the rent shall from a person who was in 1898 a resident of an established village in Hong Kong, the rent shall remain unchanged so long as the property is held by that person or by one of his lawful successors in the male line. Where lease of land not having a right of renewal expire after June 30, 1997, they shall be dealt with in accordance with the relevant land laws and policies of the Hong Kong Special Administrative Region.

3. From the entry into force of the Joint Declaration until June 30, 1997, new leases of land may be granted by the British Hong Kong Government for terms expiring not later than June 30, 2047. Such leases shall be granted at a premium and nominal rental until June 30, 1997, after which date they shall not require payment of an additional premium but an annual rent equivalent to 3% of the ratable value of the property at that date, adjusted in step with change in the ratable value thereafter, shall be charged.
4. The total amount of new land to be granted under paragraph 3 of this Annex shall be limited to 50 hectares a year (excluding land to be granted to the Hong Kong Housing Authority for public rental housing) from the entry into force of the Joint Declaration until June 30, 1997.
5. Modifications of the conditions specified in lease granted by the British Hong Kong Government may continue to be granted before July 1, 1997, at a premium equivalent to the difference between the value of the land under the previous conditions and its value under the modified conditions.
6. From the entry into force of the Joint Declaration until June 30, 1997, premium income obtained by the British Hong Kong

Government from land transactions shall, after deduction of the average cost of land production, be shared equally between the British Hong Kong Government and the future Hong Kong Special Administrative Region Government. All the income obtained by the British Hong Kong Government, including the amount of the above mentioned deduction shall be put into the Capital Works Reserved Fund for the financial of land development and public works in Hong Kong. The Hong Kong Special Administrative Region Government's share of the premium income shall be deposited in banks incorporated in Hong Kong and shall not be drawn on except for the financing of land development and public works in Hong Kong in accordance with the provisions of paragraph 7 (d) of this Annex.

7. A Land Commission shall be established in Hong Kong immediately upon the entry into force of the Joint Declaration. The Land Commission shall be composed of an equal number of officials designed respectively by the Government of the People's Republic of China and the Government of the United Kingdom together with necessary supporting staff. The officials of the two sides shall be responsible to their respective governments. The Land Commission shall be dissolved on June 30, 1997.

   The terms of reference of the Land Commission shall be:

   (a) to conduct consultation on the implementation of this Annex:
   (b) to monitor observance of the limit specified in paragraph 4 of this Annex, the amount of land granted to the Hong Kong Housing Authority for public rental housing, and the division and use of premium income referred to in paragraph 6 of this Annex:
   (c) to consider and decide on proposal from the British Hong Kong Government for increasing the limit referred to in paragraph 4 of this Annex:

(d) to examine proposals for drawing on the Hong Kong Special Administrative Region Government's share of premium income referred to in paragraph 6 of this Annex and to make recommendations to the Chinese side for decision.

Matters on which there is disagreement in the Land Commission shall be referred to the Government of the People's Republic of China and the Government of the United Kingdom for decision.

8. Specific details regarding the establishment of the Land Commission shall be finalised separately by the two sides through consultations.

Memoranda

(To Be Exchanged Between the Two Sides)

MEMORANDUM

In connection with the Joint Declaration of the Government of the United Kingdom of Great Britain and Northern Ireland and the Government of the People's Republic of China on the Question of Hong Kong to be signed this day, the Government of the United Kingdom declares that, subject to the completion of the necessary amendments to the relevant United Kingdom legislation:

(a) All persons who on June 30, 1997, are, by virtue of a connection with Hong Kong, British Dependent Territories citizens (BDTCs) under the law in force in the United Kingdom will cease to be BDTCs with effect from July 1, 1997, but will be eligible to retain an appropriate status which, without conferring the right of abode in the United Kingdom, will entitle them to continue to use passports issued by the Government of the United Kingdom. This status will be acquired by such persons only if they hold or are included in such a British passport issue before July 1, 1997, except that eligible persons born on or after January 1, 1997, but before July 1, 1997, may obtain or be included in such a passport up to December 31, 1997.

(b) No person will acquire BDTC status on or after July 1, 1997, by virtue of a connection with Hong Kong. No person born on or after July 1, 1997, will acquire the status referred to as being appropriate in sub-paragraph (a).

(c) United Kingdom consular officials in the Hong Kong Special Administrative Region and elsewhere may renew and replace passports of persons mentioned in Sub-paragraph (a) and may also issue them to persons, born before July 1, 1997, of such persons, who had previously been included in the passport of their parent.

(d) Those who have obtained or been included in passports issue by the Government of the United Kingdom under sub-paragraphs (a) and (c) will be entitled to receive, upon request, British consular service and protection when in third countries.

The Government of the People's Republic of China has received the memorandum from the Government of the United Kingdom of Great Britain and Northern Ireland dated 1984.

Under the Nationality Law of the People's Republic of China, all Hong Kong Chinese compatriots, whether they are holders of the 'British Dependent Territories citizens Passport' or not, are Chinese nationals.

Taking account of the historical background of Hong Kong and its realities, the competent authorities of the Government of the People's Republic of China will, with effect from July 1, 1997, permit Chinese nationals in Hong Kong who were previously called 'British Dependent Territories citizens' to use travel documents issued by the Government of the United Kingdom for the purpose of travelling to other states and regions.

The above Chinese national will not be entitled to British consular protection in the Hong Kong Special Administrative Region and other parts of the People's Republic of China on account of their holding the above-mentioned British travel documents.

MEMORANDUM

The Government of the People's Republic of China has received the memorandum from the Government of the United Kingdom of Great Britain and Northern Ireland dated 1984.

Under the Nationality Law of the People's Republic of China, all Hong Kong Chinese compatriots, whether they are holders of the 'British Dependent Territories citizens Passport' or not are Chinese nationals.

Taking account of the historical background of Hong Kong and its realities, the competent authorities of the Government of the People's Republic of China will with effect from July 1, 1997, permit Chinese nationals in Hong Kong who were previously called 'British Dependent Territories citizens' to use travel documents issued by the Government of the United Kingdom for the purpose of travelling to other states and regions.

The above Chinese nationals will not be entitled to British consular protection in the Hong Kong Special Administrative Region and other parts of the People's Republic of China on account of their holding the above-mentioned British travel documents.

Bibliography

PRIMARY SOURCES

The Basic Law of the Hong Kong Special Administrative Region of the People's Republic of China (Draft) (Hong Kong: Consultative Committee for the Basic Law, February, 1989), April, 1990.

Boundary and Election Commission: Report on the 1995 Legislative Council General Election, (Hong Kong: Government Printer, 1995).

British Nationality (Hong Kong) Bill 1990 and Explanatory Note (Hong Kong: Government Printer 1990).

A Draft Agreement between the Government of the United Kingdom of Great Britain and Northern Ireland and the Government of People's Republic of China on the Future of Hong Kong. (Hong Kong Government Printer 1990).

The Draft Basic Law of the Hong Kong Special Administrative Region of the People's Republic of China (For Solicitation of Opinions), (Hong Kong: Consultative Committee for the Basic Law, April, 1988).

Green Paper: A Patter of District Administration in Hong Kong (Hong Kong: Government Printer, June, 1980).

Green Paper: The Further Development of Representative Government in Hong Kong (Hong Kong: Government Printer, July 1984).

Green Paper: The 1987 Review of Development of Representative Government (Hong Kong: Government Printer, May 1987).

House of Commons (UK) Foreign Affairs Committee: Second Report on Hong Kong (London, 1989).

Our Next Five Years: The Agenda for Hong Kong (Address by the Governor the Right Honorable Christopher Pattern at the Opening of the 1992/93 Session of the Legislative Council, 7 October 1992) (Hong Kong: Government Printer, 1992).

The Origins and Current Circumstances of the Hong Kong Question (New Star Publications, Beijing, 1994).

Public Response to Green Paper: The 1987 Review of development in Representative Government, Report of the Survey Office, Part I, Report (Hong Kong: Government Printer, October 1987).

Reference Paper for the Basic Law of the Hong Kong Special Administrative Region of the People's Republic of China (Draft) (Hong Kong: Consultative Committee for the Basic Law, February, 1989).

White Paper: The Development of Representative Government: The way forward (Hong Kong: Government Printer, February, 1988).

White Paper: District Administrative in Hong Kong (Hong Kong : Government Printer, January 1981).

White Paper: The Further Development of Representative Government in Hong Kong (Hong Kong: Government Printer, November 21, 1984).

White Paper on the Annual Report on (Hong Kong to the Parliament, 1985-86, 1987, 1988, 1989) (Hong Kong: Government Printer, 1987-1990).

SECONDARY SOURCES

Blake, Gerd, (ed.), *Hong Kong Voices* (Hong Kong: Longman, 1989).

Bell. H.C.F., *Lord Palmerston*, (Longmans, 1936).

Benton, Gregor, *The Hong Kong Crisis*, (London: Pluto Press, 1983).

Blake, Clagetti, *Charles Elliot*, R. N., 1801-75 (London, 1960).

Bonavia, David, *Hong Kong 1997: The Final Settlement* (Hong Kong: *South China Morning Post*, 1985).

Burns John, P, Falkenheim Victor, C; and Lampton David. M., *Hong Kong and China in Transition* (Ontario, 1994).

Carew, Tim. *The Fall of Hong Kong* (Anthony Blond, London, 1961).

Cha, Louis, *On Hong Kong's Future: A Collection of Ming Pao's Editorial* (Translated by Stephen Wang), (Hong Kong: Ming Pao Daily News Ltd., 1984).

Chan, Rosanna, *Is the Hong Kong District Board a Channel for Popular Citizen Participation?* (Hong Kong: Research and Resource Press, 1982).

Chang Hsin-pao: *Commissioner Lin and the Opium War*, (Harvard, 1964).

Chandha, K. K. (ed)., *The MecLehose Years 1971-1982* (Hong Kong): South China Morning Post, April 1982).

Chan Ming K., (ed.), *Precarious Balance Hong Kong Between China and Britain 1842-1992* (M.E. Sharpe, New York, 1994).

Chan K; and Postiglione, Gerald, A., (eds)., *The Hong Kong Reader to Chinese Sovereignty* (M.E. Sharpe, New York, 1996).

Cheek-Milby, Kathleen. *A Legislature Comes of Age: Hong Kong's Search for Influence and Identity* (Hong Kong: Oxford University Press, 1995).

Cheek-Milby, Kathleen and Mushkat, Miron, (eds.), *Hong Kong: The Challenge for Transformation* (Hong Kong: Centre of Asian Studies, University of Hong Kong, 1989).

Cheng, Joseph, (ed.), *Hong Kong in the 1980's* (Hong Kong Summerson Eastern, 1982).

_______ (ed.), *Hong Kong in Search of a Future* (Hong Kong: Oxford University Press, 1984).

_______ (ed.), *Hong Kong in Transition* (Hong Kong: Oxford University Press, 1986).

Ching, Frank, *Hong Kong and China: For Better or for Worse* (New York: China Council of the Asia Society and the Foreign Policy Association, 1985).

Chung, Tan, *China and the Brave New World* (Allied, Delhi, 1978).

Chiu, Hungdah, Jao, Y.C. and Wu, Yuan-li eds., *The Future of Hong Kong: Toward 1997 and Beyond* (New York: Quorum Books, 1987).

Coates, Austin: *Prelude to Hong Kong*, (London, 1966).

Collins, Sir Charles, *Public Administration in Hong Kong* (London : Royal Institute of International Affairs, 1952).

Collis, Maurice: *Foreign Mud*, (London, 1946).

Costin, W.C., *Great Britain and China, 1833-1860* (London, 1937).

Cottrel, Robert, *The End of Hong Kong : The Secret Diplomacy of Imperial Retreat* (London : John Murray, 1993).

Coxall, W.N., *Parties and Pressure Groups* (London: Longman, 1985).

Dally, Peter, *Hong Kong Time Bomb* (Cheltenham : The British Anti-Communist Council, 1984).

David Shambaugh, *Greater China: The Next Superpower?* (Oxford University Press, London, 1995).

Davis, Michael C., *Constitutional Confrontation in Hong Kong* (Hong Kong, Macmillan, 1989).

Deyo, Frederic, ed., *The Political Economy of the New Asian Industrialization* (Ithaca: Cornell University Press, 1987).

Domes, Jurgen and Shaw, Yu-Ming, (ed.), *Hong Kong : A Chinese and International Concern* (Boulder: Westview Press, 1988).

Easey, Walter, *Ducking Responsibility: Britain and Hong Kong in the 1980's* (Manchester: Christian Statesman, 1980).

Edwards, George E. and Byrnes, Audrew C., (eds.), *Hong Konges Bill of Rights: The First Year* (Hong Kong: Faculty of Law, University of Hong Kong, 1993).

Emmons, Charles, *Hong Kong Prepares for 1997: Politics and Emigration in 1987* (Hong Kong: Centre for Asian Studies, University of Hong Kong, 1988).

Eitel, E.J., *Europe in China*, (Hong Kong, 1898).

Endacott, G.B., *A History of Hong Kong* (Oxford, 1958).

_______ *Government and People in Hong Kong, 1841-1962*, (Hong Kong, 1964).

Fairbank, J.K. *Trade and Development on the China Coast: The Opening of the Treaty Ports, 1842-1854* (Harvard, 1968).

Foster, Sir William, *England's Quest of Eastern Trade* (New York, 1967).

Friedman, Edward, ed., *The Politics of Democratization: Generalizing East Asia Experiences* (Boulder: West-view, 1994).

Gilbert, Rodney, *The Unequal Treaties* (London, 1929).

Harrison, Brian, (ed)., *The University of Hong Kong, the First 50 Years 1911-1961.* (Hong Kong, 1962).

Hertslet, Godfrey E.P., *China Treaties*, 2 Vols, (H.M.S.O., London 1908).

Hicks, George L., *Hong Kong Countdown* (Hong Kong: Writers and Publishers Cooperative, 1989).

Holt, Edgar, *The Opium Wars in China*, (London: Putnam, 1964).

Hughes, Richard, *Borrowed Place Borrowed Time : The Hong Kong and its Many Faces* (London : Audre Deutsch, 1976).

Ingrams, Harola. *Hong Kong*, (H.M.S.O., London 1952).

Hong Kong and 1997 : Strategies for the Future (Hong Kong : Centre of Asian Studies, University of Hong Kong, 1985).

Kumar, Janardan : *Indo-China Trade*, 1793-1833. Orient Longmans, London, 1974).

Khanna Jane. *Southern China Hong Kong, and Taiwan Evolution on a Sub-regional Economy* (Washington, D.C. 1995).

Lau, Siu-Kai and Kuan, Hsin-Chi, *The Ethos of the Hong Kong Chinese* (Hong Kong : The Chinese University Press, 1988).

Loh Christine, *Hong Kong A High Degree of Autonomy and The Basic Law.* (Hong Kong, 1995).

Lo Shiu-hing, *The Politics of Democratisation in Hong Kong*, (London, 1997).

Luk, Y. F. *Hong Kong's Economic and Financial Future.* (Washington, D.C. 1995).

Mac Gregor, John, *History of Oriental Commerce, Parliamentary Papers, 1847-48* (House of Commons, C. 947)

Marshall, P.J. *The Impeachment of Warrant Hastings,* (Oxford, 1965).

Mc Gurn, William, (ed.), *Basic Law, Basic Question : The Debate Continues* (Hong Kong : Review Publishing Company Ltd., 1988).

Mc Millen, Donald and De Golyer, Michael E., (eds.), *One Culture, Many Systems : Politics in the Reunification of China* (Hong Kong : The Chinese University Press, 1993).

Mellor, George, *British Imperial Trusteeship 1783-1850* (London : Lexington 1975).

Miners, Norman, *The Government and Politics of Hong Kong* (Hong Kong : Oxford University Press, 1995).

Morse, Hosea Baueou, *The East India Company Trading to China* Vols I-IV.

______ *The International Relations of the China Empire : The Period of Conflict 1834-1860* (London, 1910).

Moore, Barrington, TV., *Social Origins of Dictatorship and Democracy* (Boston : Beacon Press, 1966).

Morris, Jan, *Hong Kong* (New York : Viking Penguin, 1988).

Owen, D.E., *British Opium Policy in China and India*, (Yale University, 1934).

Overholt, William, H., *China : The Next Super Power*, (London, 1995).

Panikar, N.M. *Asia and Western Dominance* (London, 1953).

Patrikeeff, Felix, *Mouldering Pearl : Hong Kong at a Crossroads* (London, George Phillip, 1989).

Pelcovits, N.A. *Old China Hands and the Foreign Office* (New York, 1969).

Roberti, Mark, *The Fall of Hong Kong : Chinais Triumph and Britainis Betrayal* (New York : John Wiley and Sons, 1994).

Robinson, F.P. *The Trade of the East India Company, 1709-1812* (Cambridge, 1912).

Sayer, G.R. *Hong Kong : Birth, Adolescence and Coming of Age* (Oxford, 1937).

Scott, Ian, *Political Change and the Crisis of Legitimacy in Hong Kong* (Hong Kong, 1989).

Shawcross, William, *Kowtow*, (London : Chatta and Windus, 1989).

Steven M, Goldstein, ed., *Minidragons : Fragile Economic Mirades in the Pacific* (Boulder : Westview, 1991).

Sinclair, Kelvin, (ed.), *Who's Who in Hong Kong* (Hong Kong : South China Morning Post, 1982).

Sung Yun-Wing, *The China-Hong Kong Connection* (Cambridge, 1991).

Thatcher, Margaret, '*Margaret Thatcher : The Downing Street Years*' (New York : Harper Collins, 1993).

Trench, David. H*ong Kong and its Position in the South east Asia Region* (Hawaii : East-West Centre, 1971).

Tsang, Steve Yu:-Sang, *Democracy Shelved : Great Britain China and Attempts at Constitutional Reform* (Hong Kong : Oxford University Press 1988).

Tsim, T.L. and Luk, Bernard, eds., *The Other Hong Kong Report* (Hong Kong : The Chinese University Press 1989).

Turner, H.A. *The Last Colony : But Whose?* (Cambridge University Press, 1980).

Waley, Arthur, *The Opium War Through Chinese Eyes*. (London, 1958).

Wang, Eubao, *Hong Kong : The Politics of Transition* (Colorado : Lyun Rienner, 1995).

Wesley – smith, Peter ed., *Hong Kong's Basic Law : Problems and Prospects* (Hong Kong : Faculty of Law, University Hong Kong, 1990).

______ *Unequal Treaty 1898-1997: China, Great Britain and Hong Kong's New Territories* (Hong Kong : Oxford University Press, 1980).

Wight, Martin, *The Development Council*, 1606-1994.

Wong, Richard, Y.C. and Cheng Joseph Y.S., *The Other Hong Kong Report 1990* (Hong Kong, 1990).

ARTICLES

Baker, Hugh, "Life in the Cities : The Emergence of Hong Kong Man" : *China Quarterly*. No. 95 (September, 1983).

Burns, John P., "Immigration from China and the Future of Hong Kong (1997) and implications for Taiwan", *AEI Foreign Policy and Defence Review*, Vol. 6, No. 3 (1986).

Campbell, Duncan, "A Secret Plan for Dictatorship" *New Statesman*, December 12, 1980.

Chau, Joseph Man and Lee, Chin-Chuau, "Shifting Journalistic Paradigms: Editorial Stance and Political Transition in Hong Kong", *China Quarterly*, No. 117 (March, 1989).

Chau, Ming and Clark, David, eds. "The Drafting of the Basic Law for the Hong Kong Special Administrative Region", *Chinese Law and Government*, Vol. 22, No. 3 (Fall 1989).

Chau, Ming, K. "The 1991 Elections in Hong Kong: Democratization in the shadow of Tiananmen" in George T. Yu ed., *China in Transition: Economic, Political and Social Development* (Lanham University Press, 1993).

Chau, Ming, K. "Decolonization without Democracy: The Birth of Pluralistic Politics in Hong Kong", in Edward Freidman ed., The *Politics of Democratization Generalizing East Asian Experiences*, (West View Press, 1994).

Chau, Joseph, "Hong Kong: The Pressure to Coverage", *International Affairs*. Vol. 63, No. 2 (Spring, 1987).

_______ "The Post-1997 Government in Hong Kong: Toward a Stronger Legislative", *Asian Survey* : No. 8 (August 1989).

_______ "Prospect for Democracy in Hong Kong After the Beijing Massacre", *Australian Journal of Chines Affairs*. No. 23 (January 1990).

Cheng, Joseph Y.S., "Sino-British Negotiations on Hong Kong During Chris Pattenis Governorship", *Australian Journal of International Affairs* (Canberra, Vol. 48 No. 2, 1994).

_______ "The Democracy Movement in Hong Kong", *International Affairs*, Vol. 65, No. 3 (Summer 1989).

_______ "The Future of Hong Kong: A solution for Hong Kong People", *Asia Pacific Community* (Winter 1984).

Chaung, Jae Ho and Lo, Shire-Ling, "Beijing's Relations with the Hong Kong Special Administrative Region: An International Framework for the Post-1947 Arrangement", *Pacific Affairs*, Vol. 68, No. 2 (Sunner 1995).

Chaung, Richard, "Home Insurance for British Nationals in Hong Kong?", Asian Affairs (America) Vol.17, No.1 (Spring 1990).

Cooper, Terry L, and Lue, Terry L., "Democracy and the Administrative State : The case of Hong Kong", Public Administration Review, Vol. 50, No. 3 (May/June 1990).

Cotton, James. "Hong Kong: Conveyance of or Divergence?", Journal of North-East Asian Studies, Vol. 6, No. (4) (Winter 1987).

Dalvean, A.U. "Hong Kong's Socio-Political culture: Problems of Identity and Perception", Foreign Affairs Report (New Delhi). Vol. XXXVIII. No. 2, 1989.

Dittimer, Loweld, "Hong Kong and China's Modernization", Orbis, Vol. 30, No. 3 (Fall 1986).

Dong, L.S., "The Recruitment of Cadres and Civil Servants in Main land China", Issues and Studies, Vol. 29, No. 10 (October, 1993).

Dunn, Lydia, "Hong Kong after the Sino-British Declaration", International Affairs. (London), Vol. 61, No.8, 1985.

Finer, S.E., "Hong Kong 1997: When the Kissing has to Stop", Political Quarterly, Vol. 56 (1985).

Goodlad, Alastair, "Hong Kong: Britain's Legacy, China's Inheritance", The World Today (London), June 1994.

Harris, Peter, "Hong Kong Confronts 1997: An Assessment of the Sino-British Agreement", Pacific Affairs, Vol. 59, No. 1 (Spring 1986)

Hoadley, Stephen, "Political Participation of Hong Kong Chinese: Patterns and Trends", Asian Survey, No. 6 (June 1973).

Howe, Christopher, "Growth, Public Policy and Hong Kong's Economic relationship with China", China Quarterly (London) No. 95, 1983.

Hsin-chi Kuan, "Hong Kong in 1996", Asian Survey (Berkeley), Vol. XXXVII, No. 1, 1997.

Hsiung, James, C. "Hong Kong Settlement: Effects on Taiwan and Prospects for Peking's Reunification Bid", Asian Affairs : An American Review, Vol. 12, No. 2, 1985.

Jacobs, Piers, "Hong Kong and the modernization of China", Journal of International Affairs (London), Vol. 39, No.2, 1986.

Jao, Y.C., "The Rise of Hong Kong as Financial Centre", Asian Survey (Berkeley), Vol. XIX, No.7, 1979.

Johnson, Chalmers, "The Mousetrapping of Hong Kong: A Game in Which Nobody Wins", Asian Survey, Vol. 24, No. 9 (September 1984).

King Ambrose Yeo-chi, "Administrative Absorption of Politics in Hong Kong: Emphasis on the Grassroots Level", Asian Survey, Vol. 15, No. 5 (May 1975).

______ "The Hong Kong Talks and Hong Kong Politics", Issue and studies Vol. 22, No. 6 (June 1986).

Lam, Jermain T.M., "From submissive to the Adversarial Legislature: The Changing Role of the Hong Kong Legislative Council in the Political Transition", Asian Profile, Vol. 22, No. 1, (February 1994).

Lau, Siu, Kai, "Institutions Without Leaders: The Hong Kong Chinese View of Political Leadership", Pacific Affairs Vol. 22, No. 2 (Summer 1990).

______ Society and Politics in Hong Kong (Hong Kong: The Chinese University Press, 1982).

Lau Siu-Kai and Kuan Hsin-Chi, "Public Attitudes Towards Political Authorities and Colonial Legitimacy in Hong Kong", The Journal of Commonwealth and Comparative Politics, (London) Vol. 33, No. 3 1995.

Lau Siu-Kai and Kuan Hsin-Chi, "District Board Elections in Hong Kong" Journal of Commonwealth and Comparative Politics, Vol. 22, No. 3 (November 1984).

______ "The 1985 District Board Elections in Hong Kong: The Limits of Political Mobilisation in a Dependent Polity", Journal of Commonwealth and Comparative Politics, Vol. 25, No. 1 (March 1987).

Leung, Joan Y.H. "Fundamental Representation in Hong Kong: Institutionalisation and Legitimisation of the Business and Professional Elites", Asian Journal of Public Administration, Vol. 12, No. 2 (December 1990).

Lo, Shiu-hing, 'An Analysis of Sino-British Negotiations over Hong Kong's Political Reform', Contemporary Southern Asia, Vol. 16, No. 2 (September, 1994).

______ 'The Chinese Communist Party Elite's Conflicts over Hong Kong', China Information, Vol. VII, No. 4 (Spring 1994).

______ 'Colonial Policy-makers', Capitalist Class and China: Determinants of Electoral Reform in Hong Kong's and Macau's Legislatures', Pacific Affairs, Vol. 62, No. 2, (Summer, 1989).

______ 'Decolonization and Political Development in Hong Kong: Citizen Participation', Asian Survey, Vol. 28, No. 6 (June 1988).

______ 'Decolonization in Hong Kong: Reasons, Phases, and Limits, Issue and Studies, Vol. 26, No. 5 (May, 1990).

______ 'Political Participation in Hong Kong, South Korea, and Taiwan', Journal of Contemporary Asia, Vol. 20, No. 2 (1990).

______ "The Politics of Localization of the Civil Service in Hong Kong and Macau', Journal of Commonwealth and Comparative Politics, Vol. 33, No. 1, (March, 1995).

______ 'The Problem of Perception and Sino-British Relations over Hong Kong', Contemporary Southeast Asia, Vol. 13, No. 2 (September, 1991).

Lo, Sonny Shiu-hing and McMillan, Donald, 'A Profit of the "Pro-China Hong Kong" : Image and Perceptions', Issue and Studies, Vol. 31, No. 6 (June 1995).

Overholt, William H. 'Hong Kong and China: A New Relationship', Current History (Philadelphia) Vol. 84, No. 3.

Remmer, Karen, L., 'New Theoretical Perspective in Democratisation' Comparative Politics, Vol. 28. No. 1 (October 1995).

Scobell, Andrew, 'Hong Kong's Influence on China: The tail that wags the dog?' Asian Survey, Vol. 22, No. 2 (June, 1988).

Scott, Ian, 'Legitimact and its Discontents: Hong Kong and the Reversion to Chinese Sovereignty', Asian journal of Political Science, Vol. 1, No. 1 (June, 1988).

_______ 'Sino-British Agreement and the Political Power in Hong Kong', Asian and Pacific Community, (Winter, 1986).

Scott, Ian and Burns, John, eds., The Hong Kong Civil Service and its Future, (Hong Kong : Oxford University Press, 1988).

_______ eds., The Hong Kong Civil Service: Personnel, Politics and Practices, (Hong Kong Oxford University Press, 1988).

Shin, Doh Chull, 'On the Third Wave of Democratisation: A Synthesis and Evaluation of Recent Theory and research' World Politics, Vol. 47, No. 1 (October, 1994).

So, Alvin and Kwitko, Ludmilla, 'The New Middle Class and the Democratic Movement in Hong Kong', Journal of Contemporary Asia, Vol. 20, No. 3 (1990).

Tang, James, T.H., 'Hong Kong's International Status', Pacific review, Vol. 6, No. 3 (1993).

Huntington, Samuel P., Political Order in Changing Societies (New Haven: Yale University Press, 1968).

_______ "Will More Countries Become Democratic?" Political Science Quarterly, Vol. 99, No. 2. 1984.

Wilson, Dick, "The Dilemmas of Hong Kong in Transition", The Round Table (London, 1988).

Wong, J.Y. "The Rule of Law in Hong Kong past, Present and the Prospects for the Future", Australian Journal of International Affairs (Canberra), Vol. 46, No. 1, 1992.

Yee, Herbert and Wong, Yiu-chung, 'Hong Kong: The Politics of the Daya Bay Nuclear Plant Debate', International Affairs, Vol. 63, No. 4 (Autumn, 1987).

NEWS PAPERS AND PERIODICALS

Asian Affairs (London)
Asian Survey (Berkeley, California)
Asia Week (Hong Kong)
Beijing Review
Bulletin of Concerned Asian Scholar (New York)
China Quarterly (London)
China Report (New Delhi)
Current History (Philadelphia)

Daily Telegraph (London)
Far Eastern Economic Review (Hong Kong)
Foreign Affairs (New York)
Foreign Affairs Report (New Delhi)
Foreign Policy (New York)
Foreign Broadcast Information Service (Hong Kong)
Hong Kong Standard (Hong Kong)
India Quarterly (New Delhi)
International Affairs (London)
International Studies (New Delhi)
International Herald Tribune (Hong Kong)
Issues and Studies (Taipei)
News From China (New Delhi)
New York Times
Orbis (Philadelphia)
Observer (London)
Pacific Affairs (Vancouver)
Summary of World Broadcasts (London)
Statesman (New Delhi)
Times (London)
Washington Post.